DISPOSABLE LEADERS

RODNEY TIFFEN is Emeritus Professor in Government and International Relations at the University of Sydney. His most recent book is *Rupert Murdoch: A Reassessment* (2014). His earlier books include *How Australia Compares* (two editions, co-authored with Ross Gittins); *Diplomatic Deceits: Government, Media and East Timor*; *Scandals: Media, Politics and Corruption in Contemporary Australia*; and *News and Power*. He has authored numerous articles on mass media and Australian politics, and is editor of *Mayer on the Media: Selected Essays on Australian Media*, and co-editor (with Murray Goot) of *Australia's Gulf War*. He worked on the Hon. R Finkelstein QC's Independent Inquiry into the Media and Media Regulation in 2011/12, and as an observer during South Africa's first democratic election, in 1994.

DISPOSABLE LEADERS

MEDIA AND LEADERSHIP COUPS FROM MENZIES TO ABBOTT

RODNEY TIFFEN

NEWSOUTH

A NewSouth book

Published by
NewSouth Publishing
University of New South Wales Press Ltd
University of New South Wales
Sydney NSW 2052
AUSTRALIA
newsouthpublishing.com

© Rodney Tiffen 2017
First published 2017

10 9 8 7 6 5 4 3 2 1

National Library of Australia
Cataloguing-in-Publication entry
Creator: Tiffen, Rodney, author.
Title: Disposable leaders: Media and leadership coups from Menzies to Abbott / Rodney Tiffen.
ISBN: 9781742235202 (paperback)
    9781742242682 (ebook)
    9781742248141 (ePDF)
Notes: Includes bibliographical references and index.
Subjects: Political leadership—Australia
 Journalism—Australia—Political aspects.
 Politics in mass media.
 Australia—Politics and government.

Design Josephine Pajor-Markus
Cover design Design by Committee
Cover images BACKGROUND IMAGES Bigstock by Shutterstock; FRONT COVER
Malcolm Turnbull: Mick Tsikas / AAP; John Howard: Paul Harris / Fairfax
Syndication; Bob Hawke: AAP / National Archive Australia; Kevin Rudd: Scott
Barbour / Getty Images; Julia Gillard: Kym Smith / Newspix; Tony Abbott: Rick
Rycroft / AP Photo and Bjelke-Petersen: News Ltd / Newspix.

UNSW
AUSTRALIA

Contents

Acknowledgments

I would like to thank the team at NewSouth Publishing, especially Phillipa McGuinness and Paul O'Beirne, and Sarah Shrubb for her scrupulous copy editing. Again I am grateful for the collegiality of the departments of Media and Communications, and Government and International Relations at the University of Sydney, and to Graeme Gill and Chris Masters for their solidarity.

I would particularly like to thank John Wanna, David Clune, Mitchell Hobbs, Graeme Dobell, Judy Betts, Ross Gittins and, especially, Stephen Mills and Peter Browne for commenting on one or more of the early chapter drafts.

As always, my greatest debt is to Kathryn, for our more than four decades of marriage, in which I have always been the deputy leader.

Abbreviations

2PP   The Two-Party Preferred Vote is a measure originally developed by Malcolm Mackerras designed to capture two key facts about Australian elections: that (a) it is a preferential voting system in which the distribution of second preference votes of minor parties and independents may be crucial; and (b) the basic question in deciding who forms government is which side – Labor or the Liberal-National Party Coalition – has the majority. It is the best single measure of changes in support and likelihood of winning government. Of course that does not mean that it is the only relevant measure. It is also necessary to know the degrees of support for minor parties and independents, especially if they are in a position to win seats themselves. Nor does it show the distribution of the vote, where sometimes one party wins more seats than its share of the national vote would suggest. Since World War II there have been five occasions on which one side has captured less than 50 per cent of the 2PP and still won government.

APEC   Asia Pacific Economic Cooperation

ETS   Emissions Trading Scheme. Policies which aim to reduce greenhouse gas emissions, either through market mechanisms, such as a tax on carbon, or through cap and trade schemes. The Rudd Government's version was called the CPRS (Carbon Pollution Reduction Scheme).

PMO Prime Minister's Office: the personal staff of the Prime Minister

PMC (or DPMC) Department of Prime Minister and Cabinet

Publications referred to in the Notes

AFR   *Australian Financial Review*
Age   *The Age*
Aust   *The Australian*
Conv   *The Conversation*
CT   *The Canberra Times*
DT   *Daily Telegraph*
G   *Guardian*
IS   *Inside Story*
NYRB   *The New York Review of Books*
NYT   *New York Times*
SMH   *Sydney Morning Herald*
S Tele   *Sunday Telegraph*

CHAPTER 1

Leadership Challenges from Menzies to Abbott

'A sick feeling of repugnance and apprehension grows in me as I near Australia.'

This famous line from Robert Menzies' May 1941 diary has sometimes been used to suggest his lack of patriotism. In fact, the Prime Minister's dread at returning, his wish to 'creep quietly into the bosom of the family' after three months away discussing issues of war planning in London and North America, stemmed from the looming political conflicts awaiting him.

Menzies' apprehension was well founded. His wife had twice unsuccessfully urged him to cut short his trip because of mounting intrigues against him. A senior Minister, Percy Spender, warned Menzies that his grave was being dug. Three months later, Menzies' efforts to retrieve the situation finally collapsed, and on 29 August he resigned as Prime Minister.

The most important conflict was not with his party opponents, Labor. He was impatient with their criticisms and refusal to form a government of national unity. But relations with Labor leader John Curtin had a warmth not matched in any relationship between Prime Minister and Opposition Leader since. After his resignation, Menzies wrote, 'your political opposition has been honourable and your personal friendship a pearl of great price'. Curtin replied, 'I thank you for the consideration and courtesy which never once failed in your dealings with me.'[1]

Rather, Menzies' problems lay within his government. His grip on the leadership had never been strong. After the death of his predecessor, Joseph Lyons, Menzies had won the leadership of the United Australia Party (later transformed into the Liberal Party), only on the third ballot, and then he only narrowly defeated the 77-year-old Billy Hughes. Earle Page, leader of the Country Party (now the National Party), trying to stop Menzies' rise to the prime ministership, launched one of the most vitriolic personal attacks in Australian parliamentary history. He accused Menzies of avoiding service in World War I, of disloyalty to Lyons when the latter was sick, of being unstable, and of being unable to lead. Their personal relationship was never repaired, but the viciousness of Page's attack did more damage to him than to Menzies.

Even in the crisis of war, however, Menzies was unable to unify his government. His despairing diary entry is eloquent testimony to the personal toll taken by such internal conflicts. His fall in 1941 is a dramatic example of the old political adage that in parliament your opponents sit opposite you, while your enemies sit behind you.

Menzies was the first Prime Minister to be overthrown by his own party. It was another 30 years before it happened again – when John Gorton fell in March 1971 – and then 20 years until Paul Keating defeated Bob Hawke in December 1991. So in the century up to 2010, three sitting Prime Ministers were victims of party coups. Then in just five years three more followed – Kevin Rudd was defeated by Julia Gillard in June 2010; Rudd then defeated Gillard to resume the prime ministership three years later, in June 2013; and most recently Malcolm Turnbull defeated Tony Abbott, in September 2015.

It is not only Prime Ministers who have become more vulnerable to being displaced by their own side. In the 1960s there were no successful leadership challenges in the major parties, federal or state, but since 1970 fully 73 leaders have been ousted by their colleagues. And, as Appendix B Table 1 shows, their frequency has been increasing, with 32 this century, an average of two per year.

(All figures in this chapter refer to federal and state Liberal and Labor Party leaders, plus the Queensland Nationals, because they were the major conservative party in that state for a long period.) Of leaders whose tenure began after 1970 and finished by 2016 almost half (68/138) were victims of party coups. It has become the single most common means by which leaderships end.

Leadership challenges have become an important part of the Australian political landscape, and they frequently have profound consequences, but beyond detailed accounts of individual challenges, they have not received the analytical attention they deserve. This book has two central purposes. The first is to explore the politics of these challenges. The driving force for their increased frequency is a much more ruthless electoral pragmatism, and yet only a minority of them bring subsequent electoral success. They are usually uncertain and disruptive in process, and sometimes produce enduring legacies of personal bitterness and internal division. The book's second purpose is to analyse the pivotal role the media play in how these conflicts develop. In terms of publicity interests and strategies, of the challenges confronting media reporting of them, and of the consequences of media coverage, leadership coups are a unique conflict.

An evolving genre

Politics in 1950s Adelaide was a gentlemanly affair. The Premier, Thomas Playford, and Labor's Mick O'Halloran faced each other in four election campaigns between 1950 and 1959. More surprisingly, they dined together each week to discuss Playford's future plans for South Australia, and often praised each other publicly. O'Halloran remained Labor leader until he died in 1960. Playford wept openly when told of the death, and was a pallbearer and speaker at O'Halloran's state funeral.

To contemporary eyes it is not surprising that the victorious Playford – the longest-serving party leader in postwar Australian history – remained leader, but more unusual that O'Halloran also remained leader without serious challenge through four losing elections.

In the decades after World War II, losing an election was not necessarily grounds for a leader's being replaced or challenged. Federal Labor leaders Bert Evatt and Arthur Calwell and Victorians Clive Stoneham and Clyde Holding all lost three successive elections while remaining in place. Others survived though enjoying only mixed success. Queensland Country Party leader Frank Nicklin lost five elections from the 1940s before winning four in a row from 1957 on. John Cain Snr led Victorian Labor for almost 20 years from 1937, before dying in office. In that time he had two election victories and five losses. In contrast, only one party leader since the 1980s (Rob Borbidge, Queensland Nationals) has survived to suffer three or more electoral defeats.

Until at least the 1970s, the major route to party leadership was through seniority, and patience was considered a virtue. When Harold Holt became Prime Minister in 1966, he proudly told his wife, 'I climbed over no-one's dead body to get here.'[2] In Western Australia, Charles Court 'desperately' wanted to be Premier, but he was 'unbelievably patient', waiting until his long-reigning predecessor, David Brand, retired for health reasons, wrote Peter Kennedy, the great journalistic chronicler of WA politics.[3] Brand's successor as Premier, Labor's John Tonkin, did not become leader until he was 63, having been deputy for 15 years, and then became Premier when aged 69. Some of his junior colleagues suggested he might step down for someone younger, but he neatly deflected them, and open challenge did not occur to them.[4]

The emphasis on seniority and patience had its costs. It denied some of the most able people their chance to lead. One was Tonkin's deputy in WA Labor, Herb Graham. Many considered him the better leader, and many MPs went to him for advice and help. From early on, and continuing for two decades, there was rivalry between them, but Graham was always 'behind Tonkin in the party "pecking order"'". Graham never challenged, and Tonkin's longevity as leader meant that natural attrition just did not occur.[5]

The pace and pressure of contemporary society is one reason for the greater turnover of leaders. Appendix B Table 2 lists the 17 postwar leaders who led their party continuously for 12 years or more. Of these, ten became leader in 1960 or before, and only three (Bob Carr, Mike Rann and John Howard) became leader after 1980. The fact that leadership has become more precarious and conditional is starkly confirmed by trends in length of tenure. Those who became party leader before 1970 averaged eight years and six months in the role, while those who became leader from 1970 on averaged just under half that: four years exactly. Similarly, those who became leader before 1970 fought 3.0 elections, on average; those from 1970 on averaged just 1.2 elections as leader. Some states have moved from a three-year to a four-year election cycle, but that is only a very small part of the explanation.

The more temporary nature of party leadership is clear from these figures, but they only start to capture the greater ruthlessness. A successful leader can still lead a party to several elections, but an unsuccessful (or not likely to be successful) leader is much more quickly disposed of. In recent decades, fewer than three in ten losing leaders led their party into the next election, in contrast to six in ten in the 1950s and 1960s. Challenges became increasingly pre-emptive: among those who became leader from 1990 onwards, one-quarter (20/78) were ousted by their colleagues before they had fought a single election.

Of the 55 who became leader before 1970, their leaderships finished predominantly for personal rather than political reasons. Almost one in five (10) actually died in the role, the last such death being Queensland Country Party Premier Jack Pizzey in 1968, the second last being Harold Holt, who drowned the previous December. Of pre-1970 leaders, almost one-quarter (24%) retired because of old age, compared to just 3 per cent of the post-1970 cohort. If we combine those dying in office, those who retired as a result of

5

old age, those who resigned for a medical reason or for personal reasons, the total is 55 per cent of all the pre-1970 leaders. Since then, all those reasons combined account for just 10 per cent of leaders' departures.

The reasons for leaderships ending in recent decades are much more political. Thirty per cent resigned either after an election loss or because of poor electoral prospects, compared with 15 per cent of the earlier group, while as already noted, almost half were forcibly displaced by their own party.

A unique conflict

The other key difference between contemporary leadership struggles and those of an earlier age is the central importance of the media. As the media have become a more massive and intense presence on the political stage, skill at handling their demands has become one of the keys to political success. Beyond all specific stances, mediating all particular policies, is the pervasiveness of leaders and leadership in the news. The media also often play an important role in the conduct of challenges. These are a unique type of political conflict, and the media play a unique role in their unfolding and resolution. Seven factors which produce this uniqueness are outlined below:

1   **Leadership struggles are between ostensible allies, and so normally they need to be contained in the larger interests of the party.**

Isn't it great to lead a united political party, with a deputy I can trust, a predecessor who's a friend and a former prime minister who's a hero.

Tony Abbott, election launch 2010.[6]

Electoral strategists uniformly believe that – as John Howard said after his 1987 election loss – 'disunity is death'.[7] An internal party conflict is always subject to exploitation by opposing parties. During the 1990 election campaign, 'describing the Liberal Party as split with bitterness and hatred, Bob Hawke closed with the familiar but effective line, "A party that can't govern itself cannot govern the country"',[8] a theme which he 'repeated over and over again'.[9] By 1991 the problem was on the other side, as Paul Keating laid siege to Hawke's leadership. National Labor Party secretary Bob Hogg was mindful that 'You can't win if the party's divided.'[10] Intra-party conflicts threaten the party's fundamental purpose by undermining its electability, so the public appearance of such conflicts must be controlled, and subordinated to the pursuit of the inter-party electoral competition.

When we think of news coverage of politics, we tend to think of the most frequent conflict in the news, which is the conflict between the major political parties. In the two-sided contest to form government, the conflict is zero-sum, winner-take-all, and decided by public opinion. It is zero-sum in that if one side's prospects are improving, the other's are necessarily declining. It is winner-take-all in that there is a chasm between winning and losing. No matter how close or one-sided the result, one party is in government, the other in opposition. The publicity interests are clear: each side is constantly looking for chances to criticise the other, to magnify the appearance of conflict between them, and to discredit and destroy their opponents. There are few incentives to restraint.

The publicity interests in internal party conflicts are very different. The pressure to maintain the appearance of unity is strong, and in a disciplined party will be a primary consideration in all but the most extreme conflicts. In dealing with conflicts over policy, electorally pragmatic participants try to minimise the appearance of conflict through finding an acceptable compromise or seeking a path that enhances the leader's public standing. Similarly, the normal rhythm is that in the lead-up to an election, internal conflicts will be controlled, but afterwards they surface. On the Monday after Hawke's victory in the 1987 election, the *Sydney Morning Herald* headline was 'Now the Brawls Begin', and Mike Steketee's story detailed a leadership challenge by Peacock against Howard, as well as strong-arm factional lobbying over ministries in the Labor Government.[11]

However, parties will remain irredeemably 'poly-vocal'.[12] Major political parties are by their nature 'broad churches', coalitions of diverse outlooks and competing interests. Their representative forums are rarely completely silenced, and the party membership often have stronger views on key issues than the swinging voters the electoral strategists want to focus upon. Also, the publicity interests of incumbents and challengers often differ.

However, for some individuals other factors may loom larger than what is politically rational in a party sense. Sometimes, for some participants, factional loyalties rival party ones. After his defeat, Hawke was particularly critical of:

> one of Paul Keating's most immoderate followers, Gary Punch,
> [who] openly said in the office of one of my supporters whom
> they were trying to win over, that they would press on even if it
> meant taking the Government into Opposition. Such fanaticism
> has a certain terrifying logic.[13]

Wayne Errington and Peter van Onselen believed that key people, including perhaps the two principals, had a similar attitude in the 1980s:

> In the coming years Howard and Peacock each developed a
> core group of supporters that despised one another. For his part,
> Fraser believed that Peacock and Howard were sensible enough
> to realise that they would need each other's help to defeat Labor.
> This ignores the fact that it was in neither man's interest to
> return to government other than as leader.[14]

But it is unusual for most politicians to prefer to be leaders in opposition than members of a government, and if such an attitude were known internally they would soon lose support.

2   Leadership struggles are the most personal of all political conflicts. The contenders typically have an extensive direct personal relationship and in addition one refracted through the media.

> I think there were tears shed … I'm not enjoying this, Karl.
> It's a very difficult time.
>
> *Julie Bishop, on breakfast TV*
> *the morning after Abbott's fall* [15]

> You're a cunt, Malcolm.
>
> *Drunken Abbott staffer yelling at*
> *Turnbull as he walked past a party of*
> *Abbott supporters in Parliament House* [16]

Most political conflicts are conducted at a distance, or in stylised, limited encounters. Their conduct is relatively impersonal. Party leadership challenges, however, are unique among political conflicts because of the complexity and extent of the relationship. The contenders are not only simultaneously allies as well as antagonists, but in addition they have frequent and wide-ranging interactions with each other, and a direct, even intimate, personal relationship. Keating biographer John Edwards observed of Hawke and Keating:

> They had after all worked more closely with each other over
> the last eight years than either of them ever had with anyone
> else. Both of them believed the work they had done [together]
> was the most interesting and important they would ever do. [17]

The combination of personal affection and intractable divisions make leadership conflicts emotionally draining, and sometimes all-consuming. Gareth Evans commented on Hawke's ousting of Bill Hayden in 1983:

> There's so much agony involved in these leadership changes for
> someone who's close to them … I had a lot of respect and a lot
> of affection for Hayden and it was just terribly sad to see the
> end of that chapter of his career being played out.[18]

Eight years later, when Hawke was deposed, the scenes were even more emotional. Graham Richardson recalled, 'Emotion in the room ran high. Caucus members swarmed round Hawke and Keating and most of them had tears in their eyes.'[19] In Hawke's account:

> leadership battles are very tactile events and a lot of hugging,
> kissing and crying occurred … After the vote two lines
> formed in the Caucus room as people congratulated Paul and
> commiserated with me … I was confronted with devastated
> loyalists and the sometimes tearful faces of those who had done
> everything they could to bring me down – John Dawkins, in
> particular, wept as he thanked me for all I had done.[20]

The mixture of being simultaneously allies and antagonists would be a minefield in any situation, but in this one, the contenders have both an extensive, even intimate, direct personal relationship and also one refracted through the news media. The difficulties are magnified because news reports are biased towards highlighting the most dramatic aspects, focusing overwhelmingly on the degree of conflict between the leaders. This is often expressed with a hardness and sharpness quite different from the rhythms and fluidity of actual personal encounters.

Participants sometimes accord more political currency to the public news reports than to their actual private interactions.

Especially when there is unfavourable news coverage based on covert sources, the reports can directly affect issues of trust and workable personal relations. This sets many personal–cum–political challenges for the protagonists in terms of maintaining clarity of perception and judgment, and it is easy for embattled leaders faced with adverse publicity to retreat from their colleagues. Thus in 1989:

> disillusionment with [Opposition Leader John] Howard was profound inside the parliamentary party, but it was greatest inside the shadow ministry, where it was most dangerous. Howard had succumbed to paranoia, the natural malaise of leaders under threat. The paranoid leader cannot trust anyone and thereby runs the risk of alienating everyone.[21]

3   Leadership struggles are typically marked by public correctness and private criticism.

When there is leadership tension, and a contender seeking an opportunity to challenge, the resulting need to juggle the management of commonality and difference frequently becomes difficult. Public statements are typically framed to minimise disharmony, to achieve differentiation without open dissent, and to avoid personal criticism. Much of the material which feeds news coverage comes from leaks and background briefings, where the name of the source is not revealed. These allow considerable latitude. The hypocrisy to which it gives rise was exemplified by Steve Crabb, a Minister in the Victorian Labor Cain Government. As John Cain (Jnr) was increasingly under siege, and Crabb was manoeuvring to replace him, he was interviewed on the record by *Sydney Morning Herald* journalist John Lyons. Crabb told Lyons he would be interested in becoming Premier if Cain 'fell under the proverbial bus', and offered a series of other platitudes. As Lyons was leaving, Crabb yelled, 'It would be funny one day to compare what someone says on-the-record with what someone says off-the-record.'[22]

By their nature, leaks cause resentment and invite retaliation. Abbott denounced the leaks by his colleagues. In his speech the day after his defeat, he said, 'And if there's one piece of advice I can give to the media it's this: refuse to print self-serving claims that the person making them won't put his or her name to. Refuse to connive at dishonour by acting as the assassin's knife.' After the coup, his supporters were angry with his deputy, Julie Bishop, and 'his office had also blamed her for some of the Cabinet leaks that crippled the Prime Minister'.[23]

Equally, though, many others claimed that Abbott and his office had leaked against them. Former Howard Government Minister Peter Reith judged that:

> too many ministers have too many stories of problems with dealing with either Abbott directly or with his staff, or end up reading about them in the paper.

> There was far too much briefing of the media by the PM's office. The provision of information is bread and butter for any government, but leaking to the press as a tool for dealing with colleagues is playing with fire.[24]

One person Abbott's office made a permanent enemy of through leaking was Arthur Sinodinos. Sinodinos had agreed to stand down from the ministry while a NSW Independent Commission Against Corruption (ICAC) inquiry into his conduct was ongoing. Three days before Sinodinos was to announce his decision, the news was leaked to the media. A furious Sinodinos blamed Peta Credlin, Abbott's Chief of Staff, for the leak. He told colleagues he felt the Prime Minister's office was 'dancing on his grave' by briefing against him. 'There has always been gossip and innuendo in the past, but the leaking was never like this,' he told Fairfax Media. 'It has been on an industrial scale.'[25]

4 Much of the action in leadership struggles is subterranean, which provides challenges for the news media, and it is often impossible for the public to gauge the accuracy of reporting.

After leadership coups, there are often disputes about who said or did what, when, and with what motive, and it is often impossible for the public to know what to believe. At a time when there is no declared challenge it is even more difficult to know what is occurring. The reporting of leadership struggles presents particular tests and issues for the news media. At one level the clash of personalities, the elements of politics as blood sport, the fact that they often lend themselves to good TV coverage, gives the contests a newsworthiness that the media relish. However, because these internal conflicts are marked by a lack of transparency and frankness, it is often difficult to verify what has been occurring or have a sure sense of perspective.

In particular, it is hard to gauge momentum, even for those directly involved. It is an axiom of internal conflicts that there are more votes than people. Through wishful thinking, miscalculation and because people may be less than honest, it is easy for both sides to overestimate their support. Even in February 2015, when the spill motion against Tony Abbott was moved, his office was briefing journalists that no more than 30 MPs would vote for it. When the spill was defeated by 61 to 39, Abbott seemed shocked by the narrower margin.[26] During the long stalking of Gillard by Rudd, it was often charged that news accounts exaggerated Rudd's numbers in a coming challenge, but the situation was too murky for any observer to know with certainty.

The situation allows scope for competitive 'scoops', and journalists' status is tied to how well they know the back story behind public developments. But reporting private words and actions carries the risk of frequent public disavowals. It also means, though, that unsourced news reports are often more correct than the public, especially the partisans of the affected party, realise. And equally, reports that sound certain may be insubstantial, or may in fact indicate that no one is able to establish the truth of what occurred. For the journalists, there may be few costs – even sometimes rewards – even if a report is wrong. However it is unlikely that a story will be sustained for a lengthy period if there is not some basis for it.

5   The key group in leadership struggles is the party room, not the public.

In the 1960s, the legendary Labor machine politician Pat Kennelly said he could not understand why all these political science departments were springing up in universities. There was only one thing you had to do in politics, and it could be summed up in three words (although he took four): 'get the bloody numbers'. At the very least this overlooks, as Labor machine politicians in those days were prone to do, the fact that what produces a majority inside the party may not do so in the broader public, that sometimes there is a great disjunction between internal and the public evaluations of the rivals. Indeed it may even be that the factors that are likely to lead to success internally make success externally more difficult. This was the case with the influence of the Tea Party and Fox News on internal Republican Party politics in the 2012 election. To prevail internally meant that would-be candidates tied themselves to stances that were not likely to produce success in the presidential campaign.

The importance of coterie communication in party conflicts makes the media's role more difficult to discern. Sometimes seemingly minor stories with little prominence may have a major impact, perhaps signalling a change of allegiance or a breach of trust. On the other hand, what seems a great public success may not have the same impact internally. In 2015, soon after Abbott survived a spill motion, Turnbull appeared on the ABC TV forum *Q&A*, in what some described as a 'bravura performance'. But Mark Kenny thought that such appearances by the centrist Turnbull ran the risk of 'drifting too far from his own party base'.[27] Turnbull was consistently more popular with the public than Abbott, but faced determined internal opposition. Similarly, Rudd was much more popular with the public than Gillard, but among Labor MPs this was not the case for much of the period of tension between them. In both cases electoral desperation among colleagues seems to have been a central factor in bringing about successful challenges.

6   **Precipitating a leadership spill is a problematic and idiosyncratic process. Between elections there is no routine institutional moment for changing leaders, so a spill occurs only when there is a sufficient sense of crisis among the MPs, and the media are often implicated in bringing events to a climax.**

In most parties there is a meeting following a general election at which leadership positions are voted upon, but there is no further opportunity for a leadership vote. Typically such a vote only occurs between elections when accompanied by a sufficient sense of crisis. For the challenger, mounting a challenge is a hazardous process – how to translate latent discontent into active support, how to promote the struggle without producing accusations of disloyalty, how to force a showdown without alienating support are all full of uncertainty.

When a crisis is at its height, and speculation unstoppable, almost any public comment, or a refusal to comment, can feed the story. This can induce the feeling that there must be a resolution so that the party can move on. Even so, there is often much suspense over whether and how a spill will occur. *Sydney Morning Herald* journalist Peter Hartcher has a perhaps unique distinction in that he wrote stories almost two decades apart which were both instrumental in triggering a spill. In 1991, amid a growing crisis, Hawke decided to move John Kerin, the person who had replaced Keating as Treasurer. But the fact that factional chiefs Graham Richardson and Robert Ray had advised this was leaked to Hartcher. It meant that the reshuffle was seen as an admission of failure and a panic move,[28] and it then weakened rather than strengthened Hawke's position. In 2010 there had been considerable signs of party discontent with Rudd, but his deputy, Gillard, had refused to join the rebels. In 2010, Hartcher and Phillip Coorey wrote a story that Rudd's 'most trusted lieutenant', Alister Jordan, had been talking privately to MPs, and he concluded that Rudd 'does still enjoy solid support in caucus', and that Rudd 'does not necessarily trust the public assurances of his deputy, Julia Gillard, that she is not interested in the leadership'.[29] The story angered Gillard, and led to crisis meetings. The following morning she was elected unopposed to succeed Rudd.

7 **Leadership contests are not always the end of the story. In the short term the question is how much the media will focus on a post-mortem and how much on the way ahead. In the longer term, the issue is how united the party will be around the new leader.**

The immediate issue is how much – and for how long – news coverage will look backwards (at conflict, failure and conspiracy) or forwards (to the brighter future the successor is promising). Perhaps the most famous question in Australian interviewing history came in 1983 when the ABC's Richard Carleton asked Hawke, on the evening he had replaced Hayden as Labor leader, '[Do] you feel a little embarrassed tonight at the blood that's on your hands?' Hawke's snarling response did his cause little immediate good, but Malcolm Fraser had already solved the problem for him. By calling a federal election on the same day, Fraser ensured that the bulk of media coverage would be on the coming election rather than on the leadership change. The coincidence meant that Labor began with a strong sense of initiative, and Fraser seemed badly wrong-footed.

Although the degrees of public bitterness vary, two opposing narratives are most common. Allies of the deposed leader promote a narrative of falling victim to treacherous saboteurs (both Rudd and Abbott have referred to assassins); the challenger's supporters promote a narrative of the reluctant saviour, who only moved at the last minute and for the good of the party. In 2015, Turnbull felt that Abbott burnt the house down, and was the main contributor to his own downfall. In contrast, Abbott lamented 'the white-anting' he felt he had suffered. In the next few weeks, Abbott gave a series of interviews to his favoured outlets. When asked about his feelings towards Turnbull, he told 2GB's Ray Hadley, 'I might exercise the former Prime Minister's prerogative of silence' on that, and 'obviously a lot of dirty water passed under the bridge'.[30] He also said he refused to sack Treasurer Joe Hockey or his Chief of Staff, Peta Credlin, because 'when someone is absolutely focused on a particular objective, they're not going to be put off if they're thrown a few human sacrifices, as it were, and frankly it's wrong to feed this particular beast'.[31]

The longer-term question is whether there will be unity and reconciliation in the party, or continuing recriminations and destabilisation. Although the Hawke–Keating leadership challenge was full of bitterness, once Keating succeeded, the party united behind him. In 2010, the coup plotters seem to have assumed that Rudd would simply disappear once he was deposed. Instead he began the longest and most determined stalking of Gillard, finally becoming the first person to become Prime Minister again by replacing his successor.

The idiosyncrasies of the contenders and of their conflicts mean that leadership challenges are complex and contested events. The first part of this book traces some of the most important leadership challenges at federal level. The factors discussed above will be seen clearly at work in those challenges. The second part is organised thematically, using material from both federal and state parties, to explore the political and media issues.

CHAPTER 2

Rudd vs Gillard vs Rudd

Between 2007 and 2015, both major parties went through several leadership challenges. Both, for the first time, deposed a first-term Prime Minister. Both had the rare sight of a defeated leader later regaining the leadership by defeating the person who had overthrown them.

It would be easy to see a symmetry between these two pairs of coups and counter-coups, but the differences are just as great. There could hardly have been two more contrasting ascents to the leadership than those of Julia Gillard and Tony Abbott. In process, the overthrow of Opposition Leader Malcolm Turnbull in December 2009 was prolonged and publicly bloody. It was most immediately provoked by irreconcilable internal divisions over a central policy issue – the existence of and proper response to anthropogenic global warming. Abbott won the leadership by a single vote after a confused and messy set of party ballots. The defeated leader was not immediately prepared to bow to the shift in party policy under his successor, and polls indicated Abbott was the least preferred of the principal contenders. This is not usually a formula for political success. However, Abbott's strident oppositionism spooked an eminently spook-able Labor Government, and aided by that government's increasing dysfunctionality, the Liberals' electoral prospects improved.

The Gillard coup in June 2010 was swift and tidy in process, and its immediate reception was positive. Despite some weeks of low-level media rumbling, the challenge only became public the night before a party meeting, which then endorsed the change by a unanimous vote. Rudd gave a heart-wrenching farewell speech listing all that he was proud of, but Gillard, unlike Abbott, had an immediate honeymoon, receiving much favourable publicity about being the first female Prime Minister. Labor's polls jumped, and she initiated a series of fixes to what were perceived as the government's major problems.

The Gillard coup was, however, a brilliantly executed strategic stupidity. The plotters seemed to have little idea of the gravity of what they had done. They seemed to assume that once defeated, Rudd would simply disappear, and there would be no media or public interest in him. There was little recognition that when a government disposes of its own leader, it also seems to be disowning its own performance. Without giving time for Gillard to gain an air of prime ministerial authority or of governmental stability, Labor rushed to the polls, and the dumping of Rudd became a theme haunting their campaign. Gillard's became the first federal government to lose a parliamentary majority at its first attempt at re-election since Joseph Scullin's loss in 1931, in the depths of the Depression.

The assumption that Rudd would disappear once he was defeated was always wishful thinking. But no one could have anticipated his relentless, monomaniacal pursuit of revenge – it has no parallel in contemporary Australian politics. Having made history as the first Prime Minister to be forced from office after winning government from opposition, he then made history by becoming the first to regain the leadership by displacing his successor, which enabled him to lead Labor into its sweeping 2013 defeat by Abbott.

After the 2013 election, party leaderships were stable for a time. During the long period of intense partisan conflict leading up to his 2013 election victory, Abbott's leadership had not been challenged in the Liberal Party, and the victory had solidified his position. In late January 2015, when the government had been trailing in the

polls for more than a year, in quick succession Abbott awarded one
of his new Australian knighthoods to Prince Philip and the Queensland Liberal National Party Government went from a record majority to a shock defeat in one term. Backbench dissatisfaction with
Abbott gathered to the point where he was subjected to a leadership
spill. With no other candidate declared, Abbott comfortably defeated
'the empty chair'. Six months later, Turnbull moved decisively; the
challenge became public and was consummated within one day.

Rudd in freefall

In November 2009, Kevin Rudd seemed to have the Australian
political world at his feet; seven months later his colleagues forced
him out in an unprecedented coup. It is probably the most dramatic
fall from grace in Australian politics.

Rudd was in such a strong position because of both his political and his policy achievements. His campaign to win the 2007 election was brilliantly mounted, and his leadership was a key factor
in Labor's triumph. The smashing victory demoralised the Liberals.
Rudd's personal approval ratings, which had been high ever since
he took over as Opposition Leader in December 2006, continued
at high levels during Labor's first two years of office. For the whole
of 2008, Labor's 2PP lead was 54–46 or better in every Newspoll.[1]
The only other Prime Minister whose first-term polling has neared
Rudd's stratospheric levels was Bob Hawke.

Rudd helped position Australia internationally as a leader on
climate change. Immediately after his election, he went to the UN
Climate Change Conference in Bali, where he received a standing
ovation. He also pressed the issue at APEC. His prominence was recognised when he was one of several world leaders invited to be a
'Friend of the Chair', to help guide proceedings, at the Copenhagen Summit in December 2010.[2] His most important diplomatic
achievement was to promote the G20 as an important body, a vehicle

well suited to Australia's middle power status. But there were also downsides. Rudd, the first senior Australian politician to be fluent in Mandarin, handled relations with China poorly, needlessly alienating the regime for no gain, and making a grandiose, hollow proposal for an Asia–Pacific Community, which attracted no support.[3]

Rudd's conduct of the Apology to the Stolen Generation stands as one of the great moments in reconciliation in recent Australian history. The proceedings in the Federal Parliament were televised live to the nation. Rudd's speech, which he wrote himself, was eloquent and moving; his personal conduct with the victims exemplary and sensitive.

Rudd led the government's response to the Global Financial Crisis (GFC), the most threatening economic development to face Australia in some generations. Although later Labor's critics underplayed its seriousness, it was a huge challenge, and government policy was a central reason why Australia escaped much more lightly than other developed countries. Nobel Laureate in Economic Sciences Joseph Stiglitz concluded that 'the stimulus helped avoid a recession and saved up to 200,000 jobs'.[4] He also described Labor's response as 'the best designed stimulus package' in the world.[5] The advice of Ken Henry, Head of Treasury, was 'Go early, go hard, go households.' In an atmosphere of crisis and uncertainty, Rudd, Wayne Swan as Treasurer and the government acted decisively and constructively. They gave a cash handout of $900 to poorer households, guaranteed to keep credit flowing to the major financial institutions, and initiated a strong Keynesian program of public works to boost employment.

Even in late 2009, however, there were several looming vulnerabilities and problems. Rudd's strength was more brittle than was publicly apparent.[6] Though still largely invisible to the public, Rudd's interpersonal relations and working methods had already antagonised many of his colleagues. These occasionally came into public view, such as in an article by John Lyons on 'Captain Chaos',[7] and stories about him losing his temper with a flight attendant.

Until December 2009, there were individual casualties of Rudd's bad temper and chaotic working habits, but he still had good relations with key party members. His control freakery did produce dysfunctions in government, but probably not more so than in most governments.

December 2009 was the turning point for two reasons. First, Abbott replaced Turnbull, and while Turnbull was the much more intellectually formidable, Rudd had his measure. He found Abbott's sweeping style much more unbalancing. More important, however, was the failure of the Copenhagen Summit on climate change.

The Copenhagen Summit was the follow-up to the Kyoto convention, whose Protocol only applied to the economically affluent countries, recognising that their long industrial history meant they had contributed far more greenhouse gases to the planet. The task at Copenhagen was to reach an agreement that embraced all countries. This was always unlikely to succeed, as Rudd recognised,[8] even though concerned people around the world had an increasing sense of urgency about the issue. It was made even more unlikely by a spectacular and massive 'leak' of emails from the Climate Change Centre at the University of East Anglia. This was grist for the conspiracy theorists' mill, even though eventually it was clear, as several inquiries established, that nothing in the emails suggested that the science was compromised or in question.[9]

As a 'Friend of the Chair', Rudd poured himself energetically into the summit, and by all accounts played a very constructive role. He came back to Australia exhausted and dispirited; probably also feeling that the relative failure of the summit weakened his hand on the issue domestically. Even more basically, in Barrie Cassidy's words, 'those close to him sensed he had lost his mojo, and something quite dramatic was needed to get it back'.[10]

In the week before Christmas 2009 key government strategists met to discuss an early election. In Paul Kelly's account – others, such as Sarah Ferguson,[11] are not so unequivocal – without exception, all those present, including Gillard, Swan, John Faulkner, Mark Arbib and Karl Bitar, urged Rudd to call an early election, a double dissolution based on the Senate's rejection of the Emissions Trading Scheme (ETS) legislation. Bitar's research showed that around two-thirds of voters believed that the Liberals were not ready for power, and also that they were disunited.[12] Some present thought Rudd intended to call the election. Bitar booked advertising space. But nothing happened.

Liberal Federal Director Brian Loughnane was dreading an early election: 'My strong belief is that if an election had been held in early 2010 there would have been a further swing to Labor.'[13] He thought Labor blew its big chance. The Liberals had no agreed position on climate change. Turnbull observed of his fateful meeting with Nick Minchin and Abbott the previous November, 'When I asked them what our alternative policy was going to be they had no idea.'[14] The wounds inside the Liberal Party were still raw and the doubts about Abbott were still strong. But, argues Kelly, 'Rudd backed off – and *made* Abbott.'[15] A Labor election victory in February or March would have seen the Liberals divided and demoralised.

As important as Rudd's not calling the election was, his failure to communicate with the others was equally vital. Whatever Rudd's thoughts, he largely cut himself off from his Labor colleagues. Arbib had been an early supporter of Rudd, and played an important role in helping him win the leadership, but 'when the early election option came and went without a word, Rudd lost Arbib forever'.[16] (As Rudd's crisis developed, four meetings between the two were arranged, but all were cancelled.[17]) Faulkner also thought it was a crucial missed opportunity.[18] According to Rudd, one voice against an early election based on the emissions trading legislation was Gillard. She agrees that in January she told him that, but gives as her reason that she thought Rudd himself was not in a fit state to fight an election.[19] Kelly judged that Rudd was tactically adrift and had no re-election strategy: 'the uncertainty was corrosive, and from early 2010 Rudd's Government went into a trajectory of rapid decline'.[20]

Rudd's increasing isolation was accompanied by more faltering performances, both in private and in public. For example, he appeared on the first *Q&A* program of the year and 'performed terribly. He was cranky and condescending.'[21] At the same time, various problems were catching up with the government. There were increasing calls for action on asylum seekers. The government's gimmicky Grocery Watch program finally collapsed in February.[22] Both fair and unfair criticisms focused on the government's two major 'shovel-ready' programs, undertaken as part of the economic stimulus in 2008 – the program for building school halls,[23] and home insulation (pink batts).[24]

Rudd's energy through the early months of 2010 was devoted overwhelmingly to health and hospitals. He wanted a full federal takeover of hospitals, which no other important player in the government thought was feasible. There were severe internal conflicts, climaxing, according to Swan, at a meeting on 14 February, with Rudd losing his temper with Health Minister Nicola Roxon, Gillard, Swan and Treasury officers. But in the end Rudd had to bow to their combined view.[25] Arguably, Rudd then to some extent mishandled relations with the state Premiers. But politically, the bottom line was that health was an electoral winner for the government. Rudd promoted the package with what Cassidy called 'the longest virtually continuous road trip that any Prime Minister has ever undertaken'.[26] He skewered Abbott in a debate on health at the National Press Club; admittedly, Rudd, with many new positive announcements to make, was at an advantage. In Hartcher's judgment, 'Rudd was all smiles and softly spoken solutions; Abbott was all aggro accusations.'[27]

Rudd's obsessive concern with health policy meant there was little room for other issues, and perhaps this preoccupation was a way of avoiding what he now saw as the less palatable and increasingly uncertain politics of climate change. As Philip Chubb, the author of the best book on the subject, observed, 'Rudd began the year 2008 as the head of a national movement for change.'[28] It had been an important ingredient in Labor's 2007 victory, as Howard himself bemoaned.[29] Rudd's rhetoric was unequivocal. Tackling climate change was the 'great moral challenge of our generation'; we had to 'forge a national consensus' and examine how 'we best reorganised as a nation to deal with this'. Soon after the election he told the Parliament that 'the costs of inaction on climate change are much greater than the costs of action', and that Australia must 'seize the opportunity now to become a leader globally'.

Yet what followed was what Professor Ross Garnaut, a leading public intellectual on the issue, called 'one of the worst examples of policy making we have seen on a major issue in Australia … the way it's broken down is extraordinary'.[30] When Abbott was overthrown as Prime Minister in September 2015, despite all the spilling of political blood and all the raging controversies, climate change policy was little advanced from where it had been before the 2007 election. Labor's failure to secure enduring reform on an issue where its initial mandate was so strong is an indicator of some of the main pathologies of the Rudd Government's functioning.

After a strong start, Labor gradually lost momentum. In Chubb's words, 'Through 2009 Rudd scarcely said a word on the subject. He seemed uninterested.'[31] While Rudd and Climate Change Minister Penny Wong were doing little to bring the public with them, the critics were increasingly vocal. Climate change denialists had prominent platforms in News Corp newspapers and on commercial talk radio. And there were increasing criticisms of the alleged costs of the policy. Barnaby Joyce called it 'a new tax on ironing, a new tax on watching television, a new tax on vacuuming'. The Sunday roast would cost up to $100, he claimed. The Australian Industry Group claimed that up to one million Australian jobs were at risk. Industry groups were consistently demanding greater compensation.[32]

At this time, the Greens, environmental groups and some economists were stronger protectors of the public purse than the major parties. The Australian Conservation Foundation walked away from an agreement with the government in mid–2009 when the electricity generators' compensation was more than doubled.[33] These groups argued that the government's plans were rewarding the largest polluters, and lacked any rationale. So from the public's point of view, there were very large and unexplained figures of compensation floating around, there were increasingly strident scare campaigns, the government was being criticised from both sides, and it was itself a far from powerful advocate for its own reforms.

Post-Copenhagen, there was no longer a strong sense of international momentum, and the domestic voices of denial had become stronger. But there were raw conflicts in the opposition parties on the issue, and still probably majority support for action. Instead of acting, though, Rudd entered a prolonged period of drift. Perhaps his paralysis was reinforced by his knowledge that polls on the issue were declining.[34]

After four months, the looming budget deadline finally forced a decision. The Gang of Four (Rudd, Gillard, Swan and Lindsay Tanner) decided in early April to defer any action on an ETS. They did not immediately announce the decision, though, and it leaked out in an exclusive story by Lenore Taylor in the *Sydney Morning Herald*, which Rudd then off-handedly confirmed at a press conference.

'The shock inside and outside the government was profound,' Taylor wrote. Environment Minister Peter Garrett learned about it by reading the paper.[35] One ministerial adviser said, 'People were shattered, [and many are] still scarred to this day.' The Parliamentary Secretary for Climate Change in the Gillard Government, Mark Dreyfus, 'thought where the hell is the government going? When you've nearly got there, not to press on with things, is, to me, unforgivable.'[36] This was a critical turning point in the fate of the Labor Government, and in Rudd's demise as leader.

In early May – roughly a week after the ETS public surrender and a week before the federal budget – the government finally released the Henry Review into taxation reform, undertaken by the head of Treasury, Ken Henry. The government had been sitting on the report since late 2009. Of the Report's 138 recommendations, the government was to act immediately on just three. The most important of these was the introduction of the Resource Super Profits Tax, a tax on the very large profits being made by the major companies during the mining boom. Instead of using the Review to open up public debate on tax reform, the government engaged in a very controlled exercise: instead of introducing the mining tax as a single measure, it did so in the shadow of the imminent budget, with an election to follow within months.

Swan argues that the mining industry had been consulted,[37] but Kelly mounts a compelling case that they were taken by surprise and affronted by some of the content.[38] Certainly their reaction was instant and extreme. The industry mounted a furious advertising blitz.[39] This provoked the government to break Rudd's firm commitment before the 2007 election that in contrast to the Howard Government, it would not use public funds for partisan political advertising.[40] Although there was some negotiation going on privately, the public spectacle was of acute conflict. Rudd's comments were not conciliatory. He told a mining industry forum, for example, that 'Guys, we've got long memories.'[41] In early May leading journalist Laura Tingle wrote, 'the Government [was] stuck between a flailing Kevin Rudd' and a 'sense of pending oblivion'.[42] For Cassidy, the mining tax 'was the initative that brought all of the Labor Party's frustrations with Kevin Rudd to a head ... lack of judgment, his inability to finesse a solution, and his propensity to ignore or not even understand the damage that a runaway issue can cause in the electorate'.[43]

While Rudd was riding high in the polls, and government seemed to be working, the internal grievances had been kept in check. But now the polls dropped alarmingly. After the abandoning of the ETS, Labor's primary vote in the next Newspoll crashed from 43 per cent to 35 per cent, one of the sharpest falls ever, and a result soon confirmed by other polls. Indeed Nielsen suddenly had the ALP trailing 47–53 (2PP). In addition, 'for the first time since his election two and a half years before, more people disapproved of Kevin Rudd than approved of him'. In this period the polls were an obsessive focus for the media. In particular, *The Australian* carried 161 stories mentioning Newspoll in the three months preceding Rudd's fall, almost two a day, which is probably unprecedented for a non-election period.[44] Then, on 19 June, there was a NSW state by-election in the seat of Penrith, and it produced a staggering 25 per cent swing against Labor. Although the decaying NSW Labor Government was probably the main contributor to this record swing, Swan feels that the shock of this result hardened the determination of NSW MPs to dispose of Rudd.[45]

In Gillard's final meeting with Rudd on 23 June, telling him that she was going to challenge, she used as her reason her view that Rudd could not win an election.[46] At that time, the most recent Newspoll had Labor back in the lead 52–48 (2PP). The electoral difficulties, although far from insurmountable, contributed to apprehension among MPs, especially as they felt captive to Rudd's increasingly problematic political judgment. These tensions were the catalyst for releasing the internal discontent with Rudd's erratic and dysfunctional working habits and his lack of respect for MPs.

Treasurer Swan, who began as a friend and ally, and finished as one of Rudd's most vehement critics, thought that 'the longer we governed, the more Kevin's idiosyncratic style infected the way officials and staff interacted with him'. The way Rudd treated Cabinet and Caucus:

> meant that his prime ministership was not built to last …
> During late 2009 and early 2010 the agenda of unresolved
> matters was getting bigger, not smaller, alarming ministers and
> political advisers when we should have already begun clearing
> the decks for an election year.[47]

The head of Swan's office, Chris Barrett, wrote a 12-page analysis of Rudd's operational approach, with the basic conclusion that 'his failure on proper process led to poor policy'.[48] There were mounting complaints about policy gridlock; his office was called the black hole.[49] The emphasis on centralisation stemmed partly from Rudd's fear of leaks and wish to control; he also failed to be decisive in matters that were not top of his agenda.

Often, colleagues charged, he would keep senior groups of people waiting hours, then come in late and grumpy and treat them like schoolchildren.[50] Some insiders have charged that his 'need to be the smartest guy in the room' led to his being intolerant of debate or dispute and not listening properly to expert advice.[51] And most basically, what some have called his Jekyll and Hyde character[52] meant, according to the former head of his private office, David Epstein, that Rudd:

> treated many people badly. As prime minister he would shout at people and sometimes humiliate them. I heard him say to people, 'you'll have no future while I'm here'. He would make promises to individuals and then break them.[53]

For Swan, 'Kevin's treatment of people was extraordinarily vindictive and juvenile. And it was frequently on display.'[54]

The whispering discontent in the ranks was becoming more widespread and intense. But it seemed his survival was guaranteed, as there was no credible challenger. His deputy, Gillard, popular with both Caucus and the public, was effusive in her professions of loyalty, proclaiming, for example, that there was more chance she would replace footballer Barry Hall in her AFL team, the Bulldogs, than that she would challenge Rudd.

Then, on 23 June, Hartcher and Coorey wrote in the *Sydney Morning Herald* that Rudd's Chief of Staff, Alister Jordan, had been taking soundings in Caucus about Gillard's intentions. Angered by having her loyalty questioned, and seeing this as yet another sign of dysfunctionality, Gillard decided to confront Rudd. There are directly contradictory theories over how Hartcher got the story. Arbib thought that Rudd or his office had leaked it because Rudd was close to Hartcher;[55] the Prime Minister's office believed that

Arbib had leaked it in order to increase leadership tensions.[56]

Gillard took various soundings that day without committing herself to a challenge. Many were urging her on. The ABC TV news reported at 7pm that night that Gillard was then meeting with Rudd over the leadership. In a clip much played since, Labor MP Daryl Melham said the ABC had lost all credibility, when of course their story proved correct – the truth was that he, like most MPs, was still in the dark.

At Rudd's meeting with Gillard, with Faulkner also present, Rudd asked for more time to improve his performance. In Rudd's version, Gillard agreed, and they parted on that basis. However, she then rang Stephen Conroy and others, and they told her events had moved too far not to proceed, that the media had the story, and that there was no way anyone could credibly conceal how close they had come to a challenge. Gillard then returned to Rudd and said the challenge would proceed.

Rudd has since expressed indignation that Gillard reversed herself. However, this version undermines his picture of her as a determined assassin. It shows that Gillard was wavering until the last, reluctant to sever their four-year partnership. There has since been conjecture about when Gillard decided to challenge, and no doubt leadership had crossed her mind. It is clear that several people wanted her to, that there had been coded conversations, but if the Rudd version of their fateful meeting is true, it also reinforces the view that she was the last recruit. Until the end, the plotters were nervous that she would not stand.

When Gillard returned to her office after the meeting with Rudd, said Kelly, 'it was flooded with caucus members. It had become a spontaneous uprising. People were feral to remove Rudd.'[57] For Cassidy, 'never before have the numbers tumbled so quickly at the whiff of a leadership challenge. That's because Rudd himself drove them. His own behaviour had caused deep-seated resentment to take root.'[58]

Later that evening Rudd called a special Caucus meeting for

the next morning to resolve the issue. At first he said he would stand, but it became apparent that support for him had all but disappeared, and he withdrew, so Gillard was unanimously elected. Swan thinks that if Rudd had stood, he might have got 20 votes out of a possible 114.[59] This reflects the widespread wish for a new start, but also the momentum that had built up, and how once an outcome is clear, many MPs want the result to be decisive – and to be on the winning side.

Gillard's public justification for her action was that a good government had lost its way. Rudd gave a tearful farewell speech, enumerating all that his government had done that made him proud. He also sat through Gillard's first Parliamentary performance, hearing Abbott say it should have been the Australian people, and not a midnight knock on the door, that ended his prime ministership. As strong as the theme of sympathy for Rudd was in media coverage, there was also a honeymoon for Gillard, the first female Australian Prime Minister.

Through all of this, there had been too little thinking through either of Rudd's future or of the impact of the sudden change on public opinion. As Swan observed, explaining this speedy coup, seemingly coming out of nowhere, to 'a bewildered public would be a monumental challenge'.[60] At least Swan saw it as a problem. Cassidy quotes MP Bernie Ripoll as telling his colleagues, 'Julia has much better numbers than Kevin', as if such figures are set in stone. Another said, 'within a few months, Julia will be PM and it will seem that it was always so'.[61] But, as Rudd loyalist Bruce Hawker correctly observed, the clinical efficiency of the coup 'left the public reeling. They went to bed with a prime minister they elected and would wake up with one who had been foisted on them.'[62]

Although the polls had made Rudd vulnerable, the key to the challenge's success was his relations with his colleagues. He can blame the ambush, and rail against factional chiefs and assassins, but the larger point is how quickly and completely his support in the Caucus collapsed, among so many groups. It is also clear that the plotters' larger political judgments were clouded by the myopia of insiders.

Two seemingly contradictory conclusions are both valid: by June 2010, Rudd no longer deserved to be Prime Minister, and overthrowing him in this way was a huge mistake.

Gillard's quick-fix fixation

While those who sought Rudd's removal, including Gillard, had abundant and genuine grievances, they also shared some delusions about the speed and ease with which they could solve the government's problems. Their immediate motive was to remove or reduce the political targets available for the opposition to attack. Although in each case it could be argued that they were operating in a loaded and difficult political environment, on the three main issues – asylum seekers, global warming and the mining tax – the result was poor policy and/or a failure to dispose of the political problem.

Rudd's internal critics had bemoaned his lack of action in addressing the increasing electoral bite of asylum seekers arriving on Australia's coastline. Gillard immediately contradicted Rudd's embrace of a 'big Australia', with large-scale migration feeding very large population increases in the next few decades, instead saying that she believed in a 'sustainable Australia'. Both Gillard and Abbott committed to cutting the migration rate before the 2010 election.

Then, in one of the sillier stunts, Gillard and David Bradbury, Member for the western Sydney seat of Lindsay, were filmed wearing flak jackets in a patrol boat off Darwin, to dramatise their seriousness about stopping asylum seekers. ALP national secretary Karl Bitar had infamously sent Rudd an email saying that all policies should be subject to the 'Lindsay test' (see Chapter 10): how would the move be received in that marginal electorate? Gillard now seemed to be taking this literally, joining with Bradbury in a blatant gimmick to show action on border security.

Next Gillard announced a deal with East Timor where that country would become a regional processing centre.[63] One DFAT official who worked on the East Timor desk said that the first he knew of the policy was when he saw Gillard's lips move.[64] Almost immediately, the East Timorese Parliament rejected the idea, and Gillard's rushed deal, born of a political – not a policy – urgency, collapsed. The issue of asylum seekers remained a political headache throughout her prime ministership.

Rudd's paralysis on climate change, from the Copenhagen Summit onwards, climaxed in April with his indefinite deferral of an ETS, a decision Gillard supported. From then until the election Gillard was running scared on the issue. Labor entered the August 2010 election campaign without a clear climate change policy. Gillard insisted on community consensus as a precondition for action. Environmental groups were frustrated, and saw this as a lack of leadership. On the day of her official campaign launch, she said, 'There will be no carbon tax under the government I lead.' The centrepiece of her policy was to be a 150-person citizens' assembly that would advise the government. As Chubb notes, 'Gillard was ridiculed, her plan dismissed as leaving the government's climate change policy to a "giant focus group".'[65]

The fear of offering targets to the Liberals and News Corp was clear in an interview Gillard gave to Annabel Crabb a year after the 2010 election, explaining why she had made the promise again a day before the poll:

> Because I knew exactly what they were going to do with it. I
> mean, last campaign, every journalist in the country somehow
> persuaded themselves we were going to canter it in … All the
> scrutiny was on us. *The Australian* was feral. The [*Daily*] *Telegraph*
> was feral … I knew exactly what they were going to do with
> it if I left the door open to a carbon tax. It would have been a
> free gift for Abbott. And so I used the strongest form of words I
> could to rule out a carbon tax.[66]

The fierce opposition of the mining companies had alarmed many Caucus members. Gillard took immediate action. First she cancelled the government's advertising campaign, and the mining lobby reciprocated by dropping its advertising against the tax. In Kelly's summation, 'the government was in a weak position: Gillard needed a revised tax, she needed it fast, and she needed an agreement … that would constitute political peace'. Labor had gone from excluding the industry to making it a co-author of the tax.[67]

The scale of the surrender was initially hidden. The first announcement was that the compromise would mean that revenue would be reduced from $12 billion to $10.5 billion over four years.[68] This was steadily revised downwards until in May 2013 it was announced that in that financial year it would raise only $200 million.[69] Rarely in the history of government taxation has so much political capital been spent to earn so little revenue.

All these actions were symptomatic of a wider attitude. Afterwards political analyst Lindy Edwards commented that Labor 'has run from every fight. Rather than stand its ground, it has backed down, giving the impression Abbott's accusations were true.'[70]

The final quick fix was to rush to an election. This was a response to the feeling that without an election, without a personal mandate as Prime Minister, Gillard lacked legitimacy. This sense of urgency – and especially the idea that a short time interval was an advantage – was very much a Canberra mentality. It overlooked the fact that most of the country expected governments to govern, and that length of time in a role makes a Prime Minister look more prime ministerial. Unfortunately for Gillard and Labor, the election did not go according to plan.

The awfulness of the 2010 election

Even among the general mediocrity and sterility of Australian election campaigns, 2010 stands out as perhaps the most negative and uninspiring. Veteran journalist George Megalogenis thinks that 'elections are a form of peer-group pressure, in which leaders are bullied into being as small-minded as the public at its worst'.[71] The two major parties, both engaged in the zero-sum competition to form the next government, share key assumptions about campaigning strategy. Both are determined to reach the least attentive, swinging voters. So both parties think that endless repetition of simple themes is necessary, and both are determined to avoid all diversions and stay 'on message'. Even in the first week of the campaign, according to Cassidy, journalists were sick of Gillard's constant repetitions. One former adviser admired Abbott's and Gillard's capacity to stay focused, but asked, 'Why do they have to sound like they are talking to stroke victims?'[72] Both parties think that fear trumps hope, so there is constant attention to what a disaster the other side would be, even while they claim to be positive. This is the guiding logic in all campaigns, but even so, in 2010, for Megalogenis, 'Julia Gillard and Tony Abbott broke the democratic contract with a campaign so awful it begged a collective rebuke.'[73]

The awfulness of the election campaign stemmed directly from the leadership instability which had preceded it. Never, in recent decades at least, had a federal election been fought by two leaders whose combined tenure was less than one year. Gillard called the election for 21 August; Rudd had been deposed on 24 June, while Abbott had become leader the previous December. Gillard was only the third Prime Minister to face the electorate after forcibly deposing her predecessor. But she had been Prime Minister for less than three months, compared with the other two: 16 months for Paul Keating and 21 months for Billy McMahon. Abbott was the first new federal Opposition Leader to contest an election after there had been two leadership coups in the party in the one electoral cycle.

A government which has deposed its own leader finds it almost impossible to run on its record, and so it had to rely unusually strongly on highlighting the perils of the opposition and its leader.

Equally, an opposition whose own unity was fragile, particularly on key policies, and that was driven by the energetic oppositional style of its leader, concentrated on the weaknesses of the government. Abbott's stump speech was 15 words: 'End the waste, pay back the debt, stop the new taxes and stop the boats.'

The first week of the election campaign went as well as Labor could have hoped. The first Newspoll had Labor ahead 55–45 (2PP), but the next one cut it to 52–48. Gillard's net satisfaction rating was +29 per cent, in contrast to Rudd's last one, –19 per cent.[74] An initial focus was on whether or not the Liberals would revive the Howard Government's WorkChoices policies, but Abbott pronounced it 'dead, buried and cremated'.[75]

But from the middle of the second week, the campaign became dominated by Rudd. It began with probably the most dramatic leak in any Australian election, which transformed the campaign. Laurie Oakes, on Channel Nine, and then Hartcher in the *Sydney Morning Herald*, two of the journalists closest to Rudd, reported that in Cabinet Gillard had opposed both an increase in the pension rate and a paid parental leave scheme.[76] The drama surrounding the leak's source was as important as its content. The story opened the anti-Gillard floodgates. The *Daily Telegraph* followed up with a front page of a digitally enhanced impression of an old Julia Gillard with wrinkles and grey hair, and a story contrasting her superannuation of $2000 a week with the pension rises. Oakes described her methods as 'silly, shifty, slimy and slippery'.[77] Carney reported, 'The Age/Nielsen poll recorded a six point drop in the ALP's two party preferred vote to 48%.'[78] And Labor was fearful that the leaks would keep coming.[79] By contrast, Abbott's media conferences had become calm affairs.[80]

Desperately seeking to regain momentum, Gillard proclaimed that she was taking control, and that from then on, people would see the 'real Julia', a phrase that immediately invited the question whether it was a fake Julia the public had seen so far.

Rudd maintained his prominence in the news, by having

to go into hospital for a gall bladder operation. Putting to one side the sabotage of the leaks (which Rudd denies, but which Gillard,[81] Swan[82] and many others believe came from him), the public and media interest in Rudd was undeniable. A Nielsen poll found that more than two-thirds of voters disapproved of the way Rudd had been dumped.[83] After leaving hospital, Rudd gave an interview to Phillip Adams, insisting he could not just stand by and let Abbott slide into office, seemingly offering help while of course also implying that Gillard needed it. Eventually Gillard and Rudd bowed to the pressure and staged a meeting for the TV cameras. It was perhaps the most excruciating body language ever seen in an election campaign, as Rudd refused eye contact, looked sour and barely spoke. Both looked hugely uncomfortable.

Katharine Murphy, of *The Age*, thought that Abbott's plan of attack was to make you loathe Labor more than you feared him.[84] When the campaign moved to positive proposals such as Labor's plan for an NBN, Abbott found it more difficult. In a disastrous interview with Kerry O'Brien on the *7.30 Report*, his only comment on the NBN was to repeat that he was not a tech-head.[85] Labor had edged ahead, but Abbott finished the last week full of running, while an exhausted and exasperated Gillard became scratchier in interviews.[86]

The election result was a disaster for Labor. Expecting a comfortable victory against the 'unelectable' Abbott, they lost their parliamentary majority. As usual, explaining the result was a politically loaded exercise. Gillard supporters tended to place central emphasis on how damaging the leaks were, 'the greatest act of political bastardry in a generation';[87] Rudd supporters focused on Gillard's inferior campaigning and the disruption of the coup. Gillard rejected the idea that she should have waited until October.[88]

Would Rudd have done better at the 2010 election than Gillard? The answer is almost certainly yes. Even though by that time Rudd had accumulated some electoral liabilities – focus groups increasingly said he was arrogant and weak,[89] and the Liberals were planning aggressive advertisements against him personally[90] – he retained key advantages. First, he would not have faced the 'Rudd distraction', or the leaks which so dominated the second and third weeks. In addition, it is likely that among two key constituencies – Queensland voters and Asian Australian voters – Rudd would have had support; this was lost with his ousting. Journalist Margot Saville, studying the electorate of Bennelong, found that 'the local Asian voters had felt a strong link with the Mandarin-speaking former diplomat who has a Chinese-born son-in-law. Local leaders also told me they felt that the manner of his removal was disrespectful to the office of PM.'[91] And Rudd was the first Queensland Prime Minister since Arthur Fadden's brief reign in 1941.

Just as importantly, Labor's campaign was unduly negative for a first-term government seeking re-election; it concentrated over-whelmingly on the threat of an Abbott Government. Whatever the effect of this in 2010, it is likely that it made it a less potent tactic by 2013. With Rudd, the campaign would have focused far more on areas of strength for Labor, namely its record in the GFC and its health policy. In both these areas Rudd would have been likely to out-debate Abbott. For post-coup Labor, these were 'Kevin's issues', but they were also Labor's best issues.

The pincer attack on Gillard

From June to August 2010 – with the crucial exception of the leaks – Gillard was the principal author of her political misfortunes. She had agreed to the coup – the action which forever haunted her prime ministership; she had indulged and shared her backers' quick-fix mentality, including the rush to the polls. While her election campaigning had many strengths, it also had many weaknesses, from the 'real' Julia to the people's forum on climate change.

After her failure to win a majority of seats in the 2010 election, Gillard was always going to be in an embattled position, both against the Abbott opposition and against the Rudd forces in her own party. It might be an exaggeration to say that her fate was already sealed, but the odds against her ultimate success were very high. Ironically, from this time on, her political performance improved dramatically. Her post-election negotiations were far superior to Abbott's, and it is unlikely that either Rudd or Abbott could have navigated through a hung parliament to produce such a strong legislative performance.

The usual critique of hung parliaments is that they give too much power to the minority groups that hold the balance of power. But in the 43rd Australian Parliament, the independents in the House of Representatives all acted properly and honestly. Instead, the precarious balance of numbers brought out the worst in the two major parties. More than in most parliaments, both sides were on a permanent war footing. There was never a period of relative normalcy. One crisis simply fed into the next.

The loss of a single MP on either side could either consolidate the government's position or force an election. This was most spectacularly manifested in two scandals, both involving allegations of sexual misconduct and financial misappropriation. Labor backbencher Craig Thomson was alleged to have misused his union credit card, including paying for services at a brothel. In April 2012 the Labor Party suspended him,[92] but in other circumstances they would probably have acted more decisively and earlier. In order to shore up their numbers, Labor recruited Liberal backbencher Peter Slipper to become Speaker. Hailed as a master stroke at the time, it led to severe problems, when a member of Slipper's staff, James Ashby, alleged that Slipper had engaged in sexual harassment and misused parliamentary travel entitlements. The Liberals attacked him with the special relish reserved for defectors. The heightened political temperature also infected all policy debates, most importantly on climate change.

The two New England independents, Tony Windsor and Rob Oakeshott, favoured Labor because of that party's commitment to the NBN, to expanding educational opportunities in the regions, and to action on climate change (and presumably such factors were part of the reason their electorates had preferred them to their Coalition opponents). Their final decision was probably also influenced by Treasury's post-election disclosure of a huge $11 billion hole in the Liberals' budget plans.[93] The other two cross-benchers keeping Labor in government – Greens MP Adam Bandt and Tasmanian independent Andrew Wilkie – also wanted action on global warming. So Gillard had little choice but to pursue the issue.

In September 2010 she announced plans for a multi-party committee to build consensus on tackling climate change. The Coalition refused to join. In February 2011, Gillard and the Greens announced agreement on a carbon pricing scheme. Gillard agreed to call it a carbon 'tax' (rather than an ETS with an initial fixed price, for example), and this haunted her for the rest of her government. In July 2011 a legislative package was announced, and in November, the *Clean Energy Futures Act* passed both houses of Parliament,[94] with the carbon tax to apply from 1 July 2012. Gillard was hopeful that once the tax was a 'lived experience', combined with the compensation packages, the scare campaigns would be seen as groundless. Indeed, as forecast, it added just 0.7% to the CPI.[95]

Each step in this sequence was greeted by ferocious attacks by the opposition. In February 2011, Abbott said Gillard's move was 'an utter betrayal of the Australian people' and predicted a people's revolt. Apart from the alleged costs of the policy, Abbott zeroed in on the issue of trust. This was reinforced by shock jock Alan Jones in his confrontation with the Prime Minister: 'people are saying your name is not Julia, but Ju-Liar'. In March Abbott spoke to a No Carbon Tax rally outside Parliament, with posters proclaiming 'Bob Brown's bitch' and 'Ditch the Witch' around him.[96] (Gillard thought this should have been a career-ending move by Abbott,[97] but it did him only minor damage.) In November 2011, Abbott denounced the scenes of ALP MPs rejoicing – 'they celebrated their betrayal with a kiss' – and then vowed to repeal the tax: 'this is a pledge in blood'. Meanwhile, demonstrators in the public gallery chanted 'no mandate' and 'democracy is dead'.[98] Such was the sustained ferocity that a mid-March 2012 meeting of Ministers decided that to continue talking about climate change was playing into Abbott's hands, so they agreed to stop.[99]

The other issue that had not been resolved by Gillard's attempted quick fix before the 2010 election was asylum seekers. In May 2011 (officially signed in July) Minister for Immigration Chris Bowen proposed a new approach, tagged as 'the Malaysia solution'. The government would fly people who arrived without authorisation by boat in Australia to Malaysia for processing. Whatever the result, they would never be accepted for refugee resettlement in Australia. Advocates said it would destroy the people smugglers' business model. In return, Australia would accept 4000 refugees from Malaysia and increase its intake of refugees from 13,750 to 20,000, and provide some financial support to Malaysia. Thus it had both humanitarian and deterrent elements. The Greens and some human rights advocates criticised it as not meeting Australia's obligations as a signatory to the Refugee Convention. After losing a High Court test case, the government needed new legislation to pass the Parliament, but the opposition and the Greens combined to defeat it.

The Liberals expressed outright opposition, ostensibly on the basis of concerns about asylum seekers' human rights and worries about how they would be treated in Malaysia. At the time they were advocating that asylum seekers be sent to Nauru for processing. According to Abbott, 'Malaysia is a proven failure. Nauru is a proven success.' The opposition's central motivation was almost certainly electoral. A cable from the US embassy in Canberra, revealed by WikiLeaks, cited one unnamed 'key Liberal Party strategist' as saying that the issue of asylum seekers was 'fantastic' for the Coalition and 'the more boats that come the better'.[100] The electoral calculation was correct. The issue continued to be a running sore for Labor.[101]

While the Abbott Opposition was as negative and hyperbolic as any party in Australia's recent history, Gillard faced an added dimension because of her gender. Most infamously, Senator Bill Heffernan described the childless Gillard as someone who had chosen to remain 'barren'.[102] More blatant examples occurred in situations below the threshold of what would normally become public, such as when at a Liberal Party fundraiser for Mal Brough there was a sexist menu, and several dishes clearly referred to Gillard. Many of the worst abuses were on social media, on Facebook or YouTube, or using Photoshop. Cartoonist Larry Pickering regularly did obscene drawings of the Prime Minister.[103] It was also strongest on the fringes of mainstream media. Commercial talk radio, almost universally having male presenters, was notable for some of the listeners' comments, but also for the presenters themselves. Howard Sattler, Perth shock jock, asked Gillard on air if her partner was gay because he was a hairdresser.[104]

Prominent Sydney shock jock Alan Jones crossed several thresholds, first with the unprecedented aggression of his rhetoric. In July 2011 he said, 'The woman is off her tree, and quite frankly they should shove her and Bob Brown in a chaff bag and take them as far out to sea as they can and tell them to swim home.'[105] At a Liberal Party fundraising dinner for Young Liberals, he wore a chaff bag that was auctioned. This was meant to be a private meeting, but someone taped his remarks, which included the following, speaking of the recent death of Gillard's father: 'The old man recently died a few weeks ago of shame ... To think that he had a daughter who told lies every time she stood for Parliament. Every person in the caucus of the Labor Party knows that Julia Gillard is a liar.'[106] When this was leaked, the outrage led to the threat of an advertising boycott, which possibly cost radio station 2GB $1 million.[107]

It indirectly had a parliamentary follow-on. Abbott was making an attack on Gillard and the government for not making Slipper resign as Speaker. Abbott was on strong ground here with the disclosure of Slipper's offensive and sexist text messages. Later that day

Windsor and Oakeshott prevailed on the Speaker to resign. But Abbott was in full flight. This will be 'another day of shame for a government which should already have died of shame'. Gillard, in a moment of white-hot anger delivered a devastating rebuttal: 'I will not be lectured about sexism and misogyny by this man';[108] 'The government is not dying of shame, my father did not die of shame.'[109] The press gallery, focused on the Slipper controversy, missed the impact of the speech, which went viral, attracting 2.4 million hits on YouTube.

Dealing with this ferocious Opposition, widespread media hostility, and the uncertainties of a hung parliament would already be beyond the normal challenges faced by a government leader. In addition, though, Gillard was under siege internally by a challenger bent on revenge. Gillard supporters felt that whenever she 'began to make progress, Rudd destabilisation would erupt'.[110] Gillard biographer Jacqueline Kent thought that whenever the polls were rising, Rudd would give an interview that was subtly subversive; when they were going badly there would be some 'more in sorrow than in anger' public advice.[111]

Gillard had made Rudd Foreign Minister as part of the peace deal after the 2010 election, and for a time leadership tensions were submerged. As the parliamentary term progressed, though, there were unattributed stories in the press that a Rudd challenge was imminent. The context for these stories was that Labor was constantly struggling in the polls, that Rudd was far more popular than Gillard, and that a change of leader would give a polling boost to Labor. In September 2011, for example, polls suggested that if Rudd were leader, the government would get a 15 per cent boost in support; he was preferred to Gillard by a margin of 57 per cent to 24 per cent.[112] Nevertheless, most of these predictions proved to be inaccurate.[113] Sean Kelly, staffer for both Rudd and Gillard, thought that having missed the first challenge, the media were determined not to miss the next one, and so were ready to give credence to such claims. The news media have since come under criticism for relying on these anonymous sources, not revisiting stories which proved to be inaccurate, and not exposing the gap between public and private statements by Rudd and his supporters.

It took Rudd three challenges before his colleagues gave him a majority. The first two began in strange ways. On 18 February, after some weeks of swirling rumours, 'the holder of the most marginal seat in the country, Darren Cheeseman, demanded that Gillard stand down as she could not win the next election'.[114] This was given front-page treatment in the Sunday papers.[115] Then, possibly in revenge, a YouTube video titled 'Not a Happy Vegemite' got a lot of attention. It was made up of out-takes from Rudd trying to record a message in Mandarin. He kept messing it up, got frustrated, swore a lot, and was cranky. The Rudd camp blamed the Prime Minister's office for the video becoming public.[116] Then as Rudd left for the US, frontbencher Simon Crean said Rudd had to decide to either be a member of the team or get out.

According to the Rudd camp, Gillard's failure to defend him then was intolerable. According to Swan, Rudd 'was clearly seeking an opening for a leadership challenge',[117] and should have just brushed this off. Rudd resigned at an impromptu press conference – at 1am Washington time. Gillard immediately called a leadership ballot for 27 February. John McTernan, in Gillard's camp, was delighted at the way they had forced Rudd into a spill[118] – both sides believed 'that Rudd would lose',[119] – but Rudd was also a 'victim of the political hysteria partly induced by his own campaign'.[120] The result was an emphatic 71–31 victory for Gillard. Some pundits immediately said another challenge was inevitable.

The most remarkable aspect of this challenge was the vehemence of Gillard loyalists in their denunciations of Rudd. They used descriptions usually reserved for opponents from other parties. Senator Conroy said 'Kevin Rudd had contempt for the Cabinet, contempt for the caucus, contempt for the Parliament'. Nicola Roxon charged that Rudd never listened. Swan said that Rudd put self-interest ahead of the interests of the labour movement, and that his prime ministership was marked by dysfunctional decision-making. He also charged that Rudd sought to tear down the 2010 campaign, and that he 'undermines the government at every turn'.[121] Presumably the large margin and the overt criticism were meant to eliminate Rudd from ever being a threat again, but Gillard's continuing weakness in the polls meant she remained vulnerable. Rudd told the party room, 'We have been on track to suffer the worst electoral defeat in our history. And I refuse to stand idly by while the next generation of Labor leaders is wiped out.'[122]

At the end of January 2013, Gillard announced that the election would be on 14 September. Such a long-term declaration of the election date was unprecedented. She said she 'hoped for a period of "cool and reasoned" governing before the campaign proper'.[123] This was always a forlorn hope, but her prospects were made worse because the polls, which had recovered somewhat in the second half of 2012, now collapsed again. In March the *Australian Financial Review* reported that the Coalition had been ahead in all 27 Nielsen polls taken since the 2010 election.[124] The prospect of electoral oblivion concentrated Labor minds on the leadership.

Gillard had had little clear political air during the previous two years, but either because her political touch deserted her or because of the greater intensity of reactions during an election year, she now made several mis-steps that contributed to her downfall. Perhaps the most important was when Senator Conroy, who had been sitting on the reports of two inquiries into the media for more than a year, suddenly moved, with Gillard's blessing. Conroy gave Cabinet no warning of his proposals, and launched his Bill by issuing an ultimatum to Parliament that it must pass within a fortnight or he would withdraw it.[125] Conroy's method guaranteed failure, and increased resentments inside the government.

Swan was 'trying to bed down two of the biggest Labor reforms of the post-war era', the 'Gonski' education reforms and the NDIS (National Disability Insurance Scheme), and resented the 'nonsense' of the 'inevitable leadership challenge'.[126] Like the one 13 months earlier, this challenge erupted in a curious and uncontrolled way. Simon Crean, perhaps thinking that he could use his authority as a former leader to stabilise the situation and keep Rudd in check, called on Gillard to resign. This was on the day that Gillard had led a bipartisan apology to mothers and children separated by forced adoption, an apology which of course then disappeared from the news. Instead Gillard terminated Crean's tenure as a Minister. Crean apparently thought he had had the go-ahead from Rudd, but then Rudd refused to stand, and there was no ballot. Many commentators thought Rudd would win easily, as did Sportsbet. But Rudd was not sure he had the numbers, so he did not challenge, instead piously intoning, 'I believe in honouring my word.'[127]

The Rudd camp was insistent that Crean had spontaneously combusted. Hawker described 21 March as 'another disastrous day for our team. Crean did a curious press conference without proper consultation with our people.'[128] In turn Crean described Rudd as spineless. The government and Gillard looked more beleaguered than ever. This was compounded by a series of ministerial resignations by Rudd supporters:'The sight of one minister after another fronting the media to resign – Chris Bowen, Martin Ferguson, Kim Carr, Joel Fitzgibbon, Ed Husic, Janelle Saffin, Richard Marles and Simon Crean – while pledging loyalty looked like a Moscow show trial from the Cold War. It was appalling.'[129]

In early June there was again increasing activity. On 9 June, Cassidy announced, on the ABC's *Insiders*, that Gillard would not lead Labor to the election. Swan says he 'knew this was the call to arms for the third Rudd challenge'.[130] There were rumours that a petition calling on Gillard to stand down was circulating.

Eventually on Wednesday 26 June, Gillard called on a spill, and announced that the loser should move to the backbench and renounce all leadership ambitions. Rudd agreed. The vote was 57–45; Gillard had lost 26 Caucus votes since her victory in February 2012.[131] For many of the waverers, the reason was simply electoral, and they turned without enthusiasm. Indeed David Feeney called it a 'wretchedly difficult decision'. He told Kelly, 'We had to return Rudd in the interests of the party and government. That meant I had to vote against a woman I respect for a man I loathe.'[132] Then, unprecedented in leadership coups, seven Ministers stepped down because of the change – Gillard, Swan, Garrett, Conroy, Craig Emerson, Joe Ludwig and Greg Combet.[133]

Kevin Rudd's second coming

'History repeats itself, first as tragedy, then as farce', wrote Karl Marx of Louis Bonaparte's 1851 coup in France. Perhaps this is exemplified in the contrast in Rudd's election night speeches in 2007 and 2013. After his 2007 victory he gave a subdued performance; after the 2013 election defeat he was much more exuberant, as if celebrating a triumph. Presumably this was based on the view that he had lost by a much lesser margin than Gillard would have. Nevertheless the Coalition had achieved a 2PP vote of 53.5 per cent, considerably greater than the 52.7 per cent Rudd had had in 2007. The extent to which this vote was a repudiation of Labor more than an embrace of the Coalition is suggested by the fact that the Coalition received only 37.0 per cent of first preference votes in the Senate. This is probably the biggest gap ever between these two figures – in 1996, for example, Howard won 53.6 per cent of the House 2PP vote but 44 per cent of Senate first preference votes. In 2013 one in three voters gave their first preference in the Senate to someone other than the two main parties.

Rudd's return to the prime ministership brought an immediate upsurge of energy, although some of it may have confused movement for action, and quite soon there were worries about his overexposure.[134] Rudd tried to promote the image of a 'new' positive government,[135] and made several policy changes. He brought forward the transition from carbon tax to an ETS by a year. He reached agreement with the government of Papua New Guinea to send asylum seekers to Manus Island (and later reached an agreement to re-open Nauru). Now there would not only be off-shore processing, but also no prospect of the boat arrivals coming to Australia even if they were found to be refugees,[136] a harsher policy than Howard's, and one retained by Abbott. Rudd was also intent on party reform, giving party members, as well as Caucus, a role in the election of the leader.[137]

With some momentum, on 4 August, Rudd called the election for 7 September. But according to Kelly, Rudd's old defects returned. He 'became erratic, failed to sort his priorities … [and] engaged in a series of disconnected, almost bizarre initiatives'.[138] He made a thought bubble pledge to relocate naval assets away from Sydney in a couple of decades, drawing fierce criticism from Premier Barry O'Farrell for lack of consultation. He proposed a Northern Australian special economic zone, a policy plucked out of the air, without any preparatory work or consultation: it was full of problems, such as different tax rates in different parts of the country, and without proper costings. After this, Hawker, a veteran Labor campaigner who was working closely with Rudd as a consultant, complained about leaks from campaign headquarters and blamed lingering bad feelings over the challenge.[139] However, being hostage to silly policies from such a centralised operation was always likely to lead to leaks.

Perhaps the single biggest embarrassment came when Rudd, Treasurer Chris Bowen and Minister for Finance Penny Wong cited official data to claim a black hole in the Opposition's costings. In an unprecedented move, the secretaries of Treasury and Finance held a press conference repudiating Labor's claims, saying the departments had not costed actual Coalition policies.

It is very likely that Rudd lost fewer seats than Gillard would have.[140] By the time of her downfall, there was a hard core of voters with immovably negative views towards her. On Rudd's resumption of the leadership, Labor's polls had had an immediate jump, from trailing 43–57 (2PP) to around 50–50. But during the campaign, Rudd's approval/disapproval ratings went backwards, from a 46–45 rating down to 34–56.[141] And Abbott's simple theme of 'don't vote for three more years like the past six years'[142] was always going to resonate. Rudd had inherited a poisoned chalice, although he had done quite a bit of the poisoning himself. The News Corp newspapers were even more feral in their anti-Labor coverage than they had been in 2010, although it is hard to know what impact this had.[143]

To the end, evaluations of Rudd among Labor figures were divided. Some were scathing: veteran operator Graham Richardson said, 'I have been a member of the ALP for 47 years and I have not known a more hated figure.'[144] But more is at stake than judgments of individuals. The 2013 defeat saw an exodus of Labor talent from the Parliament – Rudd, Gillard, Roxon, Stephen Smith, Combet, Emerson, Garrett. Some others – Swan and Faulkner – withdrew from the front line. Even more basically, on the three occasions when Labor has won government federally in the last generation – 1972, 1983 and 2007 – there has been an upsurge of public interest in politics and a widespread hope that government would act as a force for social improvement. Any policy achievements of the Rudd–Gillard governments pale before the political carnage they inflicted on themselves.

CHAPTER 3

Turnbull vs Abbott vs Turnbull

Post-2007 Liberals – The agony of opposition

Following the defeat of the Howard Government, the Liberal leadership field was unusually open. Howard had lost his seat; Downer was intending to resign; Reith had departed at the 2004 election; and then the presumptive heir, Peter Costello, renounced his leadership ambitions. Malcolm Turnbull thought that Costello's 'abandonment of responsibility' was 'terrible'.[1] The bitterness of defeat, and for the next two years the apparently hopeless electoral position, was ripe for infighting and lack of leadership authority. Because Labor's acute Rudd–Gillard–Rudd problems so dominated Australian politics later, it is easy to forget just how messy and brutal the Liberals' internal politics were from 2007 to 2009.

It came down to a contest between Brendan Nelson, who had been a Minister since 2001, but was not one of the major figures in the Howard Government, and Malcolm Turnbull, who had been in Parliament only since 2004 and a Minister less than a year. For a time a third candidate was sounding out his prospects, but he withdrew when his cause looked hopeless: Tony Abbott put himself forward as someone with 'people skills'.[2] Apart from other reservations Liberal MPs might have felt about him, Abbott had had a very poor 2007 campaign. He had arrived late at the National Press Club for his debate with shadow Health Minister Nicola Roxon, and then in their post-debate handshake, a microphone clearly picked him up saying 'bullshit' to her. When anti-asbestos campaigner Bernie Banton, dying from mesothelioma, criticised Abbott for failing to keep an appointment outside his office, Abbott responded, 'just because a person is sick does not mean that he is necessarily pure of heart in all things'. Later he apologised.[3]

Nelson defeated Turnbull 45–42 in August. The key reason seems to have been that he was more acceptable to the conservative sections of the party; Turnbull's confronting views had cost him votes. As early as 2004, Turnbull had declared that Bush's invasion of Iraq would come to be seen as 'an unadulterated error'.[4] This was an accurate view, but because of its implicit criticism of the Howard Government, it was anathema to many in the Coalition. (Turnbull's clarity contrasts with Abbott's determined avoidance of all the key issues in his book *Battlelines*.)[5] Just before the vote, Turnbull told Fran Kelly, on Radio National, that he endorsed making an apology to the Stolen Generations,[6] something Howard had conspicuously refused to offer. Turnbull biographer Paddy Manning thought these comments 'were enough to shift six to ten votes from the hard right into the Nelson camp on the anyone-but-Turnbull principle'.[7]

Turnbull never gave Nelson anything remotely resembling loyalty, or even respect. After the vote Nelson gave an emotional speech about the honour of leading the Liberals. Straight afterwards, Turnbull burst into Nelson's office, 'startling the small group' there, and told him 'Brendan, that was terrible. It was funereal.'[8] Turnbull told him to toughen up. He continued to be free with his advice and criticism. Some weeks later, he rang his leader and said: 'Let's face it, Brendan. You're just no good at this. The best thing you could do is just step down.'[9] According to Manning, he told Nelson's Chief of Staff, Peter Hendy, that Hendy's job was to get Brendan to resign in the next few weeks because he was hopeless and would damage the Liberal brand, making it more difficult for Turnbull when he took over.[10]

Meanwhile, Nelson was floundering. He had an all-but-impossible threefold task: to move the post-Howard Liberals forward, to maintain unity, and to criticise the enormously popular Rudd Government. Journalist Nic Stuart thought 'the danger was that Nelson had begun sending out mixed messages right at the start of his leadership'.[11] This was most evident with his shifting positions on the Apology, where, said journalist Annabel Crabb, 'it sounded as though Nelson was arguing with himself, and not always winning, either'.[12]

Turnbull was the loosest of loose cannons. In March he publicly launched a comprehensive tax review without telling his leader.[13] By the May 2008 budget, Nelson had cut Turnbull out of opposition deliberations, convinced that anything he showed Turnbull would leak. The centrepiece of Nelson's budget response was a five per cent cut in petrol excise. Turnbull slammed this in an internal email as fiscally and environmentally irresponsible. No one was surprised when this email was leaked to the press soon after.

Nelson was sick of the undermining and the criticism. According to journalist Tony Wright, the final trigger was newspaper reports quoting anonymous sources suggesting that now that Costello had finally declared that he did not want the leadership, he – Nelson – 'was being given a month before he would be executed'. Wright wrote, 'Nelson presumed to detect the hand of Turnbull in these "execution" stories and decided to try to move first.'[14] He earmarked a date for a spill to resolve the leadership, and then found out that Turnbull had gone, with his wife, Lucy, to the Venice Biennale – without telling him. Although caught with little time to lobby his colleagues, Turnbull won 45–41.

Nelson was understandably bitter. Nelson was a doctor, and told Peter Hartcher he believed Turnbull had a 'narcissistic personality disorder' – 'He has no empathy.'[15] Nelson joined what Crabb calls 'the considerable ranks of Malcolm veterans who can't stand him'.[16]

From the beginning Turnbull acted as if his leadership were secure, even though if three people changed their minds he would be defeated. Not only had his victory margin been narrow, but the manner in which he had disposed of Nelson was not likely to inspire loyalty. Moreover, there was a group of conservatives who deeply distrusted him, and in particular opposed him on climate change. Even at this time, Crabb judged that the Liberal Party wore 'Malcolm Turnbull like a borrowed suit',[17] and she quoted Costello telling one backbencher, 'Turnbull will destroy the Liberal Party.'[18]

Turnbull immediately brought a force and credibility to opposition that had been lacking under Nelson, but he failed to bring unity or cohesion to the Liberals, and he made only limited progress in the polls. The overriding issue of the time was responding to the GFC. The high stakes did not inhibit Turnbull's wish to play politics. For example, the government announced a wholesale guarantee for the banks, but the opposition had announced a similar measure two nights earlier, and claimed credit for it. Treasurer Wayne Swan later learned that a Liberal Party loyalist in the Treasury, Godwin Grech, had leaked the news and allowed Turnbull to engage in some grandstanding.[19] Swan was critical of Turnbull's performance, claiming he 'was happy to say anything to get him through a media cycle, without thinking about the enduring impact of his words'.[20] Others judge Turnbull's policy criticisms more charitably,[21] but journalist Barrie Cassidy's judgment of the politics is surely correct: 'the public saw a potential catastrophe. They saw Rudd energetically trying to do something about it. And they saw Turnbull ... carping away on the sidelines.'[22]

Any progress Turnbull was making went into sharp reverse following one of the most bizarre episodes in Australian politics, which has been variously labelled 'utegate', the OzCar affair, and the 'Godwin Grech' affair. It began on 4 June 2009 with suggestions in a Senate Committee – through questions by Liberal frontbencher Eric Abetz to Treasury official Grech – that a car dealer in Queensland had got special treatment from the Labor Government because of its links to Rudd and Swan. It climaxed on 22 June when Federal Police raiding Grech's house discovered that the key piece of evidence – an email purportedly from the Prime Minister's office – was a fake, written by Grech himself. During those weeks, Rudd and Swan feared for their political careers, although, according to Swan, knowing they had done nothing wrong.[23] It reached a crescendo with articles in the *Daily Telegraph* by Steve Lewis, who had been dealing with Grech, and then with 'an extraordinary, hand-wringing performance'[24] by Grech in the Senate Committee, in which he appeared to – ever so reluctantly – accuse the government. Turnbull then declared that 'if the Prime Minister and Treasurer cannot immediately justify their actions to the Australian people, they have no choice but to resign'.[25]

The government and Treasury were frantically searching all emails, and then on Monday 22 June came the news that the key evidence was a fabrication, by Grech, a Liberal Party supporter intent on damaging the government. Those who had cooperated with him – Turnbull, Abetz and Lewis – were sorely embarrassed. Paul Kelly judged that Rudd's counter-attack was 'methodical, merciless and awesome to watch'.[26] The lasting consequences were a hardening of the Labor leadership's attitudes to Turnbull, and damage to Turnbull's public standing. Labor now led the Coalition 58–42 2PP; Turnbull's approval rating dropped 11 points;[27] and Rudd led Turnbull 65–18 as preferred Prime Minister.[28]

In addition to the large section of the party always hostile to him, now added to by his poor polling performance and the damage done to his political judgment and credibility by the Grech affair, Turnbull's leadership was further complicated by the strong personal antipathies swirling inside the opposition parties. Prominent backbencher Petro Georgiou described the party infighting as 'the worst he [had] seen since he started working as a political adviser in 1975'. He accused colleagues of 'cannibalising' one another.[29] Turnbull himself was not a calming influence. According to Manning, 'people started referring to "Good Malcolm", who was unbelievably clever and charming, and "Bad Malcolm", a thin-skinned bully with a short fuse who was occasionally frightening'.[30] Another of the Turnbull biographers, Crabb, thought 'It's not enough to say that Turnbull is prepared to play hard-ball. He prefers to play hard-ball – that's the point.'[31]

Turnbull's position was even further complicated by the presence of Costello, who had publicly renounced leadership ambitions, but about whom speculation continued. At one stage, Turnbull was 'forced to fend off suggestions the two were at loggerheads over the Fair Work Bill', as Liberals were 'abuzz with speculation about the former Treasurer's intentions'. The reports provided ammunition for the government to taunt the opposition – 'Come on down the front, Pete,' Rudd called when Costello interjected from his backbench seat.[32]

Former Costello staffer Niki Savva thought that after Turnbull won the leadership he 'sent an unequivocal message to Costello that if he wanted the job, he would have to "wade through blood"'. According to Savva's dramatic account, when Turnbull's leadership came under threat, 'he pressed the self-destruct button, seemingly determined to leave his successor nothing but rubble', and 'set about slaughtering his own troops, too. I have never seen anything like it, not even during the years of the Howard-Peacock war and the mad Joh-for-Canberra campaign. In retrospect they behaved like gentlemen.'[33]

Perhaps this explains Costello's scathing judgment of Turnbull in early October 2009 to Julie Bishop: 'nobody trusts Turnbull any more' and 'he's a wounded beast running on three legs'.[34] The immediate context was Turnbull's support for the Rudd Government's EST (Emissions Trading Scheme). 'Seventy per cent [of the party] want to vote it down but the leadership wants to vote it up,' said Costello. From this point on, the conflicts inside the Coalition escalated sharply, climaxing in Turnbull's fall. The core group of climate change deniers inside the Liberal and National Parties became ever more opposed to the ETS as it neared realisation and as its likely costs kept increasing. Others resented the way Turnbull took them for granted.

On 1 October, Turnbull told ABC Radio that he would not lead a party that was not as committed to effective action on climate change as he was. To many MPs, thought Cassidy, that was Turnbull personified: do it my way or not at all.[35] On 2 November, Turnbull was a guest on shock jock Alan Jones's radio program. Jones was berating Turnbull about the 'hoax' of global warming. Turnbull stood up to Jones, and dismissed his conspiracy theories. Listening in, 'Abbott thought Turnbull's leadership was terminal at that moment': 'Turnbull wasn't showing the necessary respect [to Jones].'[36] Abbott, now into his sixth position on climate change, according to David Marr's essay on him,[37] had gone back to the resistance camp. Then on *Four Corners*, on 9 November, several Coalition MPs voiced their opposition to an ETS. Senator Nick Minchin declared that he thought a majority of the Liberal Party rejected the view that human beings were the main cause of the planet warming.[38]

This was the build-up to the dramatic events at the end of the month. On Tuesday 24 November Ian McFarlane, who had been handling the Liberals' negotiations with the government, presented the party room with the proposed deal. He claimed that they had arm-twisted concessions from government, including $7 billion in industry assistance and a better deal for farmers. The meeting went for over six hours. The turning point was the speech by Andrew Robb. Robb had been the opposition's main negotiator until he resigned because of depression. He was on the conservative side of the party, but was generally thought to support the ETS package. Instead he made a powerful speech against it, one that shocked Turnbull and his allies. Joe Hockey described the speech as 'the worst act of treachery he had seen in twenty years in politics'.[39] At the end of the meeting, despite the evidence of widespread and deeply felt dissent, Turnbull made a 'leader's call' that support for the ETS package had passed. The meeting erupted. Many backbenchers were seething with anger: 'After so many hours of debate, and with so much feeling against the ETS deal, Turnbull's call precipitated a crisis.'[40]

By this time, many in the National Party were vociferously

against any ETS. Leader Warren Truss called it 'a job-destroying rabid dog that should be put down'.[41] Turnbull's chances of obtaining Coalition unity were nil. Inside the Liberal Party, those in opposition to the ETS were increasingly emboldened. Back-bencher Wilson Tuckey moved a spill motion, and the conservative Kevin Andrews, calling himself a climate sceptic, moved to challenge Turnbull. He lost 41–35. However, the closeness of this vote – against Andrews, a relative non-entity – spelled doom for Turnbull. Minchin and Abbott now confronted Turnbull, asking him to change his stand on the ETS, and announcing that they would not support it, meaning also that they would resign from the shadow cabinet.

A spill of the leadership positions was called for Tuesday 1 December. There were three candidates. Abbott was the champion for the staunch conservatives, opposed to an ETS. He now took the view that anthropogenic climate change was 'absolute crap', saw opposition to Rudd as the only way to maintain the unity of the Liberal Party, and could see a campaign against Labor's 'giant new tax on everything' as a rallying cry for the opposition.[42] Turnbull, the incumbent, was intellectually and politically committed to support-ing an ETS. The candidate in the middle was Joe Hockey. He was the most popular with the public. A poll published the day before the leadership ballot said 33 per cent favoured Hockey as leader, 30 per cent Turnbull, and just 19 per cent Abbott.[43] There were reports that Abbott offered to support Hockey if he opposed the ETS. Hockey, who had already publicly supported it, was aware that there were irreconcilable divisions in the party, and said he would make it a free vote. In effect – with all Labor's numbers plus a substantial chunk of Liberals – this would have guaranteed that the government's legis-lation passed, and so Abbott stayed in the race.

On the morning of the poll, many, including Hockey him-self, thought that Hockey would win. Unexpectedly, after the spill against his leadership succeeded, Turnbull re-contested the leadership when many had thought he would give way to Hockey.

With support fairly evenly split between the three candidates, by two votes Hockey came last, and was eliminated. He would have won if he had been one of the two final contenders. Abbott then defeated Turnbull by one vote, 42–41.

David Marr quotes one Liberal MP as then saying, 'What have we done?'[44] Labor was sure the Liberals had blundered. The day before the ballot, Anthony Albanese told the ALP Caucus: 'We've now got the Libs on the canvas and they are more internally split than any major political party since the great Labor split of the 1950s.'[45] After the vote there was elation in Rudd's office.[46] Many commentators thought that Abbott was unelectable, and indeed the combination of internal conflicts, the narrow vote, and his poor polling meant that he received more critical coverage than most successful coup leaders do.[47]

Labor thought that there would be continuing division in the Liberal Party on the central issue of the day – global warming and an ETS. This seemed to be immediately borne out. After the leadership vote, Abbott secured party opposition to Rudd's ETS by a secret ballot. Turnbull spoke eloquently in Parliament in favour of the legislation, and crossed the floor. There was then a Senate vote and two Liberal Senators crossed the floor to vote with the government, but without Greens support this was not sufficient to pass the Bill. The rest of the opposition adapted to the new leader's views.

Abbott brought a stark change of style to the opposition leadership. Whereas Turnbull had engaged with policy, Abbott engaged in trenchant and unrelenting oppositionism. Whereas Turnbull sought to debate, Abbott denounced. His was 'a strategy of continuous scorn' and, thought Marr, Abbott 'made Rudd and his Government look shabby. He's good at this. Baiting is his forte. He knows the cruel truth that the baiter is never blamed when victims lose their cool.'[48]

For Kelly, Abbott's 'elevation saved the Liberal Party': 'The conservative side strengthened its electoral base', and 'Abbott was able to unite the Liberals when, under Turnbull, they were only becoming more divided.'[49] This is a generous assessment. After the bruising events of late 2009, the Liberals had looked into the electoral abyss that continuing conflict would bring. It seems clear that many decided, in effect, that unity under any leader with whatever policies was preferable to going into the next election divided and so facing a massive defeat.

Abbott's success in the 2010 election, reducing Labor to a minority government, and thus bringing the party competition to an intense pitch from then on, combined with the Liberals' lead in the polls kept Abbott's position secure, even though his personal polling continued to be poor.[50] His smashing victory over Labor in the 2013 election gave him considerable internal authority, so he began his government with a secure hold on the leadership.

Abbott Agonistes

John Milton chose the title *Samson Agonistes* (contestant or challenger) as the title of his epic poem to highlight that at heart his Old Testament hero was a warrior, a combatant. The title of this section is to highlight that this is also the core of Tony Abbott's political approach, and central to his rise and fall. It might be amusing, but it is not germane to search for other parallels – Philistines, Delilah, Samson's blindness, or his final disaster/triumph, where he uses his strength to bring down the temple, defeating the Philistine enemies but also killing himself.

Probably more than any other Australian politician, Abbott has defined himself as a combatant. He titled his memoir *Battlelines*. On the night of his 2013 election victory, he described his Chief of Staff as 'the smartest and fiercest political warrior I have ever worked with'.[51] When he was elected to Parliament he said he looked forward to being a 'junkyard dog attacking the other side'.[52] When he was Opposition Leader, and Niki Savva suggested that he needed to turn the negativity and aggression down, he responded, 'when you have your boot on their throat you keep it there'.[53] In

Abbott's world view, warrior virtues were central. When addressing groups of soldiers, he used to sometimes quote the 18th century writer Samuel Johnson: 'every man thinks meanly of himself for not having been a soldier'.[54]

Although he has obviously matured since his student days, his approach then was also marked by relishing conflict, and by personalising it. Barbara Ramjan, who defeated him in a student election, charged that after the result was announced he came over and punched the wall on either side of her head. She said that he always stood out because he behaved offensively and rudely to opponents.[55]

His first high-profile national political campaign was driving the monarchist side for the Republican referendum. Turnbull and Abbott confronted each other on opposing sides, and Abbott's polarising style was to the fore. His strategy document for the monarchists advised:

> This battle should be presented as real Australians' greatest
> chance ever to vote against all the politicians, journalists,
> radical university students, welfare rorters, academics, the arts
> community and the rich that deep down they've always hated.[56]

He also recommended the monarchists attack Turnbull personally: 'As their public face, Turnbull is arrogant, rude and obnoxious – a filthy rich merchant banker, out of touch with real Australians. He is the Gordon Gekko of Australian politics.'[57]

Abbott carried his hyperbolic style into opposition. In order to encourage British permanent residents to take out Australian citizenship, the Hawke Government took away the voting rights of non-citizens. When such people were removed from the electoral rolls, Abbott called it 'ethnic cleansing'.[58] While pursuing the government over the home insulation program, during which there were four deaths, he accused Environment Minister Peter Garrett of 'industrial manslaughter'.[59] After Gillard foreshadowed the introduction of a carbon tax, he called for a people's revolt. 'This toxic tax based on a lie … will make every job in Australia less secure,' he said.[60] Although all oppositions tend to be shrill, perhaps the 2010–13 period was the most constantly so.

The transition from opposition to government did not soften Abbott's style. For Michelle Grattan, Abbott failed to become leader of the whole nation: 'His government is tightly wrapped in its tribalism. One reason is that Abbott's all-powerful private office, headed by Chief of Staff Peta Credlin, has a "them and us" mindset.'[61] For the first time ever, the three most recent Labor leaders were compelled to appear before Royal Commissions. The thousands of appointments to government boards were said to be undergoing a purging of all Labor appointees, irrespective of their performance or qualifications.[62]

When faced with controversy, Abbott's response was often to escalate. When the Human Rights Commission, led by Professor Gillian Triggs, published a report critical of the treatment of asylum seekers on Nauru, Abbott's response was that 'The Human Rights Commission ought to be ashamed of itself.'[63] The ABC was a recurring target.[64] Other Ministers often joined in. Immigration Minister Peter Dutton accused Fairfax newspapers of carrying out a jihad against the government.[65]

National security concerns became more central during the Abbott Government, partly because of conflicts erupting in the Middle East, partly because of the ongoing threat of terrorist attacks, and partly because the government wanted it prominent on the public agenda. In external conflicts also, Abbott's strategy was to keep the political temperature high. Sometimes the anger was justified but the expression eccentric. After the shooting down of the Malaysian airliner by Russian-backed Ukrainian rebels, resulting in more than 200 deaths, he asserted that he would 'shirt-front' Vladimir Putin.

Although before the 2013 election Abbott was reluctant to take sides in the conflicts in Syria and Iraq ('baddies versus baddies'), with the barbaric acts and apparent military successes of Islamic State in the civil wars his attitude changed. Abbott described it as a 'death cult' that was 'coming after us'.[66] In two years, the Abbott Government made a series of commitments – to participate in air strikes, to send troops to train the Iraqi Army, and to commit some special forces personnel.[67] The US Ambassador to Australia pointed out in early 2016 that for well over a year Australia had been second only to the US – greater than Britain and France, for example – in its commitment to the conflict.[68]

Abbott was always keen to link such commitments to the threat from terrorism: 'Recent attacks in Australia and elsewhere around the world show that no country is immune from terrorism.'[69] Savva, though, judged that 'it seemed that [Abbott's] mission was to keep people in a constant state of anxiety, rather than to reassure them'.[70] She cites a September 2014 intelligence review of the security of Parliament House which concluded that it needed strengthening. This was leaked in advance to the *Daily Telegraph*, which ran a front-page story, 'Red alert over plot to attack nation's leaders'. The story changed a potential vulnerability into a concrete threat, but more importantly, it did not help security to have such sensitive material splashed all over the tabloids.[71] After the Lindt Café siege in Sydney, Abbott warned of a new 'dark age' and a 'hardened cohort of Australian jihadists'.[72] Occasionally he generalised about Australia's Islamic leaders: 'I wish more … would say [that Islam is a religion of peace] more often and mean it.'[73]

These responses provoked criticism. Some thought that elevating the terrorist groups so that they appeared powerful and threatening actually helped their propaganda aims, and possibly emboldened would-be 'lone wolf' attackers. Some feared that Abbott was pursuing social divisiveness as a political strategy, and was not at all interested in winning over the bulk of Muslim citizens and leaders. Some saw little direct relationship between a small force in the Middle East and protecting Australia against terrorism.

It was difficult to disentangle where national security concerns ended and seeking partisan advantage began. In August 2015, leading Canberra journalist Laura Tingle reported that the National Security Committee of the Cabinet had asked 'for a list of national-security-related things that could be announced weekly between now and the election'.[74] In June 2015, the government proposed introducing a law that would allow the Minister for Immigration to strip citizenship from foreign fighters without there having been any involvement of the judicial system. When Labor wanted a judicial process, Abbott immediately accused them of 'rolling out the red carpet' for terrorists.[75]

If seeking to wedge Labor on these issues, or picturing itself as the custodian of national security, was the Abbott Government's electoral strategy, there is little evidence from the polling that it worked. The Abbott Government quickly fell into the worst polling performance of any first-term Australian government. William Bowe's Poll Bludger aggregation of the major polls shows the government dropping behind on a 2PP basis in December 2013,[76] less than three months after winning the election, never to lead again until after Turnbull replaced Abbott. There were ups and downs within this consistently losing pattern, such as a big drop after the May 2014 budget, which so ostentatiously broke the Coalition's election promises of no cuts to various areas of spending.

It is little wonder that Coalition MPs finished 2014 as low in spirits as they were in the polls,[77] the public data paralleled by anecdotes of donors and prominent party members expressing dismay at the government's performance. Much of the blame was put on the Prime Minister's Office, specifically his Chief of Staff, Peta Credlin, and this gained greater public focus after an incident seemingly designed to humiliate deputy Liberal leader and Foreign Minister Julie Bishop. She wanted to attend an important conference on climate change in Lima. Initially the Prime Minister's Office had refused to give her permission. However, she took the matter to Cabinet, and her colleagues agreed she should attend.

Straight afterwards, there was a leaked report that Trade Minister Andrew Robb would 'chaperone' her there, a curiously old-fashioned word from a more sexist age, perhaps intended to convey that Robb was more reliable on climate change issues.[78] As Aaron Patrick noted, 'The "chaperone" moment focused internal anger at the government's mistakes on to Credlin.'[79] The burst of criticism provoked a defence from Abbott, that if Credlin's name was spelled P-E-T-E-R rather than P-E-T-A there would be no problem. 'I think people need to take a long, hard look at themselves with some of these criticisms,'[80] the Prime Minister admonished his colleagues and other critics.

The relative political peace of summer was rudely interrupted for Liberal MPs by Abbott's Australia Day announcement of one of his new Australian knighthoods for Prince Philip. According to Savva, Abbott had expected the decision to be popular.[81] Instead, in the words of Costello, it was 'the barbecue stopper of the century. It completely hijacked Australia Day. Rarely have I heard such ridicule.'[82] While it was a dramatic demonstration of how out of touch Abbott was with the views of mainstream Australia, it was entirely consistent with his own commitment to the British monarchy. On the eve of his 2013 victory, Peter van Onselen had asked Abbott what he wanted his legacy to be and Abbott replied that he wanted to contribute to Australia's enduring links to the 'Anglosphere'.[83]

Days after the knighthood controversy, Campbell Newman's Queensland Government went from a record victory to defeat in one term, after a first-term Coalition Government in Victoria had already been defeated the previous year. Abbott addressed the National Press Club days after the Queensland loss. Although promising to be more consultative, he also asserted that his leadership should not be challenged, that 'It's the people who hire and, frankly, it's the people who should fire.'[84] Without getting into distinctions between parliamentary and presidential governments, it is sufficient to note that this is not a doctrine likely to appeal to MPs in marginal seats whose careers would be ended if the people fired their leader.

Soon after this a motion for a leadership spill was moved by two backbench MPs. The spill was remarkable in that there was no declared challenger, and the move was driven entirely by a disenchanted backbench, with no frontbenchers seeking to destabilise the leadership. Abbott defeated the empty chair 61–39, with one abstention.[85] Some thought this was a 'mortal blow'[86] for Abbott, but he promised this 'near-death' experience would make him change, and, according to Patrick, he was more consultative afterwards. Credlin's public profile was reduced, although Abbott resisted all calls to move her or Treasurer Hockey.

The first major sign of discontent within Cabinet came at the end of May 2015. In the *Sydney Morning Herald*, Hartcher gave one of the most detailed accounts of a Cabinet meeting that has ever been published.[87] It was a meeting where six Ministers challenged a proposal by Immigration Minister Peter Dutton to strip Australian citizens suspected of involvement with terrorist organisations of their citizenship by ministerial decision. It had not been listed on the Cabinet agenda and no supporting documents had been distributed. 'Here we go again, something as momentous as this and nothing before us,' said Turnbull. Dutton even said that not needing as much evidence as a normal legal process was one of the advantages of the scheme. Turnbull asked, 'Have you already told the *Daily Telegraph*?' Abbott denied having done so, but next morning the paper had the story (which means its journalist had been briefed before most of the Ministers, and before the evening Cabinet meeting). In Manning's summary, 'Cabinet had been ambushed, treated as a rubber stamp, and misled.'[88] The Hartcher leak showed a divided Cabinet and Abbott and Dutton had to retreat.[89]

Several embarrassments for the government followed in the next few months, with Speaker Bronwyn Bishop's 'Chopper-gate' gaining the most publicity. Bishop, a strong Abbott supporter, had taken a helicopter to a Liberal Party fundraiser at taxpayer expense, with the controversy lasting some weeks in July before Abbott demanded her resignation. Then in August came the conflicts inside the Coalition over whether to allow a conscience vote on same-sex marriage. Abbott held a combined meeting of the Coalition parties, rather than the more normal Liberal Party-alone meeting, to decide how to proceed. This sealed the numbers for him, but his tactics left the reformers feeling alienated. The main proponent for allowing a conscience vote, Warren Entsch, felt 'betrayed and duped' by Abbott.[90]

According to Savva, the first meeting of the group determined to make Turnbull leader only occurred on 13 August.[91] Just one month later, on 12 September, eight days before a by-election in the Western Australian seat of Canning, the *Daily Telegraph* published a front-page story of a likely ministerial reshuffle at the end of the year in which many of the older Abbott loyalists would go. Lenore Taylor reported that 'Phones ran hot … with theories of who was behind the leak and what might have motivated it.'[92] The Prime Minister publicly insisted the story was simply wrong, and rang the Ministers named. Even though the content of the leak seemed to run against Abbott's immediate interests, 'the trouble [was] that most in the Government assumed the reshuffle story was deliberately placed, given the *Telegraph*'s tendency to faithfully regurgitate the Government's line on almost everything'.[93] On such a story it was 'hard to imagine [reporter Simon] Benson taking anyone else's word': it had to be the Prime Minister's office.[94] Malcolm Turnbull described it to colleagues as 'a Credlin special': 'It was highly destabilizing at a sensitive moment.'[95]

While it took three months of politicking – barely visible to the public – for Menzies' fate to be sealed in 1941, Abbott's fall may be the fastest on record. On Monday 15 September, many newspapers carried stories that his leadership was under threat, but most were forecasting a challenge before Christmas.[96] Abbott was sufficiently confident to tell reporters he was 'not going to get caught up in Canberra gossip. I'm not going to play Canberra games.'[97] Late that morning, the ABC's Chris Uhlmann gave more specificity to the speculation, saying he had spoken to eight Ministers and six said Abbott would face a leadership spill no matter what happened in the Canning by-election. Julie Bishop met with him late in the morning, and warned him that a challenge was underway. Then after Question Time, Turnbull and Abbott had a meeting which Savva describes as 'brutal'.[98] At 4pm, Turnbull made a televised speech announcing his challenge and outlining the reasons for it; a couple of hours later Abbott followed, and called a party meeting for later that night. From then on there was rolling TV coverage. Near the time the count was announced, there were over 2500 tweets on the #spill hashtag per minute. These included many humorous tweets, such as a photo of Gillard laughing, with the caption, 'Julia Gillard Rushed to Hospital after Overdosing on Schadenfreude'.[99]

Turnbull won 54–44, and then Bishop comfortably retained the deputy's position.[100] According to Savva, Turnbull paid tribute to Abbott as a great Liberal leader, but Abbott's reply soon descended into recriminations, about being 'torn down' and about disloyalty and white-anting, and he rebutted some of Turnbull's criticisms of him ('You are wrong, Malcolm …'). Abbott's and Credlin's speeches to their staff were even more bitter, with Credlin several times calling Bishop Lady Macbeth.[101] In Abbott's public farewell speech the next day, he pledged loyalty, but the shock and bitterness were also apparent:

> We have more polls and more commentary than ever before. Mostly sour, bitter, character assassination. Poll-driven panic has produced a revolving-door prime ministership which can't be good for our country. And a febrile media culture has developed that rewards treachery.[102]

Abbott thus joined Rudd as an election-winning Prime Minister overthrown by colleagues in the first term of government. The dynamics of their downfalls provide interesting parallels and counterpoints. In both, doubts about electoral support played a role. There was far more basis for this among the Liberals. As Turnbull said when announcing his challenge, they had lost 30 Newspolls in a row, while Labor actually led in the latest Newspoll before Rudd's overthrow, although it had suffered a precipitous fall in the preceding months. Abbott has since said that he was confident of winning the next election, but there is nothing in the polling data to support this confidence.

In each case the execution was swift, with the challengers having to spend relatively little time and energy persuading colleagues to support a change, because both leaders had lost the confidence of a substantial number of MPs. In each, the challenge caught the leader unprepared and shocked by how their position had collapsed. Each, through over-confidence or through sealing themselves inside a personally agreeable cocoon, ignored the warning signs. Savva thought Abbott had received many warnings about how his performance was alienating his colleagues, but he ignored them all.[103] Turnbull was confident that 'Abbott would do the job for him. "He's burning the house down", Turnbull told supporters.'[104]

In both cases, there were widespread complaints about centralised control, about decision-making processes that were far from inclusive, and about how relations between the leader and his office were cutting across and damaging relations with colleagues (see Chapter 10). This was a major factor with Rudd, and was even more pronounced with Abbott.

The deteriorating relations between the two leaders and their colleagues were many-sided. Perhaps the most important single factor was the increasing doubt about the leader's political judgment, with backbenchers and even Cabinet Ministers feeling captive to what they increasingly saw as erratic decision-making. This was crystallised in the way Rudd abandoned the ETS and embraced a fight with the mining companies with apparently little preparation, for example, while for Abbott it was an accumulation of issues – the broken promises while denying they were broken; the constant crying wolf on national security, possibly with diminishing effect; an inability to generate a strong socio-economic narrative; and allowing side issues such as Chopper-gate to become more politically embarrassing than they needed to be.

For Rudd, another factor was his lack of respect for his colleagues: his habitual lateness, his outbursts of rudeness and abuse, and his lack of consultation. For Abbott the issue was probably more a declining level of trust. Abbott's broken promises had long been a public issue, and for a damagingly long period he denied, publicly and privately, that he had broken any: 'refusing to concede only made it look like he was lying about lying'.[105] Equally, though, the same sentiment became more widespread internally, in denying that leaks had come from his office, for example – denials which few believed.

In the end Abbott's combative outlook was counter-productive; his polarising style alienated large portions of public opinion, and then the centralised control alienated his colleagues. When told by former Minister Ian McFarlane that his colleagues had removed him because they thought if he stayed leader, they would lose, Abbott, according to Savva, replied 'Death before dishonour.'[106] However, by that time it seems likely that his warrior code was ringing hollow to his colleagues.

These pairs of leadership conflicts have dominated recent Australian politics. It is not yet clear whether they are harbingers of a continuing pattern, or a momentary aberration. Between 2013 and 2016, Bill Shorten became the first Labor leader since Kim Beazley (1998–2001) to serve a full parliamentary term as leader, while Turnbull went into the 2016 election, as leader for nine months, asking the electorate to support him in the name of 'stability'. Whether that stability results remains to be seen.

CHAPTER 4

Hawke vs Keating versus Howard vs Costello

The two conflicts

The Hawke and Howard governments shared an unwelcome similarity. Both were destabilised by a long-term tension and rivalry between the Prime Minister and the second most important member of the government. Paul Keating and Peter Costello were both Treasurers in the governments they aspired to lead. In both, each Prime Minister's periods of office began with their later contender being a close factional and personal ally. Both challengers were the obvious heir apparent from the beginning of each incumbent's tenure. Both relationships deteriorated as the challengers became increasingly frustrated at the failure to form any succession plan, and felt that the hard work of governing was being left to them.

The tensions were resolved in diametrically opposite ways. Keating mounted a frontal challenge, which paralysed the government for a long period, but eventually succeeded, and he went on to win the next election, though he lost disastrously at the following one. In contrast, Costello never challenged directly, and Howard led the government to defeat, with lack of renewal being one of the central themes in its electoral decline.

Incumbents

Hawke and Howard were both elevated to their party's leadership unanimously, and at an electorally opportune moment for the oppositions they led. In both cases their parties were keen to unify behind them to pursue electoral victory. Nevertheless, when faced with challenges to their own leadership, neither Hawke nor Howard was in a strong moral position to express outrage, because both had come to the leadership through internal machinations, having determinedly undermined rivals.

Even before Hawke entered Parliament in 1980, he had made his leadership ambitions clear. For two and a bit years after that election, Hawke's unswerving ambition to displace Hayden intermittently destabilised the party, until, in the most dramatic fashion, Hayden resigned on the very day in February 1983 that Fraser went to the Governor-General to seek an early election. Whatever Hayden's strengths and weaknesses as leader, his prospects would have been much better if Hawke had given him strong support rather than cultivated every opportunity to replace him.

Howard was a veteran of internal Liberal Party wars, in several of which he had triumphed. He had deftly parlayed himself into the deputy leadership when Andrew Peacock was vainly challenging Malcolm Fraser in 1982.[1] Then he had out-manoeuvred Peacock to win the leadership in 1985. His greatest single failure was the ambush that saw him ejected from the leadership in favour of Peacock's return by the unusually crushing margin of 44–27 in May 1989. After this Howard memorably compared his future leadership prospects to Lazarus with a triple bypass, but he still was the most eminent leader for one side in a divided party:

> Howard and Peacock taunted each other for years. It became the worst sort of leadership competition: compulsive but unresolved … They were personality opposites whose mutual

antagonism nourished the battle, while they were politicians too evenly matched to enable a convincing resolution.[2]

As the Liberals continued to flounder after John Hewson lost the 'unloseable' 1993 election, Howard's ambitions returned. According to Costello, Howard 'relentlessly pursued the leadership of the Liberal Party all through that period. He would come around and talk to you about the need for better leadership.'[3] But despite the party's disillusionment with Hewson, 'the anti-Howard mood in the party was confronting him at every turn'.[4] In 1994 Alexander Downer replaced Hewson. Downer and Costello were hailed as the Liberals' 'Dream Team' and a generational shift from the Howard–Peacock divisions. Soon, however, Downer's leadership descended into disaster, and with Peacock's 1994 departure from politics, Howard told colleagues the 'veto had been lifted'.[5] Howard returned to lead an increasingly desperate party.

Both leaders consolidated their internal authority through electoral success. Hawke and Howard are the two most successful election winners in Australian politics since the Menzies era, having won four elections each. In each case leading the party from opposition to government was the key achievement, but both faltered somewhat in their first attempt at re-election. Hawke, after achieving record approval ratings and facing a seemingly weak opposition, called an early election with an inordinately long (seven-week) campaign, and against all predictions, his government suffered a swing against it. His performance in the 1987 and 1990 elections was much better, but by this time not only were Keating's ambitions burning brightly, but several of the campaign professionals did not believe Hawke could win again.

Howard's triumphant 1996 victory was followed in 1998 (the GST election) by a line-ball result. His government was re-elected with a 2PP vote of just 48.9 per cent, the lowest winning percentage in Australian postwar history. The election was so close that his pollsters told him on the day that they thought he would lose. From then, and through the introduction of the GST and the government's travails over Pauline Hanson, the independent right-wing populist Member of Parliament, both the government and Howard's leadership looked to be in some danger. In early 2001 all the omens were pointing towards a Labor victory.

The 2001 election transformed Howard's stature. From being the target of Hawke's and Keating's epithet of 'little John-nie Howard', he was now en route to becoming George Bush's 'man of steel'. Helped by his determination not to allow the asylum seekers rescued by the ship MV *Tampa* to land, in August, and the atmosphere following the September 11 attacks in New York, he brought the Liberals back from the brink of defeat to an emphatic victory. Moreover, the issues now dominating the public agenda – the threat of terrorism and asylum seekers – were not Costello's natural strengths. Howard's triumph in the 2004 election, where he increased the government's majority for the second successive election – a feat that no government had achieved since the 1960s – reinforced his unchallengeable position in the party.

The incumbents shared a further trait. Both were determined to remain. Both came to see themselves as essential to each of their party's electoral success:

> Every success he had within the government and the Australian
> economy strengthened the Prime Minister, and gradually
> persuaded Hawke, whom Keating still believed to be a far
> inferior intellect and politician to himself, of his great success in
> office and the wisdom of remaining in it.[6]

Hawke was in no doubt about his central role: 'according to all the independent evidence I was the one who got the party across the line, certainly on the last two occasions, probably three, and perhaps all four of them'.[7]

Even as the Labor Government struggled with the depths of the recession, its decline in the polls, and the favourable media and public reaction to Hewson's *Fightback!* program, unveiled in late 1991, Hawke's faith in his own abilities and indispensability never wavered: 'There was no way I could embrace the idea of a staged exit … What was driving me was the need for Labor to remain in government at a critical time in our history.'[8] 'The key to Hawke's psychology,' thought Paul Kelly, was the messiah mentality: 'he had fused his own prime ministership … with Labor's self-interest'.[9]

Although less grandly expressed, some commentators have ascribed to Howard a similar outlook. Two months before the 2007 election, Shaun Carney wrote, 'Then there's Howard, the ceaseless intriguer, the man for whom being Prime Minister is everything. He cannot let go.'[10] Howard certainly had the view that his electoral victories gave him the right to decide his leadership future. He told Peter Hartcher:

> After the 2004 election, Peter's mistake was to not realise what had happened, and that is that I had won four elections. Really, his attitude then should have been, publicly and privately, to have said, 'Well, you have won four elections, and you have earned the right to retire at a time of your own choosing, and you are under no pressure from me, or any people around me.' You know, if he had adopted that attitude, I'd have retired during the last term.[11]

While some have taken such comments as meaning that at times Howard came close to retiring, Costello does not believe it: 'The fact remained that when it came to the crunch he always decided against it. There was always a reason why he would stay.'[12]

A less popular challenger against a more popular leader

Both challengers always saw themselves as the logical next leader. This was most obvious with Costello. When the Howard–Costello leadership team began in 1995, Costello, according to his biographer, Shaun Carney, could probably have won the leadership, as he could have a year earlier against Downer. Each time, Costello allowed the other contender to become leader free of challenge. This possibly heightened his later sense of entitlement: 'Costello has been viewed – and he has viewed himself – as the future of the Liberal Party for more than 25 years.'[13] Similarly, long-serving Keating staff member Barbara Ward told the ABC that a primary concern of Keating's in the Hawke–Hayden machinations was positioning himself as the next leader.[14]

Another central feature of both struggles was that they involved a less popular figure pitting himself against a more popular one. In this sense the challenges ran against conventional political wisdom about the importance of leadership in electoral success. The challenges were the opposite of the sort of challenge Hawke had waged against Hayden, where Hawke's public popularity – and hence greater electability – was paraded as the essential qualification to become leader.

In contrast, just before Keating won the leadership in December 1991, the poll on preferred Prime Minister had him at 12 per cent – compared with Hewson, at over 80 per cent.[15] Labor's electoral fortunes had been in severe decline, and according to Gareth Evans, the choice for the electorate, between Hawke and Keating, was like a choice between arsenic and strychnine.[16] Nevertheless, the Caucus chose the less publicly popular contender. Similarly the polls:

> showed Peter Costello to be less popular than his leader. And this was the nub of the Liberals' problem. There was not one scintilla of polling evidence that the Australian electorate liked Costello any better than it liked Howard.[17]

Former leader John Hewson was even more blunt in 2009, telling Costello it was time to retire:

Peter, enough is enough … All the polling I've ever seen or heard of – Liberal, Labor or from whatever – has had you as unelectable.[18]

Why were the challengers so much less popular than their leaders? One ingredient is the nature of the roles they occupied. The two roles – Prime Minister and Treasurer – generate differences of perspective. It is unusual for treasurers to have a warm and positive public image. Typically they see themselves as custodians of policy purity, while prime ministers are more electorally attuned, and so more prone to compromise or to allow political prerogatives to override financial discipline. Thus Keating and other economic Ministers used to refer to Hawke as 'old jelly back',[19] while a recurring theme in Costello's post-election defeat comments has been his difficulty in stopping Howard's spendthrift tendencies.[20]

A curious parallel between the two struggles is that both incumbents were helped in prolonging their tenure by Saddam Hussein. More precisely, the two wars against Saddam, and their preceding crises, allowed both leaders to appear as international statesmen, as strong leaders, as more rounded figures than their economically limited Treasurers. This particularly frustrated Keating, who during the Gulf War compared Hawke to Napoleon without the hat. He also thought that his bid for the leadership was gaining momentum in late 1990, but that 'the war changed the thinking about my leadership from being an expectation to an act of sedition'.[21]

But most basically, the public image of the two challengers was determined by their personal styles. Both Keating and Costello were the main parliamentary aggressors, the head-kickers, for their parties, and while this often increased their popularity with their colleagues, it did not always help their public image. For example, Costello attacked Kim Beazley, then Deputy Prime Minister in the Keating Government, whose father had also been a federal Labor Minister, and who was very active in the Moral Rearmament Movement, in a deeply personal way: 'You, a fat man with a famous name, have gone around in Australian life trying to play off the honesty of your father. But every time you back this Prime Minister you hook yourself in deeper and deeper with his lies and dishonesty.'[22] According to Derek Parker, Keating's terms of abuse towards the opposition included 'sleazebags, frauds, harlots, pigs, cheats, criminals, clot, fop, scumbag, scum, muck, perfumed gigolos, ghouls, vandals, mindless, brain-damaged, swill, thugs and crooks'.[23] Carney's comment on Costello applied equally to Keating: 'It was with this sort of over-the-top rhetoric that Costello earned himself a reputation as a formidable parliamentary performer for the Liberals … but it also fashioned and limited Costello's image in the public eye.'[24]

To leave it at that, however, is an over-simplification. Both were the most effective aggressors on their side of politics. It was not just the violence of their language – Australian party politics produces many 'phoney toughs' and a surfeit of hollow rhetoric. Rather, Costello and Keating were notable for their capacity to target the political 'jugular' in a sustained way. Howard's long-serving Chief of Staff, Arthur Sinodinos, praised Costello because 'he framed the Coalition's narrative on Kim Beazley's black hole and hung it around Labor's neck for years, so much so that Labor was virtually intimidated into surrendering the Hawke-Keating economic legacy'.[25]

If the challenger was a less popular leader, what was driving their challenge? Initially it should be remembered that although both lagged in the personal popularity polls, each challenge gained momentum as the government trailed in the party to party polls. So as the Labor Government was floundering with the recession, Keating's prospects brightened. Kelly notes, 'Keating's adviser, Don Russell, had long ago asserted: "The caucus will only turn to Keating when it feels the Government is completely demoralised".'[26] Similarly as the Liberals' prospects looked increasingly hopeless in 2006–07, speculation about a leadership change was raised as offering some hope.

The two sides both sought to use the media to project their contrasting narratives – renewal versus indispensability, substance versus popularity. Hawke 'regarded his legitimacy as leader as self-evident, verified by three election wins', but Keating also thought 'the legitimacy of his [own] leadership claim was beyond dispute; he privately called himself the "real prime minister"'.[27] The leader deposed by Hawke, Bill Hayden, later wrote that in the years when Labor achieved most, Hawke was Prime Minister, but Keating was the leader.[28]

The personal relationships

The two pairs of contenders had very different personal relationships. Although both relationships deteriorated over time, and trust declined in both, Hawke and Keating seem to have had a much more intense relationship, with far more communication between them, than Howard and Costello. And that greater degree of communication extended to discussing the leadership itself; Howard and Costello seem to have shrunk from talking about it.

By mid-1983 'the Hawke–Keating bond was sealed and their relationship reached its zenith. Often, late at night, Keating would walk up the stairs to Hawke's office, just above his own, and they would chat into the early hours.'[29] Over the next five years, their personal relationship deteriorated. Hawke later wrote that their 1988 post-budget confrontation 'essentially spelled the end of our friendship, although not the end of our working relationship'.[30]

But each of the crises in this relationship was marked by long and extensive conversations. In 1990, for example, 'they talked on and on and stopped only when exhausted by the talk and the futility of it'.[31] As early as a New Year's Eve party in 1987, six months into Labor's third term:

Keating asked Hawke if he was considering standing aside from the Prime Ministership at any stage during the Bicentennial year. It was a bold approach, and caught Hawke unawares. Hawke met it not with outright refusal but with an ambiguous wait-and-see response.[32]

Likewise, the day Keating began his public challenge to Hawke, in May 1991, he went into Hawke's office and said, 'I always told you I'd let you know when I was going to come at you, and now it's on.'[33]

The Howard–Costello relationship was a stark contrast. From quite early in Howard's tenure, Howard was determined to maintain his political and psychological ascendancy in the party, and to nip any challenge from Costello in the bud. For the first several years, there was little public indication of tension between them. But as early as 1998, according to the accounts of Costello biographers Carney and Tracey Aubin, the internal tensions were palpable. At the 1998 election launch, 'Howard all but publicly snubbed Costello', structuring the rhythm of his remarks so there could not be separate applause for the Treasurer, and instead elaborately lauding Tim Fischer, leader of the Nationals. Carney is clear: 'It was an insult and Costello did not need any encouragement to see it that way.'[34] Howard:

> never missed an opportunity to undercut his deputy if he
> suspected that Costello's ambitions were beginning to blaze too
> brightly. If Costello erred … Howard was quick to take the role
> of fixer and facilitator, the wise head putting right what his less
> experienced deputy had mishandled.[35]

But these tensions only very occasionally – and partially – became publicly visible.

While the Hawkes and Keatings socialised together at the Prime Minister's Lodge in that government's early years, John and Janette never dined privately with Peter and Tanya Costello, even though various other Ministers and their spouses were sometimes invited.[36]

Over the years the social distance between them increased, so that by the 2007 election campaign, Michelle Grattan was able to write: 'Howard and Costello neither like nor respect each other. Howard tried hard for as long as practicable to encourage a possible alternative successor; Costello despises the way Howard has clung to the leadership.'[37]

Perhaps the most puzzling aspect of this limited personal relationship was the paucity of their direct communications over the leadership. When Howard made his statement in 2000 about making a decision on his sixty-fourth birthday (see below), Costello felt Howard was sending him a message – be patient, I know I have to go, and it will be some time in the next term – but never pursued it directly with him.[38] Costello's memoirs give several examples of this reticence:

> Howard and I did not discuss the leadership again in 2002 …
> I did not want to push him … It would not be helpful.
>
> On 25 February 2003 he told me he had not yet made up
> his mind.
>
> But if, at any time, he was intending to step down in December
> 2006, he never communicated that to me.

During the 2007 APEC summit Liberal leadership crisis, Costello writes that Howard 'said nothing about it to me'.[39] And from the other side of the fence, even after the election, Costello did not tell Howard of his plans:

> The oddest thing is that if he had already made up his mind to
> leave if the Coalition lost, why did he let the Prime Minister
> endorse him so strongly? Were the conversations between them
> so sparse that this salient fact could not be communicated?[40]

Hawke vs Keating media coverage

Paul Keating saw the turning point in his relationship with Hawke when Hawke was in agony after he discovered in 1984 that his daughter had a severe heroin addiction:

> Before the official dinner for [Malaysian Prime Minister] Mahathir, Hawke broke down again with Keating as he told the treasurer about Rosslyn. Hawke was in tears and Keating was nearly in tears as the terrible story tumbled out. Keating always remembered these events. Years later he dated this as the night when Hawke stopped being prime minister.[41]

It is a harsh judgment, and an illustration of how sharing a personal vulnerability became a political liability.

As noted, the two had initially had a close relationship, and a clear hierarchy, as Hawke was riding high in the polls and Keating was mastering the challenges of Treasury. But Hawke's performance in the 1984 election was mediocre, and the government lost ground. Then Hawke and Keating took different views during the 1985 tax summit, when Keating's favoured Option C (a version of a Goods and Services Tax) was defeated. In public Hawke and Keating remained models of public correctness.

'Banana Republic'

Keating took an increasingly high profile in asserting the difficulties of economic management, sometimes to Hawke's chagrin. Although tensions between them remained largely beyond public view, one flash point was precipitated by Keating's reference to Australia being in danger of becoming a 'banana republic' on John Laws' radio program on 14 May 1986.[42] It led immediately to a fall in the Australian dollar, and a political furore. His statement produced a crisis that Keating had not intended, but which he moved quickly to exploit in terms of moving for a stronger policy to confront the economic problems.

At the time Hawke was in Japan, en route to China. 'As the Hawke party received the full details of Keating's remarks and the market reaction, they were appalled ... Hawke's advisers went into white fury. Their target was Keating.' They felt Keating had set up Hawke, who quite unfairly was getting a bad press, looking weak and indecisive, 'engulfed in this upheaval, from which he was removed'.[43] Eventually Hawke gave a non-attributable background briefing. He said he had given Deputy Prime Minister Lionel Bowen a series of instructions to convene a meeting and assume control until his return. Next morning papers had banner headlines such as 'Hawke pushes Keating aside'.[44]

That day Hawke had a phone hook-up with his Ministers where he reiterated these points:

> Keating sat, newspaper on lap, ticking off the points as Hawke
> made them. After Hawke had finished, Keating angrily accused
> him of inspiring the newspaper reports. The ministers saw
> Keating's temper flaring. 'Be careful, the Chinese will be
> listening,' they cautioned. 'Fuck the Chinese,' Keating replied.

And launched into his tirade. 'The Chinese listeners received a graphic insight into ALP politics.'[45]

The public relationship between them was quickly healed, although the episode increased the wariness in their personal relations. Keating was not able to directly criticise Hawke, whom instead he praised while criticising the 'Manchu Court' around him, referring to the advisers Bob Hogg and Peter Barron (both of whom became Keating supporters in the 1990–91 conflicts).

'We would miss him.'

Increasingly Keating felt he was doing the hard work of government, but was not getting the recognition he merited. After successfully maintaining the appearance of unity and close cooperation until after the 1987 election victory, Hawke and Keating were 'in more or less open warfare through 1988'.[46] In terms of gathering numbers, the period was a failure for Keating, but when Hawke's discipline faltered after the 1988 budget with his boastful put-downs of the Treasurer, the resulting crisis produced the secret Kirribilli agreement to hand over the leadership in the government's next term.

In 1988, there were many media reports suggesting that Hawke's time was past and Keating's was here,[47] and 'Keating continued to think he could use the media to blast Hawke out of office.'[48] His essential strategy seemed to be to act like the real leader. For example, at the Hobart Federal Conference of the Labor Party, Keating performed brilliantly, overshadowing Hawke in the public forums. However, Hawke showed restraint. His advisers told him there was no challenge in Caucus, and that nothing could happen at the conference – 'It was all in the media. And he should not respond to a challenge that existed only in the media.'[49] And at this stage the push indeed existed largely in Keating's mind. The overwhelming feeling in Caucus was that they wanted the Hawke–Keating team to continue. Hawke recalled that 'according to Richardson, Paul might have had five votes in Caucus'.[50]

Keating presented the 1988 budget with an air of triumph, as the one that 'brings home the bacon'. However, the next day Hawke made a series of inflammatory statements. Rather disingenuously, Hawke's memoirs contend that 'I was bending over backwards to contain a particular line of questioning which owed its origin to Paul Keating himself.'[51] But next morning's headlines had the correct tone: 'PM takes shot at Keating'. Stephen Mills notes that with Hawke's approval back up to 60 per cent, he 'had the confidence to try once and for all to lance the boil of the Keating challenge'. In the course of his usual round of post-budget media interviews, Hawke started launching darts at Keating. Hawke said he didn't want Keating to leave but conceded that 'it's a possibility', and if he did 'we would miss him'.[52] While he was 58 and Keating was only 44, Hawke said, 'I still feel young, only feel about 44 … don't get upset by that, Paul … It's clear that the party and the people want me as Prime Minister … I think their judgment is the correct one.'[53]

Hawke was in a position of strength, both with the public and within the party, and had clearly grown impatient with Keating's continuing assertion of his leadership credentials and ambitions. However, equally clearly, he did not anticipate the strength of Keating's reaction, which he thought 'was in fact hysterical and, to my mind, illogical and self-deluding'.[54] Keating went to Hawke's office and confronted him, lambasting him for distracting attention from the budget, which should have been a triumph for the government. Kelly notes that 'Richardson now moved into damage control.' He told Hawke to get back on TV as soon as possible. Hawke went live on Channel Nine's *A Current Affair* and gushed over Keating – what a magnificent contribution he had made, the best Treasurer this country has had, the best Treasurer in the world. Moreover, his ambition to be Prime Minister was totally legitimate and if Hawke went under a bus, Keating would make an admirable Prime Minister.[55]

But Keating was not assuaged, and their private confrontation continued, until it was resolved by their Kirribilli agreement. The agreement, settled at the Prime Minister's Sydney residence, was not written down, but it was a solemn promise made in front of two witnesses, Peter Abeles and Bill Kelty, that Hawke would step down in the next term of government. The Kirribilli agreement has entered into Australian political folklore. It has become symbolic because of its arrogance, its presumption that the leadership was theirs to decide. It has also become symbolic of that government's

84

penchant for back-room secret deals and lack of transparency. Kelly again: 'Hawke and Keating had made a pledge, both lied about it [during the 1990 election campaign], and then Hawke dishonoured the pledge by refusing to quit.'[56] In the parliamentary debate that followed the revelation of the Kirribilli pact, Opposition Leader Hewson accused them of trading the prime ministership like a sack of potatoes, and claimed that Hawke's integrity had been fatally undermined. Hawke was struggling, as Kelly again notes: 'At one stage Hawke left the fantastic implication that his misrepresenta- tion was justified because it would be bad for this country if the Coalition had won the election.'[57] Hawke's post-budget put-down of Keating had backfired, and Keating was only finally placated by the agreed plan for Hawke's departure.

'Placido Domingo'

From the Kirribilli agreement – indeed from the weeks leading up to it – until after the March 1990 election, Keating was disci- plined in his public and private loyalty to Hawke. It was only after the election, and with no sign that Hawke was going to act on the agreement, that he again began active destabilisation.

The irony is that while the years 1986–88 were probably the peak of Keating's stature inside the government, 1990, the year in which Keating began his drive for the leadership, was politically his worst year as Treasurer: 'As the economy slid into recession Keating became an isolated figure – from business, the media and the ALP.'[58] The recession broke two years of promises by Hawke and Keating that Australia would have a soft landing, and that their economic policies were working. Keating's biggest mistake came on 29 November 1990, when he used the phrase that would haunt him for the rest of his career, that 'this is a recession that Australia had to have'.[59]

Inside the Cabinet, Keating suffered from his manic behav- iour on the issue of telecommunications reform. Not only did his powers of persuasion fail to convince his colleagues, but the personal way in which he confronted the Minister, Beazley, alienated many. It climaxed with him losing his temper and walking out of a Cabinet meeting when he was defeated.[60] This only helped support Hawke's numbers in Caucus. Kelly again: 'The irony is that Keating's fury only accentuated the growing Cabinet majority for Hawke.'[61] According to Hawke, when Keating came to talk to him about the leadership in October, saying he was frustrated, 'his level of frustration was matched by my increasing impatience with his behaviour'.[62]

Hawke had shown no sign of moving to fulfil the Kirribilli agreement, but his stated reason for ultimately renouncing it was a speech Keating gave in December 1990. Keating was the guest speaker at the press gallery's end-of-year dinner. The content of the speech at this annual event is officially off the record, but with an audience of around 120 journalists, if something newsworthy is said it soon finds its way not only into political gossip in Canberra but into the news media as well. Keating was in an emotional state – 'exceptionally maudlin', he later told ABC TV – because of the death the previous day of the head of Treasury, Chris Higgins, who had died suddenly and completely unexpectedly, aged 47.[63] He was a close colleague of Keating's, and Keating had been with him earlier on the day he died.

As John Edwards wrote, 'He lauded Higgins as a participator in public policy, and went on to speak about the importance of political leadership, the importance of being right rather than popular, and of changing things.'[64] Keating told the gallery that they had to choose between 'being participators or merely voyeurs'. The trouble with Australia, he said, was that it had never had a great leader, 'not one'. Australia was 'teetering on the brink' of becoming a great nation. But it needed a leader who could communicate a vision, and not go round 'tripping over television cables in shopping centres' (as Hawke had done recently). Then he referred to himself as doing the Placido Domingo, always giving his best performance, trying to marry the politics and the economics.

The contents of this off-the-record event were plastered all over the Sunday newspapers. Keating had not mentioned Hawke's name, but the speech was widely interpreted as a plea to the gallery to support his leadership credentials against Hawke's. Even before the press reports appeared, the gist of the speech was reported to Hawke.

Hawke's reaction was at least as furious as Keating's had been in 1988: 'Paul's performance was vainglorious and arrogant, disloyal and contemptuous of everyone on the political stage but himself … disingenuous, churlish and inaccurate.' The speech heightened Hawke's concern at what he saw as Keating's 'deficiencies of judgement and character'.[65] And as Edwards noted, 'There was no doubt an element of Hawke looking for an excuse to repudiate a promise that to him had become more objectionable as its due date came closer',[66] but by seeming to belittle Hawke, Keating removed any option of 'retirement with dignity'.[67] Kelly observed that 'Hawke felt that Keating wanted to destroy his place in history as a prelude to stealing his job.'[68]

Keating's intentions remain unclear, possibly even to himself, in what was after all a largely *ex tempore* speech, delivered at a moment of emotional vulnerability. Later, he told Richardson privately that he did not intend it as an attack on Hawke,[69] although Richardson does not seem to believe this. Keating staff member Tom Mockridge thought that Keating wanted the gallery to be thinking harder about the role of leadership: 'That is very different altogether from saying that he wanted the Sunday newspapers screaming about it', but 'it's an imprecise business'.[70] There seems little doubt that Keating launched much more of a showdown with Hawke than he intended, one that destroyed any chance, small as it may have been given Hawke's intransigence, of a managed transition.

Things only got worse for Keating, with the recession and then having to watch from the sidelines as Hawke led the country during the First Gulf War. So when the public Keating campaign finally began in May 1991, it had been preceded by 14 months when he had not been building his popularity with either the public or the party.

Keating's first challenge. On Thursday, 30 May 1991, straight after Keating told Hawke he was going to launch a challenge, Richardson went to Laurie Oakes, who broke the Kirribilli story on Channel Nine that evening. Keating hoped the agreement would legitimise his challenge,[71] given its formal and unconditional nature. The Keating camp knew its impact would be great. Indeed, beforehand they referred to its revelation as the thermonuclear option.[72] Kelly, though, judged that they made 'a terrible tactical mistake' by releasing the Kirribilli story simultaneously with the declaration of the challenge.[73] It did catch the Hawke forces unprepared, however. Staff efforts 'to develop various forms of words on the point were, frankly, more ingenious than convincing' thought Mills.[74]

In his memoirs, Hawke is somewhat defensive:

> Looking back now, it is easy to characterise the agreement as a mistake, particularly when one considers its personal and political consequences. But what concerned me then was the importance to the party of maintaining an effective relationship between Keating and myself … for the greater good of the party and the country.[75]

He does not discuss the issue of whether having made the agreement, he should have kept it.

The revelation was followed by immediate action, both sides moving into campaigning mode. The Hawke forces attempted to bring on a leadership ballot without delay. They called a meeting for early Friday, but misplayed their hand, making themselves look silly. At the meeting Hawke invited the challenger to move that the position be declared vacant, a vote taken on a show of hands. Others responded that that was not what Hayden had done in 1982, and that there should be a secret ballot. Keating then said, 'If that's what I have to do then I'll do it at a time of my choosing. Not now.'[76] So the meeting was adjourned after 15 minutes. In Hawke's account, 'the Keating camp walked out and the meeting ended in anti-climax'.[77] But in reality Hawke had lost his chance to humiliate Keating. Realising their mistake, the Hawke forces sought to reconvene the meeting, but the Keating supporters had already scattered. As a result, Hawke endured some damaging publicity and Keating was able to spend the weekend rallying more votes, perhaps four more, so that the next week the vote was a respectable 56–44.

The party in Keating's office on the night of the loss was jubilant, with his supporters always saying they knew it would take two challenges – a classic example of how the private behaviour contrasted with the public words. Keating now retired to the backbench, replaced as Treasurer by Agriculture Minister John Kerin and as Deputy Leader by Brian Howe, both high achievers in the government, but neither with the internal authority or external aggression that Keating embodied.

Backbencher Keating. It was hard now for Keating to advance his cause. As Edwards wrote:

> Paul could not appear to be disloyal to the party. He could
> not attack the government or overtly do anything that would
> deepen the appearance of a split and diminish its slim chances of
> victory. He proceeded with great caution.

Whether out of strategic choice or necessity, he 'seemed content to allow circumstances to evolve'.[78]

His first major public intervention came after the budget – in the continuing recession, it had not been well received. Keating called for the easing of interest rates and more expansionary policies. It may have been true, as Edwards observed, that 'the August budget was an unconvincing Treasury document', but it closely followed the policy settings which Keating had insisted on before his resignation.[79] With considerable justification, Hawke commented that 'to argue that the Kerin Budget and the government were at fault reached notes on the scale of hypocrisy beyond Placido Domingo at his best'.[80] But as he also observed,[81] 'the worsening economy was sapping the morale of the Government'.

Whatever the hypocrisies involved, it was a strategic necessity for Keating. Kerin became a proxy target, and undermining him was a means of undermining Hawke. Interestingly, in the lead-up to the June vote, when trying to woo his support, Keating told Kerin he was deputy material.[82] But now, as Hawke's Treasurer, his tenure 'was doomed from the start, not simply because he inherited from his predecessor an economy in recession but because the insidious and incessant campaign against him by Keating and his supporters finally destroyed his confidence'.[83] In Hawke's view, 'John Kerin, who is by nature slow to anger, was in turn infuriated and depressed as stories emerged of pro-Keating forces feeding the press gallery with ammunition to attack him.'[84]

Keating's other major policy criticism came as Hawke and the state Premiers were moving towards new federal financial arrangements. Although he had been involved in the preliminaries, in an address at the National Press Club on 22 October 1991 Keating said the new proposals would mean a lack of federal financial control over taxation levels, and hence an abdication of responsibility for economic management.[85] A promising attempt to rationalise Australian federal–state relations was thus a casualty of Keating's challenge. The temperature within the party reached a new high soon after this, but then there was a truce: 'The arm twisting in Caucus ceased. The leaks to the media dried up.'[86] But it was a temporary reprieve.

The next turning point came when John Hewson launched *Fightback!* on 21 November. Labor was shocked by its positive reception in the media.[87] Neither Hawke, nor Howe, nor Kerin was able to puncture the opposition's appeal. 'Labor acted like a divided, demoralised and beaten unit,' wrote Kelly.[88] During this period Keating maintained a strategic silence.

In December events moved quickly. Kerin, at a press conference, was unable to remember what a particular acronym stood for, and his fumble received heavy media coverage. In normal circumstances this momentary memory lapse would be trivial, but in the circumstances of the time it provoked a major crisis. Hawke concluded that the pressures and attacks had sapped Kerin's confidence and decided to move him from Treasury.[89]

But control of events was taken out of his hands by a 'page one story by Peter Hartcher in the *Sydney Morning Herald* of 6 December which revealed the Richardson-Ray advice to Hawke' to undertake a ministerial reshuffle.[90] According to Hawke staffer Mills, it seemed 'the leak had come from Richardson – who else would put the story out?'[91] It meant that the reshuffle was seen as an admission of failure and a panic move,[92] and it weakened rather than strengthened Hawke's position. As Kelly commented, 'just as Hawke had reassessed Kerin … the reshuffle had given the party a licence to reassess its leader'.[93]

Hawke was increasingly beleaguered, unable to combat either the recession or *Fightback!* politically. He later wrote, 'I knew I could destroy [Hewson] and his repugnant ideology' and he felt he had laid out a basic line of attack against *Fightback!* which, with time, would have succeeded; and that the timing of developments was fortunate for Keating.[94] However, no developments at the time give any credence to the Hawke view.

There was a parade of defectors from Hawke to Keating and Richardson got them all to inform the media, seeking a self-affirming sense of momentum. A Morgan Poll had the Coalition leading 52.5 to 31.5 and Hawke's approval rating at 26 per cent, almost 50 points below the peaks of his heady early days in government.[95]

In the penultimate act, a group of six Ministers – Beazley, Robert Ray, Evans, Michael Duffy, Nick Bolkus and Gerry Hand,

Hawke's closest supporters – decided to approach him. They told him that he had lost majority support, and that although they would work for him in any contest, it was their view that the situation was irretrievable. They urged him to resign. Hawke stared down the six, and said he would continue. As Hawke said, 'news of the meetings with the six ministers leaked to the media, which by now was in a frenzy'.[96] The press were predicting Hawke's demise. With a sense of high drama, but also inevitability, a Caucus meeting was called, and Keating won.

This transition was notable for how quickly the government recovered a sense of unity. Despite the intensity and length of the struggle, the leading Hawke supporters established good relations with Keating and the party regained at speed its sense of purpose. Despite the easing of the recession, an opposition led by a more politically adept leader than Hewson might have at some stage more successfully blocked the government's march. Nonetheless, it was only on the very eve of the 1993 election that Labor edged ahead.

Howard vs Costello media coverage

One obvious but important difference between the two leadership struggles was that the Hawke–Keating conflict occurred first, and that the Howard–Costello relationship was always seen in its light. Commentators were waiting for Costello to 'do a Keating', and he has often been dubbed with titles such as the 'poor man's Keating'.

However, a very different picture emerges from the ebb and flow of tensions between Howard and Costello. Hartcher correctly referred to the way uncertainty about the Prime Minister's intentions left the government 'vulnerable to one of its periodic convulsions' on the question. He thought the 'general pattern was for one paroxysm a year'.[97] But there is no pattern, except for some increasing frequency the longer Howard's tenure continued. The lack of pattern is the point – there are incidents, but they do not amount to any gathering momentum or logical progression of any kind. Rather, they show that, in Grattan's phrase, 'leadership issues have a lot in common with malaria. The symptoms keep recurring.'[98] The leadership tensions did considerable damage to the government, but emerged at unpredictable times, and without offering any hope of renewal or improvement.

Howard went through three phases in talking about his possible retirement. The first began on his sixty-first birthday, in July 2000, when in an expansive radio interview with Philip Clark[99] he canvassed the possibility of retiring on his sixty-fourth birthday, conceding that nothing lasts forever, but reiterating his good health and his enjoyment of the job. This had some pluses as a formula, but created a lot of expectation about what would happen when he turned 64, not least in Costello. After Howard decided to go on, he adopted a new retirement mantra, that he would stay as long as the party wanted him, the voters wanted him, and it was in the best interests of the party that he stay. This was a mantra that he used on countless occasions in the next several years.[100] It had the advantage of not setting expectations about a particular date. It also had the appearance of altruism, picturing his decision as fulfilling the wishes and needs of his colleagues, but as Judith Brett points out, its undertone was defiant, saying that if you want me to leave, you will have to throw me out.[101] This formula lasted until just before the 2007 election campaign when, as we will see below, amid much awkwardness, he said that he would leave some time into the next term.

'Mean and tricky'. According to Costello's biographers,[102] tensions between the two were present almost from the beginning, but the first decisive event only came in 2001. In May came a leak which Carney called 'a defining moment of Costello's career'.[103] In early 2001, Howard's electoral position looked hopeless – a series of state election and federal by-election losses and consistently disastrous polls had pundits predicting his demise, and there was increasing disillusion inside the Liberal Party. By this time Costello had slightly softened his hard right image by differentiating himself from Howard's social conservatism on the republic, by making gestures towards Aboriginal reconciliation and by being more directly critical of Pauline Hanson's One Nation Party. As Howard's and the government's situation was deteriorating, there was increasing restlessness on the backbench.

Then a memo, written by Liberal Party President Shane Stone, a close Howard ally, analysing the government's problems (most dramatically, that it appeared 'mean and tricky') was leaked to Oakes. The memo purported to be an analysis of their electoral prospects following the Coalition's loss in the Queensland state election in February: 'The tone of the note was almost fawning, suggesting [Howard] was seen as guilty of the government's transgressions chiefly through association with Costello.' Indeed at one stage Costello was referred to disparagingly as 'Guess who?'[104] The report's analysis could be read as a determined attempt to shift the blame for the government's problems away from its leader.

When Costello returned from overseas, he met with a very apologetic Stone, who maintained that:

> he had only ever prepared one original of his memo, which he
> had given to John Howard. He insisted adamantly that even
> he did not have a copy. I pointed out to him that if he had not
> leaked the document, he was effectively saying that the leak
> came from the Prime Minister's office.[105]

An investigation was ordered into the source of the leak, but it was never reported. Costello was openly scornful in 2007: 'As far as I know they're still doing it ... It's a long investigation, this one.'[106] Of course the source and motive of the leak were already clear to Costello. Carney notes:

The Stone memo, and Howard's handling of it, confirmed to Costello's friends and supporters what they had suspected since the Government's fortunes had soured three months earlier: that the paranoia Howard had long shown towards his former nemesis Peacock had now been transferred in its entirety to Costello.[107]

Howard's 'Athens Declaration'. Intense coverage followed what the media dubbed Howard's Athens Declaration in late April 2005. During an official tour in Greece, the Prime Minister was asked about his election prospects against the newly re-elected Labor leader Kim Beazley. In a chest-thumping response, Howard declared his ability and intention to defeat Beazley again. The statement prompted 'the usual round of anonymous empty threats from Costello supporters and fulsome praise of his deputy from Howard'.[108] As recalled by Costello:

> The next day's [*Australian*] headline was "Howard issues challenge to deputy". [Its chief correspondent Dennis] Shanahan wrote: "It's on. The Liberal leadership challenge has begun. But it is not Peter Costello challenging John Howard. Rather it is John Howard fronting up to Peter Costello."[109]

Costello was furious. He already felt that the Prime Minister had reneged on a commitment to resign in the previous two terms of government. While his public response was a low-key but disapproving statement about it being unhelpful for this to overshadow the budget,[110] a rash of stories attributed to Costello supporters appeared, attacking this 'unprovoked declaration of war', this 'destructive act of indulgence'. There were hints that he was not prepared to remain as Treasurer until the next election, and that Costello supporters had set the Prime Minister a deadline.[111] Everyone knew where these stories had come from, although Costello never confirmed them in any public statement. Because of the way Howard had provoked the reactions, he was powerless to discipline his deputy's supporters. After the election, Howard, with some justification, said that he'd answered the question the only way he could, unless he was going to announce an intention to retire. It was normal practice for a Prime Minister to declare his confidence in winning the next election.[112] Moreover, although the furore had arisen from what seemed to be a savage 'beat-up' by *The Australian*, it was the atmosphere of distrust and suspicion from Costello and his followers towards Howard's continuing tenure that allowed it to escalate.

The McLachlan note. The McLachlan note has similarities to the Kirribilli agreement, in that it purported to be a secret agreement about leadership succession. It became public in July 2006, but involved events almost 12 years earlier, in December 1994. At that time, Downer's leadership of the Liberal opposition was in terminal decline, and Howard wanted to succeed him unchallenged, which required deputy leader Costello agreeing not to run. As Howard said, 'I wanted to be drafted.'[113] Ian McLachlan, then Liberal Party President and later Minister for Defence in the Howard Government, was seeking to facilitate the change of leadership. The three of them – Howard, Costello and McLachlan – had a meeting on 5 December 1994. In the light of later events, it is important to remember that, as Costello has pointed out, McLachlan was 'there on behalf of Howard'.[114]

> According to Costello and McLachlan, Howard agreed to hand the Liberal leadership over to Costello after one and a half terms if he took over from Downer and was successful at the next election. They both considered it a deal … Howard doesn't deny the substance of the conversation but strongly disagrees that any deals were made.[115]

Costello is dismissive of this wordplay: 'It is a sterile argument whether there was an undertaking, an understanding, an arrangement, an agreement or a deal. What was said was said. There is no dispute about it. People can interpret it for themselves.'[116]

After the meeting, McLachlan, at Costello's suggestion,[117] made a note of what had been agreed, which he carried around in his wallet from then on. When McLachlan left Parliament in October 1998, he told Howard that he had an obligation to Costello to fulfil and reminded him of the December 1994 meeting, and Howard's commitment to hand over after a term and a half. Howard said he didn't remember it like that. Hartcher notes, 'This rankled with McLachlan. And it stayed on his mind.'[118] After Howard announced on his sixty-fourth birthday, in 2003, that he intended to continue, Costello said to McLachlan that he believed Howard would never retire. The latter replied that he could not believe this because of Howard's promise to Costello. McLachlan grew increasingly angry on Costello's behalf: 'For a year or two he vented his indignation in conversations with other retired Liberal politicians about the deal he had witnessed and the note he carried in his wallet ... At at least one dinner he pulled it out and handed it around.'[119]

On 9 July 2006, the 1994 meeting and McLachlan's note became public in a story by Glenn Milne in the *Sunday Telegraph*. According to Hartcher, 'McLachlan hoped that the disclosure of this arrangement would serve as a catalyst. He hoped it would orce a resolution',[120] but Costello claims he had already told McLachlan 'It won't help me.'[121] He also knew that because he had been friendly with Milne over the years, it would be insinuated that he was the source.

Howard gave an interview denying there had been a deal, which was interpreted as denying McLachlan's account. 'Incensed at Howard's intransigence, McLachlan released to the media the handwritten note he had been nursing like a grudge.'[122] Costello said he felt that the interpretation placed on Howard's words was casting aspersions on McLachlan's integrity and his own, and decided to call an all-in press conference.[123] The following day there was a Cabinet meeting in Sydney. Hartcher wrote: 'Howard avoided the cameras and entered through a back way. Costello walked in the front door and paused dramatically in front of the expectant reporters.' Then he uttered the phrase which did both him and Howard considerable damage: 'My parents always told me that, if you have done nothing wrong, you have got nothing to fear by telling the truth. I told the truth.' As Hartcher rightly observed, 'By invoking the memory of childhood innocence he had, in effect, accused the Prime Minister of lying.'[124]

According to Errington and van Onselen, 'Voters preferred Howard's obfuscation to Costello's whining. The Treasurer came out of the affair looking churlish and petty, not least to many of his own colleagues.'[125] The incident prompted Howard to declare:

My soundings tell me that the strong view in the party is that the current leadership team, with me as leader and Peter Costello as deputy leader, should remain in place through to the next election ... I will commit to leading the party to the next election.

Costello was scorned by many commentators.

Some of Peter Costello's sympathisers have complained in recent months that the Treasurer was sick of being a plinth, a mere platform to support the statue of the great leader, John Howard ... John Howard has called Peter Costello's bluff, and guess what? It turns out there was nothing there. Years of Costello's posturing and positioning were exposed to have been empty braggadocio ... His capitulation to John Howard was total and abject.[126]

Did the disclosure of the McLachlan note make Howard commit to staying on until the next election when otherwise he would have resigned? Howard's followers say yes; Costello's followers say no. Errington and van Onselen say that Howard 'wanted to leave a decision about his future until the end of the year and make an announcement around Christmas after consulting with family and close friends'. But after this incident, 'Howard was determined to hang on to the leadership.'[127] After the 2007 election, at the press gallery Christmas dinner, Alexander Downer, feeling liberated from the need for diplomatic language, claimed 'it was Howard's intention to hand over to Costello in 2006, until he felt pressured to do so by the treasurer's supporters'. Howard decided to stay on, said Downer, because the Costello supporters were 'fucking rude' to him.[128] The battles continued, however, as immediately one of Costello's supporters told another journalist, 'Mr Howard had proved that he never intended to step down.'[129]

Why did the McLachlan revelation not have as great an impact as the Kirribilli revelation? A central reason is the difference in content. Kirribilli involved a formal and unequivocal agreement, while some ambiguity surrounded the nature of the agreement between Howard and Costello. In 2008, Howard told Hartcher he never believed there was a pact and neither did Costello, as evidenced by the fact that in the intervening years Costello never referred to it.[130] In Howard's view it was closer to such meetings as Hawke's with Keating in 1982, where the floating of an expectation, a canvassing of a future likelihood, a statement of intentions were aired – something rather less than an unequivocal promise.

Probably most important, however, was that the disclosure of the Kirribilli agreement was very self-consciously the first shot in a campaign, and was immediately followed by lobbying by the Keating forces. The McLachlan note became public when it did, not because of Costello's actions, but because of Milne's active investigations. The Costello forces had not prepared the ground and were not prepared to follow up. Costello's estimate was that if he had challenged he would have got just over one-third of the 110 votes.[131] So the only tangible result of the revelation of the

McLachlan note was a public commitment by Howard to remain as leader, and in the eyes of Liberal pollster and strategist Mark Textor, both were wounded: 'Howard looked like a liar ... and Costello seemed hopeless.'[132]

2007 – Countdown to defeat. As the election drew closer, and it was clear that the Liberals needed to be united to avoid defeat, political logic would dictate that all contenders had a common interest in unity. As Grattan wrote:

> [Liberal Party] colleagues know leadership talk is poison. The party does not have an interest in change – and that includes the Costello forces. Costello hasn't the numbers, and polls show he would be less popular than Howard. Any eruption of leadership tension would make an election loss more likely. Costello wants to be PM but not for a few months [and then] a defeat for which he'd likely cop the blame. His best hope is to continue partnering the man he neither likes nor respects.[133]

But despite all political logic pointing in the opposite direction, the leadership issue re-emerged several times in 2007.

The first time came in July with the publication of Errington and van Onselen's biography of Howard. Costello had been interviewed on the record twice by the authors, and as they said, 'Costello's view of the Prime Minister's achievements in politics, stretching back to the Fraser years, is clouded by his frustration over the leadership.' Costello thought that Treasurer Howard had not been a great reformer, and that his tenure 'was not a success in terms of interest rates and inflation'. In the interview 'Costello mimicked Howard's voice as well as his slight mumble when discussing an uncomfortable subject, indicating that Howard bounces around the topic in such instances.'[134] Again, in his dealings with these authors, Costello had not advanced his own leadership prospects, but had given ammunition to Labor.

A second occasion followed a round of interviews to mark Costello's fiftieth birthday in August. During an interview on the Channel Nine *Today* program Costello poured scorn on a story in the *Bulletin* that reported that he had said that Howard couldn't win but the government could – that is, they had to switch to him – and further that if a change wasn't made he would challenge. Costello rubbished the report and then denied it, accusing the journalist of relying on third-hand gossip. However, that night Michael Brissenden, on the *7.30 Report*, said that he was one of three journalists, along with the *Bulletin*'s Tony Wright and Paul Daley, present at a dinner when Costello had said these things. He then further revealed that the day after the dinner Costello's press secretary had rung them and in some desperation pleaded that they treat Costello's comments the night before not as 'on background', here meaning that the comments could be reported but without identifying the source, but as 'off the record', meaning its content would not be reported at all, but was simply for the journalists' information. Brissenden's report went to air as Costello was hosting a large birthday drinks party.

Initially there were denials. Downer appeared on *Lateline* saying, 'I mean, you know, get real. At the end of the day, the Treasurer, who is a man of decency and integrity, has denied it.'[135] But after a day or two of bluster and obfuscation, and when it emerged that all three journalists were saying the same thing, Costello shifted ground and said the important thing was that he hadn't mounted any challenge and in fact had continued working well with Howard.

A great debate then arose over journalistic ethics: had the journalists acted unethically first in not reporting what was said at the time, and then later in revealing it? Brissenden said that the crucial factor was that by his outright denial Costello was misleading the public, so continued silence would mean that he, as a reporter, was in effect conniving in this misinformation. Others charged that having agreed not to report they should continue not to do so. Nevertheless the controversy simply underlined that Costello had indeed said what the journalists claimed.

The climax of these pre-election leadership tensions came with the APEC summit in early September. The upheavals in the Liberal Party that week dwarfed all that had gone before. Costello later called it 'the week of madness', and Nick Minchin called it 'a horrible mess'.[136]

No doubt when it was planned, the APEC summit was intended to be a pre-election boost to the Liberals. It was the greatest gathering of world leaders ever in Australia. But it did not go to plan. Rudd upstaged an uncomfortable-looking Howard and Downer by speaking Mandarin to a beaming Chinese leadership. Then *The Chaser* TV show penetrated security, arriving at the hotel where many leaders were staying with one of their team dressed as Osama bin Laden. They were only stopped after they had given themselves up. What made it one of the most remarkable weeks in Australian politics were the ructions at the heart of the government.

This week of panic, the greatest loss of internal cohesion during Howard's reign, was probably triggered by sampling error. At the beginning of the week, the fortnightly Newspoll showed that the government's position had deteriorated sharply, moving from 45–55 2PP to a disastrous 41–59. A fortnight later, after two weeks of less than glowing publicity for the Liberal Party, Newspoll showed it back at 45–55,[137] the figure it had been hovering around for most of the year. As with most explanations centring around straws and camels' backs, however, the key is to look at what else was happening. In particular, the Liberals had been hoping that as the election neared, and Rudd had been Labor leader for longer, the polls would start to equalise – but here was an apparent movement in the wrong direction, from very bad to even worse.

It should be remembered when reading the apparent poll rebound that it was only from the middle of the following week that reports started to appear in the media about the extraordinary goings-on inside the government. The stories quickly gathered momentum as journalists started to realise the extent of what had occurred, but some of it only became public after the election. Nevertheless, from the week after APEC the Liberals' disarray was publicly visible.

That disarray began because 'when John Howard read the poll published on Tuesday, 4 September 2007, at the beginning of the week of the Sydney APEC summit, all the energy drained out of him and all his fight left him'.[138] He authorised Downer and Abbott to undertake consultations about whether the Cabinet felt their election prospects would be better if he resigned. Downer convened a secret meeting of all the Cabinet Ministers who were in Sydney.

Both also contacted Costello, who was in Melbourne. He indicated his readiness to assume the leadership, even so close to the election. And as he later wrote, 'You cannot hold a meeting of nine Cabinet Ministers to discuss whether the Prime Minister should go and then expect it not to leak.'[139] But equally, he thought that it was not a problem because it would be a prelude to Howard's departure.[140]

The meeting in a Sydney hotel room ran for two hours. Hartcher's reporting of it goes like this: 'Downer told the group of ministers Howard believed the government would lose the election and he will lose Bennelong … Here was their leader … sending a signal of despair.'[141] No alternative to Howard except Costello was canvassed, although several Ministers expressed reservations about him, including about their own dealings with him. According to Downer, 'everyone knew the dilemma was that the public had stopped listening to Howard but they couldn't stand Peter Costello';[142] 'If at the end of all the consultations a formal vote had been taken … it would have resolved 11 to 3 in favour of his immediate resignation … It was a stunning collapse of confidence, in direct response to Howard's own crisis of confidence',[143] and as Costello noted, every one of these people was a Minister appointed by Howard.

Although a clear majority of Ministers wanted Howard to go, they also agreed that it had to be his decision: 'Any appearance of a putsch would make the government's electoral standing even more dismal.'[144] And this proved to be the problem. Howard insisted he would only go if the Ministers publicly asked him to: 'Howard wanted his Ministers not only to carry the full burden of blame but to grant him immunity from being called a coward.'[145] And so, at the end of all this, the status quo prevailed.

Both contenders acted strangely during this extraordinary week. As Costello later said to Howard, '"If your position was that you wouldn't go voluntarily, why did you ask their opinion?" There was no answer.'[146] In turn, given the stakes, Costello's own passivity was remarkable. He spent his time isolated from the main developments, drafting a speech he would never deliver, and did nothing to influence the outcome. He and Howard never spoke directly.

As the news reports started, the Liberal Party met, but according to Costello no one questioned Howard about the leadership. At this meeting, Howard changed his formula and told the party room he would retire some time in the next term after winning the election. That evening, 12 September, he was interviewed by Kerry O'Brien on the *7.30 Report*. He spoke of the Downer meeting as trivial and said Ministers' views were equivocal: 'What matters is, the party had decided that they want me to stay.' Then he made the public announcement: 'I would expect well into my term … I would probably, certainly, form the view, well into my term, that it makes sense for me to retire.'[147]

According to Costello, Howard's responses to interviews exacerbated the internal tensions. An interview on *Today Tonight* 'outraged Howard's ministers. He had asked their advice and they had told him he should go. Now he was saying he had consulted his family and they had told him to stay … Ministers were extremely angry. They were being portrayed as disloyal for giving him a view when he had asked for it.'[148]

Far more important than injured Liberal feelings, however, was that this set up a nightmare scenario for the party going into the 2007 election campaign, and Rudd was able to charge that Howard could promise anything because he wasn't going to stick around. Labor could exploit 'both the departure of Howard and the prospective arrival of Costello PM'.[149]

* * * * *

The Liberals' defeat raises two questions that can never be definitively answered. Would a managed transition to Costello have saved the government? And, should Costello have 'done a Keating'? The answer to the first is possibly, the answer to the second is almost definitely not. Political commentators are prone to macho narratives:

> Costello has no one to blame but himself … If you want power, you must do everything possible to get it, not sit back and hope it falls into your lap. Because it won't. Someone hungrier, more ambitious, more determined, will come along and take it.[150]

It is often forgotten just how close the Keating challenge came to disaster. The process was very damaging. Many Labor Ministers described 1991 as a wasted year.[151] At the struggle's conclusion, the vote was very close. Only two Caucus members changing their vote would have changed the result.[152] If the challenge had failed, not only Keating would have been lost to the government – so would John Dawkins and perhaps other Ministers. There would have been a very strong sense of the government haemorrhaging, of decay rather than renewal. It would have been very hard to rebound from the damage of a contest between – according to one ALP person – an egomaniac and a megalomaniac.[153]

Even then the Keating challenge owed more to psychology than to rational political strategy, according to Edwards. In May 1991 Keating 'was going ahead anyway because now he just could not endure remaining in what he called the "chicken coop" of the ministerial wing office'.[154] Costello apparently never felt that intensity of frustration.

A Costello challenge would likely have failed, and so left the government floundering even more badly. But even if he had won, the resultant blood-letting would also have more likely damaged than helped the government's cause. Costello's analysis that any transition had to be managed and consensual is rational and persuasive.

The problem is that he did not pursue the strategy it dictated. In his analysis his only path to the leadership was through Howard's brain. Howard had to be convinced that he should leave. But Costello seems to never have seriously attempted to persuade Howard, or to have had any strategy for doing so, either by himself or with the help of others.

Moreover, given Howard's intransigence, Costello did not act in a sufficiently disciplined way. Although 'he never seriously planned nor organised a challenge to Howard', he sometimes 'talked big to journalists over dinners'.[155] His increasing resentment towards Howard led him into small, often seemingly self-indulgent, acts of public rebellion. Howard's announcement that he would continue past his sixty-fourth birthday, was not 'my happiest day'. In 1999 he had said that he had only 'another budget or two in me',[156] but of course then stayed. After the leaking of the McLachlan note, he said his parents had said to tell the truth, which some sympathisers thought made him look 'wussy' and whining. The net result of all these small eruptions was a picture of a man full of frustration and sulkiness.

All four of these people – Hawke, Keating, Howard and Costello – are substantial figures; all were devoted to public service. Yet all had their public standing diminished by their involvement in these internecine conflicts. All were exposed as allowing ego to cloud their perception and their judgment. All were involved in at least some incidents where their honesty was publicly compromised.

CHAPTER 5

Duelling Amateurs – Gorton vs McMahon

All politics has become more professional, and its practices more sophisticated. This is most tangible in election campaigning,[1] as the parties very deliberately learn not only from their own victories and defeats, but by watching their sister parties in other English-speaking democracies. There are now ensembles of professionals – in party head offices, in advertising and polling, as spin doctors and speechwriters – who are focused on campaigning techniques and strategies. This battery of experts makes the evaluation of a leader's performance and prospects more scientifically based, although polling and focus group data is often afforded a certainty it does not deserve.

Most basically, there is cumulative learning. All leadership changes add to the conventional wisdom, although some lessons are over-learned. For example, Peter Hartcher reflected that 'the Liberal Party watched in frozen, wide-eyed terror as Howard took them through the slow-motion disaster of the 2007 election loss'. Their failure to act then was part of the reason for Labor moving so ruthlessly against Rudd in 2010: 'no political party will again hesitate to remove a leader it believes may be failing'.[2] But the Rudd–Gillard conflicts then themselves became part of the conventional wisdom. In 2015, when Abbott was faced with a spill motion, he declared, 'This *Game of Thrones* circus, which the Labor Party gave us, is never going to be reproduced by this Coalition.'[3]

The first part of this more professional calculation is whether a challenge should be mounted, which is based on whether or not a change of leader will make electoral success more likely. The second part is the increased sophistication in the mounting of such coups: knowing when publicity will help and when secrecy is paramount, being more certain of the numbers inside the party room, knowing when a first unsuccessful attempt will be a necessary preliminary destabilisation before ultimate success. The greater professionalism of the contemporary era can be better appreciated by considering the relative amateurism of some leadership conflicts a generation ago.

Leadership conflicts in the age of black and white television

Gough Whitlam 1968. After Arthur Calwell led Labor to one of its worst election losses, in 1966, the party had started to regain political initiative under Whitlam. Whitlam thought – correctly – that the executive's undemocratic control of the party, especially in Victoria, was an obstacle to winning a federal election. This non-parliamentary control of Labor policy had already done the party great damage, in 1963, when Calwell and Whitlam were photographed under a street lamp, waiting for the National Conference to decide on party policy towards US bases in northwest Australia. In a damning phrase, Menzies charged that Labor was under the control of '36 faceless men'. In April 1968, after another rebuff from the National Executive, Whitlam wrote a 1700-word letter to his fellow MPs, resigning the leadership in order to re-contest it. As Graham Freudenberg noted, however, 'Beyond his letter, Whitlam did very little on his own behalf.'[4] Several days later, Jim Cairns announced his intention to contest the leadership as well, asking the question, 'Whose party is it – ours or his?' The Cairns appeal resonated with the many MPs who thought Whitlam was becoming too arrogant.[5] Whitlam won 38–32, a much narrower margin than he had achieved the previous year when succeeding to the leadership.

It is difficult to know what Whitlam was trying to achieve with his resignation. Perhaps he was seeking to strengthen the case for intervention in the Victorian branch. However, if anything, it weakened his leverage. This leadership contest is clearly from a more amateur age, in that few leaders today would resign their position without much more preparation and calculation than had occurred in this case: none would be content to leave their lobbying to a single letter to their colleagues.

It is also a leadership struggle from another era in that its central aspect is a power struggle between the parliamentary leader and the extra-parliamentary organs of the party. Whatever the rights and wrongs of the various moves in the Labor Party Split of the 1950s, it had a devastating impact on the party's effectiveness, especially federally and in Victoria and Queensland. John Cain Jnr, who in 1982 became the first Labor Premier of Victoria since his father was defeated in 1955, said 'the party was institutionalized in Opposition; there was no chance of doing anything'. In his attempts, as an ally of Whitlam, to reform the party in the late 1960s, Cain co-authored a pamphlet titled 'Do you want Labor to be Out of Office for the Rest of Your Life?'[6]

In Queensland, the party took even longer to become electorally pragmatic and effective. After the 1957 split, it remained out of office until December 1989. As late as 1987, then state secretary Peter Beattie charged that too often the party seemed satisfied with the spoils of defeat. From 1958 to 1974, the party had only two leaders, John Duggan and Jack Houston. Only rarely did either look likely to win an election (Houston in 1966 came closest); their power base was the union-dominated state executive.

In 1974, Ed Casey, an MP and future leader, charged that Houston was taking instructions from the state executive of the ALP, and had even dispensed with meetings of the shadow Cabinet and Caucus. There followed a sudden party-room coup by

Houston's deputy, Percy Tucker. As John Wanna and Tracey Arklay point out, 'The momentum for the change had come entirely from within the parliamentary caucus – not from the ... unions.'[7] Electorally, the coup was a failure. Labor went down to a worse defeat when Joh Bjelke-Petersen was running his campaign as Queensland's champion against the socialist, centralist Whitlam Government, with Tucker losing his own seat. From 1974, Labor had a revolving leadership: six leaders in 16 years.[8] Even when ex-federal party president, Tom Burns, renowned for his 'easy-going and calm demeanour', briefly became leader, he found 'he could not run the gauntlet of the internal disunity ailing the ALP'.

Joh Bjelke-Petersen 1970. Frank Nicklin, who had been leader of the Queensland Country Party since 1941 and Premier since 1957, finally retired in January 1968. He was succeeded by his deputy, Jack Pizzey, who died of a heart attack just six months later. Bjelke-Petersen, deputy leader of the party, won the ballot to succeed Pizzey, but he was barely known to the public. His early performance was hardly inspiring. However, helped by the gerrymander, he won the 1969 election: the Country Party won 26 seats with 21.0 per cent of the primary vote, the Liberals 19 seats from 23.7 per cent of the vote and the Labor Party 31 seats with 45.0 per cent of the vote.[9]

The government continued to flounder, losing a by-election and flagging in the polls. Some of Bjelke-Petersen's colleagues blamed him, with his awkward style and wooden public persona, and his gift for attracting controversy. The discontent gathered, and on 20 October 1970, a group of four MPs told the Premier that they had majority support to win a spill motion the following morning.[10] Joh was shocked but sprang into action, telephoning all his colleagues. The following morning there was a tied vote; the tie was achieved by the Premier voting for himself, and claiming to have the proxy of one absentee, a claim most observers doubt. He then won on his own casting vote.

After this narrow result, there was speculation about further moves – that some MPs might vote in favour of a Labor no-confidence motion, or more probably that the process would be repeated in a joint party-room vote, where, thanks to the votes of Liberal members, Joh would lose and be replaced as Premier by the Liberal leader, Gordon Chalk. The Country Party President, Robert Sparkes, who had his own severe doubts about Joh's capacities, decisively intervened to protect the party's role as the major partner in the governing coalition, and firmly told his party's potential rebels that they had had their chance and lost, and that any further action would result in their being denied preselection.[11]

It is impossible today that any party would allow a leader to also be the returning officer for a leadership ballot, or that they would feel honour bound to advise a leader of a coming coup … without also using publicity to help generate momentum. Bjelke-Petersen remained Premier for the next 17 years.

Gorton vs McMahon

The prevailing amateurism in leadership and leadership changes of those times is illustrated by the ascent, the tenure and the fall of John Gorton as Prime Minister. After Harold Holt drowned on 17 December 1967, the Liberal Party, which had been in government continuously for 18 years, suddenly had no obvious successor. Its deputy leader, William (Billy) McMahon, was widely distrusted and disliked in the party, and then was publicly blackballed by John McEwen, the leader of their coalition partner, the Country Party. As John Howard commented, 'none of the candidates was particularly well known'.[12] There were two leading contenders: John Gorton, who had only two months before become government leader in the Senate, and who had held few senior portfolios, and Paul Hasluck, Minister for External Affairs. Hasluck was initially reluctant to stand. When he did decide to stand, his single act was to write a letter to his 80 colleagues announcing that he was a candidate. He refused to lobby further on his own behalf.[13] Hasluck knew that his loss, and particularly his failure to campaign for himself, disappointed his followers, but he said that had he behaved otherwise, 'I would have had to become cynically disrespectful to my party and assume that they could be cajoled and corrupted.'[14]

Gorton felt no such inhibitions, and lobbied strongly for himself. His great asset was that he was a very good television performer, informal and friendly. As Howard recognised, 'The popular link with the Australian people was the decisive factor that delivered him the office. In that sense, he was our first "presidential" Prime Minister.'[15] For Freudenberg:

> Gorton was the first Prime Minister of the television age. Alone of all the candidates he realized that, in the extraordinary circumstances existing in the nation, the numbers in the party room could be influenced by pressure from the people. And ... his chief weapon was television.[16]

Gorton became Prime Minister on 10 January 1968.

Journalist Wallace Brown believed that 'no person came to the office of Prime Minister of Australia supported by greater good will ... and no Prime Minister squandered immense popularity quite as quickly'.[17] Brown speculates that the initial goodwill may have come from the trauma of Holt's drowning, the drama of the McEwen veto, and also because Gorton was a fresh face, with a laconic style, and an interesting background as a fighter pilot, a farmer and an Oxford graduate. Moreover, as Gorton's biographer, Ian Hancock, observed, he had 'many admirable qualities: the irreverence, the candour, the charm and the warmth, the cleverness of mind, the engaging informality and the quirky sense of humour'.[18] Yet his prime ministership was attended by continuing controversies. In 1969 he suffered one of the biggest swings in Australian history – over seven per cent in 2PP terms. He then faced an unsuccessful leadership challenge, and was overthrown in a coup just three years after becoming Prime Minister. What explains this dramatic fall from grace?

Three factors are central. The first is that through his failure to consult, and his arrogance, Gorton was in frequent conflict with several of the key power bases any Liberal Prime Minister at that time needed to work well with. Howard thought that Gorton's belief that it was his link with the Australian people that won his victory 'helped to explain his treatment of many of his senior colleagues, his unilateral policy pronouncements and his cavalier attitude towards power centres within his own party'.[19] His aggressive style made relations with the Democratic Labor Party (DLP), which held the balance of power in the Senate, and with the states, more difficult. He had several conflicts with Liberal state Premiers such as Henry Bolte and Robert Askin, and frequently surprised his more conservative colleagues with comments made without any consultation. As journalist Bruce Juddery observed, 'no politician in Australian history was more assiduous in putting weapons into the hands of his enemies than John Gorton'.[20]

The second, related, reason is policy incoherence. Gorton seemed unable to move from expressing a general sentiment to a detailed policy position or set of principles. Both Hancock and Hasluck observe that Gorton was much more intelligent than his predecessor, Holt,[21] although Hasluck added that he was mentally undisciplined and had poor work habits. What stands out from the Gorton era is the way he would express an opinion, but as little more than a thought bubble. For example, on foreign investment, he said:

> Until very recently, it has seemed to me that the posture of
> Australia in seeking overseas capital has been the posture of a
> puppy lying on its back with all legs in the air and its stomach
> exposed and saying, 'please, please, give us capital. Tickle my
> tummy – on any conditions'.[22]

Around the same time, after consulting almost no one, and certainly no other member of Cabinet, he went against Treasury advice and blocked a foreign takeover of the insurance company MLC. In addition to his unilateral and seemingly arbitrary decisions, Gorton was often underprepared. At an international meeting, for example, he referred to Malaya rather than Malaysia,[23] causing great offence, and then refused to retract or correct himself.

Such stubbornness was part of the third reason – what can euphemistically be called his unconventional personal style. In one famous story, the leader of the DLP, Senator Vince Gair, said to the Prime Minister as he was about to leave for the United States, 'Good luck, behave yourself,' and the PM replied, 'John Grey Gorton will bloody well behave precisely as John Grey Gorton bloody well decides he wants to behave.'[24] This unapologetic style extended also to his consumption of alcohol. It is possible that Gorton drank more alcohol more often than any previous Prime Minister, except perhaps the very first, Edmund Barton, who had been nicknamed 'Tosspot Toby' by *Truth* newspaper. Gorton's relations with women also caused much gossip. His colleague, Sir Alexander Downer, wrote that Gorton 'sometimes exuberantly flirted with other men's wives'.[25] Gorton told Hancock that he had had 'two or three' extra-marital affairs, including one while he was Prime Minister.[26] This gossip became more intense in late 1968, when, after a press gallery function, he took the only female journalist and the youngest in the press gallery, Geraldine Willesee, with him on a midnight visit to see the US Ambassador. The following March this became a brief but intense controversy, when Liberal backbench MP Edward St John publicly criticised Gorton for it.

All these factors led to a steady erosion in his support. His greatest claim to leadership, his popularity with the public, was destroyed at the 1969 election. There followed the unprecedented spectacle of a freshly re-elected Prime Minister facing a party-room challenge. The conservative David Fairbairn declared his candidacy, as did McMahon, but Gorton survived. In 1970 there was a stand-alone half-Senate election – the upshot of Menzies' opportunistic calling of a House of Representatives–only election in 1963 – and the government's position did not improve.

Murdoch vs Packer

The conflict between Gorton and McMahon gains added interest because it pitted the young bull, Rupert Murdoch, against the old bull, Frank Packer. While the views of proprietors have often played an important role in Australian election coverage, it is very unusual for a proprietor to be tied to one contender rather than another within a party, or for rival proprietors to be supporting different candidates.

McMahon was an old friend of Packer's and a regular guest at his Sunday night dinners.[27] Packer was initially inclined to support him as Holt's successor, but was eventually persuaded that McMahon had no hope. McMahon's political arch-enemy, Country Party leader John McEwen, publicly vetoed him – an unprecedented action. Murdoch, who had become very close to McEwen, then engaged in his first big political coup. In the lead-up to the vote, McEwen gave Murdoch an ASIO dossier which became the basis for a front-page story in Murdoch's *Australian* saying McMahon's relationship with the lobbyist Max Newton was a threat to national security, because Newton was doing work for the Japanese trade organisation JETRO. A few days later, the paper reproduced the contract between Newton, who had been its first editor, and JETRO.[28] McMahon withdrew from the race, and Gorton won, with Packer, owner of the *Daily Telegraph* and Channel Nine in Sydney and Melbourne, also supporting him.

As Gorton upset various Liberal constituencies, there were occasional murmurings about his presidential and unorthodox style in Packer publications, but they were muted, with Packer solidly supporting the government in the 1969 election. After that election brought the huge swing to Whitlam's ALP, the Liberals' discontent with Gorton became greater and more public, with the post-election challenge to his leadership. Fortified by discussions with the Packers, McMahon belatedly, but unsuccessfully, ran.[29]

From this point on, the *Daily Telegraph's* political correspondent, Alan Reid – nicknamed 'Packer's Paladin', after a popular TV series about a gunslinger – was one of those determined to be rid of Gorton. One of the main anti-Gorton MPs, Peter Howson, kept a diary, in which there are many references to Reid and his involvement. When Howson observed in December 1969 that 'obviously the press campaign is starting to affect' Gorton, Reid's response was that 'the press must redouble their efforts'.[30]

Climax

After a long, slow build-up of tensions within the Liberal Party, in just nine days in March 1971, a disagreement between the Army and the Minister for Defence, Malcolm Fraser, over the civil aid program in South Vietnam 'escalated into a political crisis which ended in the resignation of the Prime Minister'.[31] Competing background briefings to journalists by Gorton and Fraser led to a sudden spectacular eruption. The Packer press was centrally implicated in these events. Defence Minister Fraser had briefed one Packer journalist about his dissatisfaction with the Army and its efforts in civil aid; Alan Ramsey, of Murdoch's *Australian*, had been given a similar briefing. When advised of the conflict between Fraser and the Army chief, Sir Thomas Daly, Gorton effectively took the side of the Army chief. Ramsey went to see Gorton about what he knew were Daly's criticisms of Fraser. Gorton did not deny knowing about Daly's complaints, so when Gorton disavowed knowledge of them in parliament, Ramsey dramatically – and famously – called out 'liar' from the press gallery.

On the Sunday evening, Packer's Channel Nine had a program called *Meet the Press*. The chair, and all three panellists, were Packer employees. They pressed the line that if Fraser did not resign, he would become Gorton's puppet.[32] The following day Fraser resigned. Also on that day, Reid paid his first ever visit to Whitlam's office. As Whitlam's speechwriter, Freudenberg, recalled that meeting, Reid's motive was to help defeat Gorton – he advised Labor not to move a motion of no confidence in the government as this would force the Liberals to unite. Reid later disputed Freudenberg's account, and said he was just having a general talk about tactics.[33]

Gorton fell on the Wednesday. Fraser made a dramatic resignation speech to parliament. He accused Gorton of disloyalty to a senior Minister, and attacked his 'unreasoned drive to get his own way' and the damage he had done to the Liberal Party by casting 'aside the stability and direction of earlier times'. He concluded, 'I do not believe he is fit to hold the great office of Prime Minister, and I cannot serve in his Government.'[34]

The Liberal Party was so evenly split at the subsequent meeting that a vote of confidence in favour of Gorton was tied 33–all. Gorton then pronounced that that was not a vote of confidence and resigned. He was 'sick of them', 'had had enough'.[35] But that left a problem. As Howard wrote, 'Yet, if Gorton were pulled down, who else was there? It became an exercise in unplanned chaos.'[36] The person whom Menzies referred to privately as 'that little bastard McMahon'[37] was elected leader.

The meeting was not yet finished, though. There still had to be a ballot for deputy leader. Gorton stood, and won, and became Minister for Defence, replacing Fraser. So after the meeting, as Hancock put it, the 'Liberal Party was to be led by a man who was neither liked nor respected by most of its federal parliamentary members, and whose deputy regarded him with ill-disguised contempt'.[38] Both the process and outcome helped Labor. It is little wonder that after the meeting the ALP national secretary, Mick Young, and the president, Tom Burns, 'were caught between disbelief and hilarity, shouting the non-members' bar for as long as it stayed open'.[39]

The strength, and longevity, of the feelings aroused by the coup could be seen at the memorial service following Gorton's death in 2002. Tom Hughes, his former Attorney-General, and later successful barrister, gave the eulogy, which revisited the events of Gorton's defeat, charging Fraser, who was sitting in the congregation, with treachery. When Hughes had finished, Whitlam, sitting next to the Frasers, put his hand on Malcolm's shoulder, and said, 'Let not your heart be troubled, comrade.'[40] Close observers still disagree about the central events. Ramsey thinks that Gorton was disloyal to Fraser, and others think that Gorton was trying to take Fraser down a peg or two. On the other side, Hancock remains primarily critical of Fraser, and pictures Gorton's actions as stemming from loyalty to the Army.

Long-term internal conflict

The passions aroused by the original events were compounded by the personal failings of Gorton's successor. McMahon was, perhaps uniquely, lacking the qualities needed to unify the party.

His first problems were with allocating ministries. His need to reward supporters necessitated punishing opponents. The number of demotions led former Labor leader Arthur Calwell to quip that McMahon's government was 'the only ruling party we have ever seen with [its own] Shadow Cabinet'.[41]

The key problem, however, was that 'McMahon was trusted by virtually none of his peers.'[42] Hasluck, whose public persona was staid and proper, wrote some private personal observations on his colleagues which were collected and published, after his death, by his son Nicholas. Few of his portraits are flattering, but the picture of McMahon is by far the most savage:

> The longer one is associated with [McMahon] the deeper
> the contempt for him grows and I find it hard to allow him
> any merit. Disloyal, devious, dishonest, untrustworthy, petty,
> cowardly … a contemptible creature.

> I can scarcely imagine anyone less fitted to be Prime Minister of
> Australia in a major crisis.[43]

Hasluck had earlier written that he would be unwilling to serve in any government led by McMahon 'because I did not trust or respect him, had a deep contempt for his political methods' and had 'learnt to expect disloyalty and betrayal from him'.[44]

McMahon had been dubbed 'Billy the Leak'. According to Laurie Oakes, 'McMahon rang journalists at all hours of the day and night leaking information extraordinarily damaging to [Gorton] and the Government.'[45] Wallace Brown, who described McMahon as 'a telephone addict' and the 'grand master of the art of the often devious leak', gave an example of McMahon leaking him some material from Cabinet one night and then the following night leaking him that he had told Cabinet how appalled he was that the story had leaked.[46]

It is thus ironic that McMahon's grounds for forcing Gorton's resignation from the ministry in August 1971 were that Gorton had breached Cabinet solidarity. In July, Packer journalist Alan Reid published a very one-sided book, *The Gorton Experiment*. Hancock thought that many of the book's anti-Gorton stories came from McMahon, and that Reid's gifts as a storyteller and eye for authoritative-sounding detail hid the book's many inaccuracies.[47] Gorton was sufficiently provoked to defend himself, and engaged theatrical entrepreneur Harry M Miller as his agent. Miller negotiated with Murdoch for Gorton to publish six articles in reply, for a fee of $60,000.[48] After the first, McMahon spent several days ensuring that he had the numbers inside the party room, and then demanded Gorton's resignation – arguing that Gorton had breached

Cabinet solidarity by complaining that others had breached Cabinet solidarity against him. In the parliamentary debate that followed, Whitlam, to almost universal amusement, captured all McMahon's weaknesses with the telling phrase – 'Tiberius with a telephone'.[49]

The longer McMahon was Prime Minister, the more Gorton's prime ministership acquired a retrospective rosy glow. Hancock found that Labor's Clyde Cameron and National Party leader Doug Anthony both believed that if Gorton had remained Prime Minister he would have won the 1972 election. Rupert Murdoch also maintained that his newspapers 'would have supported the re-election of a Gorton Government in 1972. And he would have won!'[50] There is nothing in Gorton's actual record as leader to support such musings. In late 1971, a Melbourne businessman started a 'Get Gorton Back Committee', but the government was too bitterly divided for anyone to unite them as they marched to their 1972 defeat.

Although they lost government for the first time in 23 years, the 2PP swing at this election was just 2.5 per cent. However, this meant that the total swing between 1966 and 1972 was 9.6 per cent. McMahon muttered on election night that at least he didn't lose as many seats as Gorton had.

* * * * *

This is a coup from an earlier, more amateur age in several ways:

- Compared with more contemporary resignation speeches, the notable feature of Fraser's is not only that it forced a showdown, but that it closed off any possibility of later reconciliation. It created a permanently alienated section of the party, and it provided much ammunition for the government's critics. In effect, it discredited the conduct of the whole government.
- The sympathy for Gorton in the party room led them to adopt an arrangement – making Gorton McMahon's deputy

and a senior Minister – that was bound to fail, and which indeed did fall apart a few months later.

• As is also sometimes the case with more contemporary coups, the actions were much more a repudiation of Gorton than an embrace of McMahon, more a wish to escape from a troubled past and present than to create a workable future.

Packer succeeded in making his candidate Prime Minister, but in the process contributed to that government being displaced by the dreaded Labor Party 21 months later. The reporting of the Liberal and Coalition ructions of the post-Menzies governments was central in building the independence and authority of the press gallery. A new generation of better-educated reporters helped to break free from the journalistic torpor of the Menzies era, but also, because of the obvious collapse of cohesion among the conservatives, it was harder for proprietors to impose their editorial certainty or judgments. It ushered in a golden period of Australian newspaper reporting of federal politics, sustained by editors such as Graham Perkin and Adrian Deamer. This continued into the Whitlam period, with that government's lack of discipline, until the lead-up to the 1975 election campaign, at which point the gallery's *glasnost* ended.

CHAPTER 6

Leadership Coups and Desperate Oppositions

'When there is no tiger in the mountain even a monkey can be king.'

Many Australian voters would see this Chinese proverb as an apt description of their political leaders – and indeed, sometimes, in some parties, the talent pool does seem very shallow. However, when examining opposition leaders, the reverse can also be true – even a potential tiger finds it hard not to look like a monkey. Opposition leaders are three times more likely to be deposed than government leaders. Occasionally these coups are momentous, but often they come and go with little apparent effect. Sometimes a leadership change energises an opposition, but there is also much scope for futile leadership conflict, and there are many cases where a leadership coup has simply made the party's task more hopeless, becoming part of a syndrome of ineffectual opposition.

Opposition leaders lack the authority that victory gives. They have little patronage or largesse to distribute. Governments take actions and so make news, while oppositions are largely reduced to reacting and criticising. The skills opposition leaders require are different from those needed for being head of government. For example, Paul Kelly judged that Bill Hayden's:

ability was to take an issue, master it, balance the economics and the politics, work through to a final position and then steer the policy through the party and the community. But in opposition there was none of this. Opposition was only images, shadows and impressions.[1]

The demands of the inter-party competition and of intra-party success may not coincide. For most of the electoral cycle, the government not only has most of the news-generating capacity, but the opposition will often want to delay its own release of policies to maximise electoral impact. According to Peter Collins, Jeff Kennett 'argued that there was no point putting out detailed policy documents well in advance of an election campaign ... Your opponents steal and sometimes implement your good ideas and beat you to death with your bad ones.' Kennett instead had a tightly planned campaign in which policies would be released leading up to the election; Collins says Howard emulated this in 1996.[2] Unfortunately for Collins, he was deposed as leader before he got the chance to put this plan into practice.

A further source of tensions in opposition can be the smallness of the numbers. This can mean, first, that it takes only a couple of individuals changing their allegiance to affect the balance of the numbers, but it also sometimes seems to add piquancy and intensity to internal tensions. In the 2001 Queensland election, Labor won a massive majority. It left the minority opposition party, the Liberals, with just three seats out of 89. David Watson resigned as leader, and with former leader Joan Sheldon being the only other Liberal MP, Bob Quinn became leader by default. Later, when the Queensland Liberals' numbers had swelled to eight, they were tied 4–all over who should be leader. The ten-day impasse saw walkouts and the public trading of insults. Visiting Monty Python star Eric Idle offered to take over the leadership, but denied that the Liberal stoush was Pythonesque – the comedy series had a much bigger following than the Liberals, he said. Eventually Mark McArdle became leader, after what all the participants described as a very painful and embarrassing week.[3] At one stage, the small Tasmanian

Liberal party room dealt with its divisions more directly. When Sue Napier became leader the 10-member Caucus was evenly split, with sometimes frayed tempers. At one meeting, reportedly, Ray Groom punched Bob Cheek, giving him a black eye.[4]

Opposition not only lacks the perks of government, it also lacks its discipline and focus. One common conflict is between those who want simply to concentrate on what they see as the immediate tasks, criticising the government and doing what is needed to win the next election, and those who want to use the period in opposition for more extensive reconsideration of the party's platform and processes. According to Mark Latham, Kim Beazley as Opposition Leader told the shadow ministry that '"opposition is all about pissing on them and pissing off" – a hit and run style of politics'.[5] Latham, though, thought it was a time for a more fundamental rethinking of policy.

On the other hand, such internal preoccupations can lead to a displacement in the priority of conflicts – from the external to the internal. This is most likely when the participants feel the battle for the soul of the party is more important than electoral success. In the decades following World War II this was the stance of some in the left wing of the Labor Party: they aimed to maintain its socialist principles, and in particular to resist any attempts to give public money to private schools. Since the 1980s, however, such ideological fervour has been more to the fore in the Liberal Party. After the defeat of the Fraser Government, one group, the dries, who supported Howard:

> had no wish to court popularity. They did not expect to win
> the 1984 election and were not about to help Andrew Peacock
> become prime minister. In fact they felt the party had further
> seats to lose before it could start to rebuild.[6]

At bottom, though, being in opposition is in itself dispiriting – 'Opposition politics feels like the dog shit on the boot of democracy.'[7] Latham thought that 'the frustrations of opposition' were part of the reason MPs engaged in intrigues: 'Many Labor MPs find they have little constructive work with which to occupy their day, so gossiping with colleagues and big-noting themselves with journalists ... become a way of life.'[8] Especially for oppositions whose expectations of victory have been disappointed, and who see only futility ahead, a sense of despair can lead to desperate measures. But more often than not they fail to improve the party's prospects: in 2002 the Victorian Liberal opposition was flagging in the polls. Robert Doyle successfully challenged Denis Napthine for the leadership, claiming that the party was 'facing political oblivion' if it stayed under Napthine's leadership.[9] Under Doyle, the party went on to its worst ever Victorian defeat.

It is easy to forget now, but for a couple of years it looked likely that Bronwyn Bishop could become leader of the Liberal Party. Bishop became a Senator in 1987, and immediately achieved considerable prominence with her energy, her thirst for publicity, and her gift for drama. Her hectoring, belligerent questioning of public servants – columnist Alan Ramsey dubbed her the 'Arnold Schwarzenegger of the estimates committee system'[10] – gave her notoriety, and her frequently false accusations and unfair insinuations did not seem to damage her. She cultivated a Thatcheresque aura of certainty, conservatism and strength. In one speech she said:

> Wherever you look in modern Australia someone is applying a
> wet blanket to our lives. In most states we can smoke marijuana
> to our heart's content but heaven help us if we try to smoke
> tobacco in the workplace ... the economic and moral busy-
> bodies are standing in our way.[11]

After the Hewson Liberals lost the 'unloseable' 1993 election, morale within the party was very low. Bishop took the chance offered by a by-election in Mackellar to move to the House of Representatives and advance her prime ministerial ambitions, of which she was making no secret. She had many powerful supporters, including Kerry Packer, Alan Jones, Harry M Miller, Ita Buttrose, Rodney Adler and Leonie Kramer. An opinion poll found that she had double Hewson's support to be party leader.[12]

Her standing with her parliamentary colleagues was much lower. Many were appalled by her behaviour, and increasingly doubted her intellectual capacity to master complex briefs, or move beyond clichés. She won the by-election in Mackellar, a blue-ribbon seat, but her performance was judged mediocre. Soon afterwards, the other Liberal leadership pretenders moved against Hewson, and the 'new generation' Downer–Costello ticket was elected.

With the advent of Alexander Downer to the leadership in May 1994, Bishop's leadership ambitions collapsed. Even though Downer himself failed as leader, and was replaced by Howard early the following year, Bishop by then had dropped out of all leadership speculation. After Howard's 1996 victory, Bishop was in the outer ministry, not the Cabinet, and was dropped altogether after the 2001 election. Abbott made her Speaker of the House of Representatives after his 2013 victory, but she was forced to resign because of the 'Chopper-gate' expenses scandal in the lead-up to Abbott's defeat by Turnbull. Her rapid rise is testimony to the desire of an opposition to break a losing pattern; her failure and career decline indicate that colleagues' judgments about a contender's performance and ability are still central.

Leaders and electoral success

Parties' electoral ruthlessness has been the primary driver of leadership instability, but how often did a leadership change lead to victory? The idea that a leadership coup could bring electoral success gained currency with three cases in quick succession in the early 1980s. John Cain, Brian Burke and Bob Hawke defeated incumbent party leaders and then went on to win, respectively, the 1982

Victorian, 1983 WA and 1983 federal elections. But this is far from common.

When dealing with the impact of leadership change and electoral victory, we are necessarily delving into the realm of counterfactuals – would the same result have occurred if things had been different? We can anchor our speculations on some evidence, such as polling trends, but there will never be certainty.

Bill Hayden, after losing the leadership to Bob Hawke in 1983, famously said that given the state of the country, a drover's dog could lead Labor to victory. Although there is always room for contention over specific judgments, at least sometimes when a leadership change preceded victory, that victory would have happened anyway. In the lead-up to the 1993 WA election, Carmen Lawrence's Government was heading for almost certain defeat because of the legacy of 'WA Inc.', a scandal involving Labor's business dealings with some large WA corporations, which were exposed extensively and over a long period by a Royal Commission. Richard Court thought the Liberals were not doing as well as they should be doing with all Labor's problems. He mounted a challenge against Barry MacKinnon. It failed, but he tried again, and succeeded. MacKinnon thought he would definitely have won the election, and resented Court's opportunism. MacKinnon retired from politics at the election that made Court Premier,[13] an election which he indeed could almost certainly have won.

The following are the 15 successful challenges that were followed by electoral victories in which, in my judgment, the party did substantially better than it otherwise would have done, where the change was an important contributor to the victory or to its scope. Other observers might include others. The list does not include instances where the party improved, but not sufficiently to win: for example, after the Dowd–Greiner coup, the NSW Liberals did better but still lost. In each case, I surmise how much difference the new leader made, and also, even more problematically, how events might have proceeded if the leadership change had not taken place.

1   **Neville Wran, NSW, 1973.** After Robert Askin scored
    the Coalition's fourth successive victory over Labor, Wran
    challenged Pat Hills. During this term, the NSW Coalition
    Government performed much less ably. Moreover, Wran
    pursued it with much more energy and acuity than Hills
    could have mustered.[14] Despite the electoral backlash
    against the Whitlam federal government in 1975, Labor
    won the 1976 state election by a single seat. The switch to
    Wran improved Labor's prospects, and it is unlikely that this
    narrowest of victories would have been achieved with any
    other leader.

2   **Malcolm Fraser, Federal, 1975.** Whitlam clearly had an
    ascendancy over Bill Snedden. If Snedden had continued, it
    is impossible to know what other events would have been
    different. John Howard thought that when Fraser replaced
    Snedden he 'changed the mood of the party immediately …
    The mainstream of the Liberal Party knew that it had done
    the right thing by going for Fraser. He sounded strong and
    looked like a winner.'[15] Fraser won in 1975; Snedden may not
    have, but under him there may not have been a constitutional
    crisis and hence no 1975 election.

3   **John Cain, Victoria, 1981.** Cain's predecessor, Frank
    Wilkes, had sharply cut the Hamer Government's majority
    in the 1979 election, helped by that decaying government's
    land scandals, and very possibly would have gone on to win
    the 1982 election. Cain, however, gave the opposition a new
    boost of energy, broader appeal, and probably a larger victory.

4   **Brian Burke, WA, 1981.** Burke replaced Ron Davies as
    Leader of the Opposition in WA. Ray O'Connor replaced the
    forceful Charles Court, his predecessor as Premier, and this

made Labor's task easier. However, Burke was a consummate political performer, and it is far from clear that Labor would have won if Davies had remained leader.

5 **Bob Hawke, Federal, 1983.** Under Hayden Labor had made great gains against the Fraser Government in the 1980 election, but many senior figures in Labor believed he could not go the extra distance required to win government. Hawke had much higher polling figures than Hayden, and his accession to the leadership made Labor's victory certain, including in the eyes of Fraser.[16] Hayden believes he also would have won, and perhaps he would have. Hawke's victory was probably more sweeping than Hayden could have achieved, though.

6 **Wayne Goss, Queensland, 1988.** Under Neville Warburton, Labor had not performed well at the 1986 Queensland election, with Joh Bjelke-Petersen's National Party able to govern in its own right afterwards. After the scandals revealed by the Fitzgerald inquiry, the bizarre, forced resignation of Joh, and the division in the National Party that led it to overthrow Mike Ahern for Russell Cooper (see Chapter 7), it is likely that many leaders could have won for Labor. But almost certainly Goss performed much better than Warburton would have.

7 **Ray Groom, Tasmania, 1991.** It is likely that the Liberals only won the 1992 Tasmanian election because Groom replaced Robin Gray, but the background is more complicated and contentious. Gray had won the 1982 and 1986 elections, but lost in 1989. There was a hung parliament with a Labor–Greens majority. Initially, Gray refused to resign, and asked the Governor to call fresh elections. The Governor refused and Labor formed government with the support

of the Greens. The conservative side was not yet ready to accept the outcome, however. Edmund Rouse, chairman of the Gunns forestry company, and owner of the *Launceston Examiner*,[17] sought to bribe a Labor backbencher to cross the floor. The MP, Jim Cox, reported the attempt to the police. There was a Royal Commission, and ultimately Rouse was sentenced to three years' gaol. Gray was found not to have a legal case to answer, but the Commission strongly criticised the quality of his evidence. Groom then defeated Gray. Groom, a former AFL star and federal MP, went on to win a Liberal landslide. That would have been very unlikely under Gray, who was by then an extremely divisive figure.

8   **Jeff Kennett, Victoria, 1991.** This is a problematic inclusion because Kennett consistently had high disapproval ratings. Kennett's career as Opposition Leader was dramatic. When he became Liberal leader in 1982, after Cain's Labor had won their decisive victory, he announced to the assembled media, 'I represent risk.'[18] It became apparent that part of that risk was to himself. Kennett was only 34, the youngest member of the parliamentary party, and was immediately in trouble. He labelled Hawke's 1983 Economic Summit 'Mr Hawke's version of the Grand Council of Fascists'. Then he referred to John Cain as 'not the sort of man you would trust your daughters with'.[19] 'Cartoonist Ron Tandberg took to caricaturing Kennett with a foot permanently fixed in his mouth', and in the 1985 election campaign, an ALP advertisement portrayed him as a bull in a china shop.[20] His propensity for gaffes and his high disapproval ratings meant that in the next four years, he faced four challenges to his leadership.[21] One of these was tied and he survived on his own casting vote; another he won by a single vote. Eventually, in May 1989, 'Kennett's enemies in the party were rising as one against him', and they coalesced around

a single candidate: 'the cautious, unassuming figure of' Alan
Brown.[22] Despite losing the leadership, Kennett maintained a
high media profile, behaving as a leader in exile. While doing
a summer shift for radio station 3AW, he even 'interviewed'
himself about his leadership ambitions. As the Victorian
Labor Government disintegrated, the Liberals led Labor by
30 per cent in the polls. Nevertheless, party disaffection with
the cautious, low-profile Brown 'had reached critical mass'.
Kennett's supporters successfully moved a spill motion,[23]
and in April 1991 Kennett returned to the leadership. After
the problems of the Cain–Kirner Labor governments, it is
all but certain that the Victorian Liberal Party would have
won the 1992 election no matter who was leading it, but the
move back from Brown to Kennett was high risk. Kennett
was still a polarising figure. Indeed Labor thought he was
their best chance of survival. Joan Kirner delayed the 1992
election for as long as possible, giving Kennett maximum
time to self-destruct. She consistently out-polled him in
popularity. Kennett not only put in a disciplined and focused
performance, but the campaign he helped orchestrate went
straight for the jugular. For months he hammered the theme
of Labor as 'the guilty party'. No one can be certain, of
course, but it is likely that despite his higher disapproval
ratings, Kennett won a more decisive victory than Brown
would have.

9   **Dean Brown, South Australia, 1992.** The South Australian
Labor Government was heading for defeat because of the
scandals centred on the State Bank of South Australia. The
Liberals felt that Opposition Leader Dale Baker was not
cutting through, however, and he was convinced to resign. To
some surprise, Brown defeated Baker's preferred candidate,
John Olsen. Brown then won a handsome election victory. It
is likely Baker and Olsen would also have won, but possibly

not by as much.

10 **John Howard, Federal, 1995.** When the Liberals elected a new leadership team of Alexander Downer and Peter Costello, it was hailed as a generational shift. But the hapless Downer's approval rating plunged from 53 per cent to 20 per cent in five months.[24] Despite the unpopularity of the Keating Government, it is unlikely that Downer could have led the Liberals to victory. After Howard became leader, the Coalition went on to a smashing victory in 1996.

11 **Steve Bracks, Victoria, 1999.** In February 1999, Labor's prospects against Jeff Kennett's Government appeared poor. Nearly all pundits expected Kennett to win the election later that year.[25] Labor dissatisfaction led to John Brumby being replaced by Bracks: 'Bracks's genial, steady style proved a refreshing counterpoint to the increasingly bombastic approach of the incumbent.'[26] Kennett blithely alienated several key constituencies, and Bracks secured a surprise victory. It is possible, but not likely, that Labor would also have won with Brumby.

12 **Kevin Rudd, Federal, 2006.** After Howard's third election victory, in 2004, Labor's morale was low. Kim Beazley's leadership was competent, rather than inspiring. The advent of Rudd brought an immediate boost in the polls for Labor – he was a fresh face, and brought the promise of a generational change. In the ten polls preceding Rudd's elevation, Labor had averaged 51 per cent (2PP), while in the next ten it averaged 57 per cent.[27] It is possible that Beazley would also have won the 2007 election, as the Howard Government had accumulated many political liabilities, but that victory was more certain – and larger – under Rudd.

13 **Barry O'Farrell, New South Wales, 2007.** After the

Liberals' disastrous performance in the 2007 NSW election,
O'Farrell challenged Peter Debnam, who promptly resigned.
The next four years brought a catalogue of catastrophes for
the Iemma/Rees/Keneally Labor governments. In contrast,
the O'Farrell-led Liberals presented an image of stability
and competence, and went on to one of the most smashing
election victories in NSW history. Debnam possibly would
have won given the Labor Government's failings, but certainly
not on the scale O'Farrell did.

14 **Colin Barnett, Western Australia, 2008.** The WA Liberals
went through four leadership changes in the 2005–08
election cycle, only to arrive back where they started. After he
lost to Geoff Gallop, Barnett resigned the leadership, and was
replaced by Matt Birney. A number of public gaffes (including
a reference to the Pope's wife) did not help Birney's cause.
A year later, Paul Omodei beat him in a party-room vote.
In December 2007, Alan Carpenter (who had replaced
Gallop) led Omodei in a poll as preferred Premier 63–13.
Omodei's response was to promise to 'land a right hook'
on anyone asking him to stand aside. In January 2008 Troy
Buswell won the leadership, but Omodei stated that Buswell
was 'not a fit and proper person to lead the party'. Buswell's
leadership only lasted seven months, and was marked by
mishaps and embarrassments. He had gained publicity for
snapping a woman's bra strap, and for sniffing the seat a female
staff member had just vacated. The party was in turmoil
because of Buswell's indiscretions. Under pressure he stood
down. Meanwhile, Barnett had decided to leave politics
completely, and a new candidate was already endorsed for his
seat. Instead, within days, Barnett was unanimously elected
Opposition Leader. The next day, Premier Alan Carpenter
called a snap poll to catch the Liberals unprepared. It did.
They had almost no money and their policy development

was minimal. But Carpenter's ploy meant that, as in 1983 with Hawke, the Liberals immediately united behind Barnett, and the media focused on the election ahead rather than on the Liberals' comical goings-on. Moreover, Barnett was already a familiar public figure. Barnett himself believes that 'a significant number of voters saw Carpenter's election timing as opportunistic'.[28] Barnett won the 2008 election by a wafer-thin margin. The Liberals' farcical leadership merry-go-round in opposition was hardly textbook political strategy, but eventually it resulted in a new era in government for them.

15 **Campbell Newman, Queensland, 2011.** When Newman launched his Queensland Liberal National Party (LNP) leadership bid, the incumbent Opposition Leader, John-Paul Langbroek, had his party leading Labor 55–45 on a 2PP basis. It was claimed that private party polling – that unseen staple of leadership challenges – showed the party would do much better with Newman as leader. Newman, at the time Lord Mayor of Brisbane, became leader of the LNP in Queensland in March 2011. He was the first person to become leader without being a Member of Parliament. Later that day, Langbroek and his deputy, Lawrence Springborg, resigned, having earlier said they would not do so. It is not clear what the numbers would have been in the party room if they had not stood down. Newman went on to secure a spectacular victory (and an equally spectacular loss three years later). The conservatives' majority was probably larger than it otherwise would have been because of the sense of momentum the leadership change brought.

Remembering always that leadership is but one element in determining election outcomes, of the 54 leadership coups in opposition parties, these are the 15 where – in my view – the change substantially helped the party win the next election. There is a similar number where it probably harmed the party's chances – either because the change was to a less capable leader or because the process of the change reinforced public doubts about the party's capacities. In the other cases the leadership coup would probably have made little difference. This hardly supports a conclusion that changing the leader is a sure route to electoral success. Moreover, even in about half of these 15 success stories it is likely that the party would have won anyway. In some – such as Howard replacing Downer and Barnett replacing Buswell – it was necessary for the party to dispense with someone lacking public respect. In other cases, there was a clear step up either in intellectual fire-power or in presentational force, and in those cases the change made the victory larger, or at least more certain, an important consideration for MPs caught up in the suspense of the moment, and whose careers hang by the election result.

The sense of desperation in opposition parties makes them fertile ground for leadership intrigues. However, many of the forced leadership changes that occur reinforce the picture of an ineffectual opposition. On the other hand, just over a quarter of the coups probably contributed substantially to success at the next election.

CHAPTER 7

Leadership Coups and Disintegrating Governments

Leadership challenges are much less frequent in government than in opposition (they are less than a quarter of the successful challenges listed in Appendix B Table 1), but they have produced some of the most dramatic and consequential conflicts in recent Australian history. Leadership coups in government are typically extremely threatening and disruptive. A challenge is tangible evidence that even some of the government's members are dissatisfied with their leader's performance, a public admission that there have been serious errors, or a 'losing of the way'. They also involve, much more sharply, issues of legitimacy, as the party room is replacing someone the public had expected to lead the government when they voted for it.

Not surprisingly, such coups are strongly associated with failure at the next election. Of the 17 leadership challenges that occurred in the major governing party (see Appendix B Table 3), only Turnbull and Keating won the next election outright; three others (Gillard, Olsen and Weatherill) survived as leaders of a minority government, and the other 12 lost government. Of course this does not mean that the party would have won the next election if it had not changed leaders. A forced leadership change is nearly always a recognition that there is a crisis. While leaders are implicated to varying degrees in the plight of a failing government – so that replacing them is sometimes necessary – in the majority of cases a leadership coup has made the situation worse, not better.

This chapter examines three main themes. First it looks at that small number of forced leadership changes that have probably helped the government's electoral prospects. Then it examines the apparently growing trend towards challenges to leaders in their first term of government. While winning government from opposition normally affords successful leaders a degree of authority and gratitude from their colleagues, several in recent years have found themselves deposed by their colleagues before facing their first re-election. Finally, and most usually, challenges occur in long-established governments, and these are often a symptom of – and then, ironically, a stimulus to – government disintegration.

First it should be noted that there are two leadership coups that are neither in opposition nor in the major governing party. The Liberals were the junior partners in the Bjelke Petersen–led Coalition government in Queensland. The longer he was Premier, the more dictatorial Joh's rule within the government became. Many Liberals bridled at his policies, his appointments, and the bullying, wilful style with which he conducted relations with them.[1] They were torn between their desire to be in government and their discontent with the Premier. Llew Edwards replaced the docile William Knox as leader in 1978 largely because the Liberals wanted a stronger voice in government.

The second coup sprang from the same sentiment, but its consequences were much more dramatic, as the Premier ruthlessly exploited it to reduce the Liberals to an irrelevant rump. Terry White was part of a Liberal Party ginger group that wanted to assert Liberal values, such as electoral reform and a well-functioning parliament. When White crossed the floor in August 1983 to support a motion to bring forward debate on forming a parliamentary public accounts committee, Edwards sacked him from the ministry, with Bjelke-Petersen's strong support. White then called a spill motion, and defeated Edwards.

Immediately White and his new deputy, Angus Innes, went to Bjelke-Petersen's office. The Premier kept them waiting an hour, in full view of the media. Eventually he admitted them, and informed them that he would not appoint White as Deputy Premier. White then pulled the Liberals out of the coalition. Bjelke-Petersen called an election, and with parliament prorogued there was no opportunity for Labor and Liberals to unite against the Nationals. The National Party and the Liberal Party contested the 1983 election independently, with the Liberals short of money, and lacking a strong and coherent policy platform of their own. The Nationals won 41 of 82 seats. Two former Liberal Ministers – Brian Austin and Don Lane – then defected to the Nationals. This left just six Liberals to sit in opposition. White resigned, and Knox was elected again to lead the remnant party in opposition. It is tempting to say that White then sought solace in drugs, but rather more accurately, he left politics and set up one of Australia's largest pharmacy chains.

Beneficial government coups?

There are just five leadership coups in government which arguably substantially helped the government's electoral prospects. Two of these – the accessions of Keating and Turnbull – have been considered at length in earlier chapters. In each case a government which had been consistently trailing in the polls managed to narrowly win the next election. Both times the new leader re-energised the government, although in Keating's case, the long challenge and the political paralysis it wrought also did considerable damage to the government.

Another coup that possibly helped the government was Jay Weatherill's overthrow of Mike Rann in South Australia. This was the least disruptive of all the government leadership coups. Rann, having been Labor leader for 17 years and Premier for nine, was intending to step down on the 10th anniversary of becoming Premier, in March 2012. He had won his third election in March 2010, but soon after that the polls, both for party vote and for approval of Rann's performance, deteriorated sharply. In late July 2011 there were reports 'that the left and right factions had formally decided to replace Rann with Education Minister Jay Weatherill'.[2] Rann was angry, but acquiesced, and effected a somewhat prolonged exit, finally resigning as Premier in October. Rann resented being forced to resign sooner than he planned,[3] but it seemed to leave no bitter residue in the party or the electorate. Some thought that Rann's eye had been on retirement, and that the government had been drifting. Weatherill gave it a sense of renewal. Helped by the lopsided pattern of electoral support, he was – unexpectedly – able to hold on to a minority government after the next election, although the Liberals won more votes.

Two other forced leadership changes may have benefited the government, but because the government's situation was so bad, or because it had ongoing difficulties, the new leader was not able to retrieve the situation. It was a necessary move for the NSW Liberals to replace the erratic Tom Lewis with the more solid Eric Willis, but it failed to help their cause. Robert Askin, in 1965, became the first conservative leader to win a NSW election in 24 years. Just under ten years later, he retired as the longest-serving NSW Premier, having dominated the government he led. Most expected his deputy of 16 years, Willis, to succeed him, even though many MPs found Willis 'dry, academic and humourless'. Askin had promised to support Willis, but after Willis declined to support Askin for a higher knighthood, he threw his support behind the more amenable Lewis. Askin also thought Lewis was better on TV.[4]

Willis was so confident of victory that he did not campaign strongly. Indeed he went into the meeting expecting to succeed and was shattered by the outcome.[5] Soon after becoming Premier, Lewis broke the convention for replacing Senators – where they come from the same party – when he refused to appoint Labor's nominee after Senator Lionel Murphy went to the High Court. Liberals all over the country were split over this. At the subsequent joint sitting of the NSW Houses of Parliament that ratifies such appointments,

Labor created uproar and Lewis lost all semblance of control.

Liberal MPs' doubts continued to grow as their accident-prone leader continued his mis-steps. Just before Fraser's sweeping federal victory in December 1975, the NSW Liberals suffered a swing of 9 per cent at a by-election.[6] Party polling which showed a negative net approval 32–50 for Lewis and a positive net approval of 50–25 for Opposition Leader Neville Wran was leaked in January.[7] Soon afterwards, Lewis walked into a party meeting, suspecting nothing, and a spill motion succeeded by 22–11. Willis was unanimously elected to succeed him.

A few months later Willis called an election, seven months earlier than he needed to, apparently worried by the likely unpopularity of Fraser's federal government. His gamble failed. Wran won the election on 1 May 1976 by a single seat, with two seats decided by fewer than 100 votes. He then turned this barest of majorities into the 'Wranslides' of 1978 and 1981.

Peter Dowding and his successor, Carmen Lawrence, were both victims of Brian Burke's WA Inc. scandal – about the dealings between the Labor Government and various large corporations, most notably Laurie Connell's failing merchant bank, Rothwells. Dowding inherited a situation he would never have initiated, but then made it much worse. Against expectations, Dowding led Labor to an election victory in 1989, its loss of primary votes not being matched by a loss of seats. But within six months the party's state secretary, Stephen Smith, had decided that Dowding had to go before the next election.[8] The problem was that as Rothwells' losses continued to worsen, threatening the recovery of the government money already invested, Dowding's response was to commit still more. The party political rationale for such spending was clear, given that Burke and Dowding had mortgaged their government's welfare to Rothwells' survival. But there was no public policy rationale. It was the government's, not the state's, welfare that was being advanced. The editor of the *West Australian*, Paul Murray, called it 'the era of the big lies'.[9]

In early 1990, a principal of Rothwells, Tony Lloyd, was found guilty of a $15 million fraud, having claimed in the trial that he had acted on instructions from Dowding. This was the trigger for Smith and a group of Labor MPs to force Dowding out immediately. Stories in the press accurately reported that Smith had the numbers to make Dowding resign, and that Lawrence would succeed him.[10] Lawrence's performance as Premier was mixed, but even if it had been brilliant, the weight of WA Inc. was too great for her to win the next election.

First-term governments

In recent years there have been four leadership coups in first-term governments. In each case there was centralisation around the leader, and a sense of exclusion among others.

The first such first-term coup was when John Olsen displaced Dean Brown as Liberal Premier of South Australia. The challenge was mounted when the government was still travelling well electorally, although some of its members felt frustrated by its lack of decisiveness. The conservatives in the party dubbed the Premier 'Dean Beige'.[11] The key factor, however, seems to be that Olsen, perhaps still resenting his unexpected defeat for the opposition leadership by Brown in 1992, moved the moment he knew he had the numbers (after two moderates, possibly because of disappointed ambition, defected from Brown).

The coup had its own damaging aftermath. There were rumours that as part of his effort to destabilise Brown, Olsen had leaked Cabinet documents to the Opposition Leader, Mike Rann. Rann confirmed this in Parliament under privilege. Outside parliament Olsen called him a liar. Rann immediately sued Olsen, and the court case helped to keep the Liberals' internal conflicts in the public eye[12] in the months leading up to the 1997 election. The government lost 14 seats, and so moved from having a large majority to being a minority government, relying on the support of two independents to stay in office.

The coup against Ted Baillieu, in Victoria, resembled that against Rudd in some of its themes, notably dissatisfaction with the centralisation of power in the leader's office, the feeling that as a result there was a mounting backlog of decisions not taken, and increasing electoral worries. In Baillieu's case, however, there was none of the personal animus occasioned by arrogant and aggressive behaviour. As with the coup against Rudd, the discontents were slow in building but swift in execution, and the immediate reception for the new leader was positive; however, the initial boost in the polls did not last.

The immediate events leading to Baillieu's fall occurred rapidly and unexpectedly, but it was the longer term context that made him vulnerable. Baillieu had won government with a bare one seat majority in 2010. Soon, however, his government was consistently trailing in the polls.[13] Labor labelled him a 'do nothing Premier', a charge which was more potent because of the state's mediocre economic performance – it moved into recession the week he fell.

At the weekly meeting of MPs held the day before Baillieu resigned, many 'vented their anger over the distractions from the business of governing. A senior minister told *The Age* Mr Baillieu was now just "one or two stuff-ups" away from a leadership challenge.'[14] The previous week the *Herald-Sun* had revealed that a former staffer, who had been forced to resign because of his role in a plot to undermine former Police Commissioner Simon Overland, had secretly taped conversations with Baillieu's Chief of Staff, Tony Nutt, and party secretary Damien Mantach. The Liberals had offered him cash ($22,500), accommodation and assistance in obtaining employment with the Liberal 'family'.[15] The day after the Liberals' meeting, the member for Frankston, Geoff Shaw, resigned from the party, thus making it a minority government. Shaw, as well as being erratic and a self-publicist, was an evangelical Christian who wanted the government to introduce tougher abortion laws;

he was also under investigation for misuse of public funds. None of this messy mix of controversies was Baillieu's fault, but according to political logic he was responsible for fixing them.

Baillieu then gave a stirring speech to the party room on the need for loyalty, but he could see by the body language that he had lost considerable support,[16] and as the day went on, he gained a clearer idea of possible moves against him. A spill motion probably would not have succeeded, but Baillieu chose to resign rather than be the focus of ongoing conflict. At 7pm, in a shock to almost everyone, he announced his resignation in an emotional speech, a speech that was also strongly supportive of his successor, Denis Napthine.

Senior Liberals sought to minimise the drama of the leadership change, describing it simply as a 'circuit breaker' and a 'rebooting' moment.[17] The immediate polls were not damaging: Napthine was preferred over Baillieu 45–37, but Labor was still ahead 52–48 on a 2PP basis, and the public was evenly split, 44–44, on their approval of the way Baillieu was replaced as Premier.[18] Over time, however, the government failed to improve its performance and Labor won the 2014 election.

Leadership coups and the disintegration of long-term state governments

Perhaps the most damaging conflicts come when the leadership challenge is the product of an explosive mix of electoral desperation and policy exhaustion. Sometimes there seems to be one immobilising issue which cannot be overcome, either because of ideological conflict or because of practical difficulties, and which affects relationships throughout the government. The four most dramatic and consequential leadership coups – in each case involving a state government which had once been cohesive and electorally dominant, but which later fell into decay and division – are considered below in order of how damaging they were. There then follows the somewhat different but equally devastating case of the Queensland Nationals.

4. Dick Hamer. The managed transition from Victorian Liberal Henry Bolte to Dick Hamer in 1972 was one of the most successful in a long-reigning government. It was a marked change of style, from the plain-speaking, confrontational Bolte to the more urbane and tolerant Hamer, but it seemed to be very much in tune with the changing times. Hamer secured two clear victories, in 1973 and 1976, the latter with a record majority.

However, he won the 1979 election with just a one-seat majority.[19] His government had been greatly weakened by what was called 'the lands scandals'. From then on what had been Hamer's political strengths started to become weaknesses. Instead of seeming calm, he seemed passive; instead of tolerant, weak. There was pressure from business groups wanting more pro-business policies, and he was facing a revitalised Labor opposition.[20] As Victoria's economic prospects and the Liberals' electoral prospects both declined, there was an increasing sense of urgency in parliamentary ranks.

The issue that crystallised the sense of crisis was a casino. Hamer made two unsuccessful attempts to introduce one. His failure heightened the impression of 'division and vacillation' in the government, according to Liberal MP Kevin Foley.[21] In March 1981, polls showed the Liberals trailing Labor by 10 percentage points: 'Extraordinary, almost farcical events followed.'[22] A young, ambitious Minister, Ian Smith, abruptly intervened by moving a Private Member's Bill to introduce a casino. Hamer sacked Smith for breaching Cabinet solidarity, but after Smith apologised Hamer reinstated him. In May Hamer left for the United States. His young Housing Minister, Jeff Kennett, had sent a letter to all Cabinet Ministers urging Hamer not to go, but to stay and seek a better housing deal from the Fraser federal government Not surprisingly, while Hamer was away, the letter leaked.[23] Polls now showed the

Liberals trailing by 20 percentage points. Smith, in a media interview, said that the party was 'numb with fright' at the prospect of facing the next election under Hamer. Hamer cut short his trip, and resigned on his return. Hamer's successor was his longstanding and loyal deputy Lindsay Thompson, who lost the election the following year. The leadership crisis only deepened the sense that this was a government whose time had passed.

3. Doug Lowe. Also an initially successful Premier, Doug Lowe was the victim of changing political priorities, which created new but strong and enduring divisions within the old Labor constituency in Tasmania. The Labor Party governed Tasmania for 45 of the 48 years from 1934 to 1982. In a state chronically beset by economic stagnation and high unemployment, the key to Labor's continuing success was government involvement in supporting economic development. From soon after World War II, it was realised that one of Tasmania's competitive advantages was the ability to produce relatively cheap energy through developing hydroelectric power. The HEC (Hydro-Electric Commission, known as the Hydro) became one of the most powerful organisations in the state. The first challenge to this consensual view came in the early 1970s, with protests against the flooding of Lake Pedder. But the Premier, 'Electric Eric' Reece, overrode those concerns.[24] However, in 1978 the Hydro announced its plan to build a dam on the Gordon River below the Franklin, which would flood the Franklin Valley. This outraged environmentalists. The Tasmanian Wilderness Society mounted a vigorous 'No Dams' campaign.

Lowe, increasingly sympathetic to the environmentalists' view, sought an alternative site, but his suggested compromise was rejected by both sides. From early on, the Cabinet was internally divided over the Franklin Dam proposal. Lowe forwarded to the Fraser Government a proposal to place much of Southwestern Tasmania on the World Heritage List; this angered his opponents. To resolve the deadlock, the Tasmanian Government decided to hold a referendum. Lowe found the state party conference 'a gut-wrenching affair'. Harry Holgate mounted an initial challenge to Lowe's leadership, which Lowe defeated. He then demoted Holgate to a more junior ranking in the Cabinet, although later he thought this had 'cemented among my opponents … a level of bitterness which was to work to my extreme disadvantage'. Then members of the environmental faction broke ranks, with one Minister, Andrew Lohrey, publicly advocating for a coal-fired power station instead. After Lowe required his resignation, Lohrey also became an implacable enemy. As the situation unravelled further, Lowe's 'feeling of isolation was unbelievable … I was to plummet into the depths of despair.'[25]

In November 1981, Holgate replaced Lowe by a 12–9 vote. Lowe joined the cross-benches, charging that the state branch was controlled 'by an elite clique of the trade union movement'.[26] The state Labor Party executive ruled that there would be no 'No Dams' option on the referendum – possibly the last time a party state executive overruled an elected government on a policy issue. The referendum produced a very big informal vote, with 45 per cent writing in 'No Dams' on their ballot paper. Holgate postponed the election as long as he could, but then went down to the Liberals.

After the overthrow of Lowe and the government's manipulation of the dams referendum process, Labor had forfeited the environmental vote. But neither could it compete with the strong pro-development stance of the Liberals under Robin Gray. In 1982 Gray joined with a militant left-wing trade unionist to form the Organisation for Tasmanian Development. The triangular 'No Dams' sticker had become very popular; theirs were rather less tolerant, with slogans such as 'Keep warm this winter: Burn a Greenie'. Former Labor Premier Reece joined them at a rally, where Gray described his former Labor opponent as the 'greatest living Tasmanian'.

Gray won the election easily, and ordered that the dam proceed. The Wilderness Society started blockading the site. After

Hawke's 1983 election victory, the federal government stopped the dam, winning a High Court challenge to its constitutional power to do so. The plan was never revived. In Paul Kelly's view,[27] Hawke's stance on this, the first environmental test of the 1980s, set the scene for a continuing advantage over the federal Liberals, whose distaste for exercising federal power over the states gave it a disadvantage. The consequences in Tasmanian politics were more mixed, and in the short term damaged Labor. But the environmental constituency was an enduring one. The actions on these issues helped to give birth to the Greens, and to create its first two national leaders, Bob Brown and Christine Milne.

2. John Cain. In 1982, John Cain became the first Labor Premier in Victoria since 1955; later he became the first Labor leader to win three successive Victorian elections. Despite early successes, both in economic performance and politically, Cain's downfall was even more dramatic than Hamer's:

> The final years of Cain's premiership were a catalogue of crisis – financial disasters, poisonous intra-party division and debilitating conflict with public sector unions. He resigned in 1990, his authority in the party exhausted and support in the electorate broken.[28]

At first, Cain led a cohesive team. He wrote: 'We were leak-free from June 1983 to late 1989 – something which frustrated the media.' But 'by early 1990 we were a disunited, shambling government racked by lack of trust in each other'.[29]

Although the Hawke–Keating economic reforms were important and necessary, the teething problems of the period are often forgotten. Bank deregulation highlighted the managerial limitations of existing banks; it was a period where corporate buccaneers and greenmail (buying strategic shareholdings with the aim of being bought out at a great profit) thrived; and the ambiguities of public–private partnerships set traps for some governments. Combined with the Cain Government's activist approach to economic stimulus, these behaviours led to a series of problems. The first involved the VEDC (Victorian Economic Development Corporation). Several of the businesses to which it had made loans failed. Then the debts of Tricontinental, the merchant banking arm of the State Bank of Victoria, started to become public, with the amount beginning at $150 million and climbing to $900 million. Government Ministers were not directly involved, but large sums of public money were lost. Then the Pyramid Building Society collapsed. Cain had reassured investors that this would not happen, and then refused to bail them out after it did.

These issues were compounded by intransigent demands from public sector unions, whose industrial action was alienating the public. The problems of the government exacerbated old factional divisions, and the earlier unity was fracturing, especially as some of Cain's closest colleagues either retired or were politically wounded. He thought that 'the net loss of talent [from Cabinet] was considerable. But more importantly, the sum total of commitment to the government was substantially diminished.'[30] There was further factional brawling over the 1990 budget, with Cain being overturned on key points. Finally, 'on 7 August, bitter and dejected, [Cain] announced his resignation'.[31] Liberal leader Jeff Kennett scored a decisive victory over Joan Kirner, Cain's replacement, two years later.

1. Morris Iemma. Rarely have any governments collapsed as completely as the NSW Labor Governments of 2007–11. Iemma won the 2007 election in New South Wales at a time when, after 12 years in government, many would have expected the electoral pendulum to be swinging back towards the Liberals. But 'from the moment he was re-elected, scarcely anything went right for [him]'.[32] Less than 18 months later he was forced to resign. His successor, Nathan Rees, was deposed 15 months later, and then his successor, Kristina Keneally, led the Labor Government to a massive defeat: 'The Coalition won a record victory on 26 March. Its two-party preferred vote was 64.2 per cent, a swing of 16.9 per cent.' Its 'primary vote was 51.2 per cent compared with Labor's 25.6 per cent'.[33]

Three factors explain this extraordinary disintegration. The first was the increasing assertiveness of the Labor Party's state secretaries, Mark Arbib and then Karl Bitar, and their firm view, from within months of the 2007 victory, that Iemma could not win another election and had to go. Earlier they had supported him. An unnamed senior Minister told Kate McClymont and Linton Besser that one reason they supported Iemma as Carr's replacement was that they could influence him, that 'Iemma is a blank sheet of paper and [we] can write our words on it.'[34] Although at the end of 2007 Labor still led in the polls,[35] the state secretary, at that time Arbib, had decided that Iemma, and all the most prominent Ministers in the government – Michael Costa, Reba Meagher, Frank Sartor – would take the party to annihilation. Rodney Cavalier, a Minister under both Neville Wran and Barry Unsworth, reported that Arbib thought that 'The only option was a cleanskin.'[36] They fixed upon Nathan Rees, who had been in Parliament for only 18 months, had held only junior portfolios, and was virtually unknown to the public. The *Sydney Morning Herald* editorial called the new ministry 'the C team'.[37] Rees's dependence on the state secretary was shown immediately, when he volunteered at a press conference that Bitar was vetting the ministerial selections.[38]

The second factor was the increasing power within the party of a corrupt group, centred on Eddie Obeid, who were intent on using the apparatus of government to profit themselves and their associates. Obeid and Joe Tripodi controlled the 'Terrigals', the majority group in the right-wing faction in Caucus. In all three leadership changes – the accessions of Iemma, Rees and Keneally – Obeid and Tripodi were brokers for the winning side. According to the *Daily Telegraph*'s Simon Benson, Obeid and Tripodi were 'Iemma's praetorian guards'.[39] As McClymont and Besser report, 'By 2008, Obeid was at the zenith of his powers. He had unprecedented access to Carr's successor, Morris Iemma';[40] and Sartor thought that Tripodi's power had greatly increased under Rees.[41]

The third factor was the pernicious influence of Treasurer Michael Costa. Iemma had a close alliance with him. Nearly all other Ministers had bad relationships with Costa, who had transferred the absolutist dogma of his Trotskyist youth to an equally absolutist neo-liberalism, which detested all government regulation of the market. Cavalier again: 'He did not brook opposition. His method of arguing crossed the border into bullying.'[42] He was arrogantly dismissive of all differing views: he thought the Reserve Bank Governor Glenn Stevens was an 'idiot',[43] and when Rudd explained to COAG the federal government's strategies to address the GFC, 'Costa burst out laughing', which – understandably – angered Rudd.[44]

Iemma and Costa were determined to privatise electricity: this was their solution to the state's financial issues and future electricity generation needs. It was something they had conspicuously failed to mention before the election.[45] Indeed, according to Benson, 'Iemma and Costa had hoped to keep the sale entirely away from parliament.'[46] Not only did opinion polls show majorities opposing the move, but Iemma could not get support either from the trade unions or in the Labor Party. Iemma and Costa confronted the 2008 state Labor conference on the issue, but the result was a disaster for them. Eventually a motion opposing the sale was carried, overwhelmingly: 702–107. Moreover, the sight of Costa haranguing his party allies, and calling them a joke, made for dramatic and damaging television: 'From his performance on that weekend, scarcely a soul did not conclude that Costa was other than stark, raving bonkers.'[47]

Undaunted, on the following Monday, Iemma and Costa 'insisted they would plough on regardless' and ignore the conference.[48] Costa charged that members of his own party had not got used to the fact that the Berlin Wall had come down.[49] The various deadlocks continued for a couple of months. Eventually Iemma sought to reshuffle his ministry, but he was unable to get his own way, and resigned.

Rees's leadership failed to lift Labor's prospects. Increasingly frustrated, and increasingly concerned by what he saw as the corruption inside the government, he persuaded state conference to give him the power to appoint his own Ministers, rather than let the Caucus, meaning the factions, 'elect' them. He immediately sacked Tripodi and Ian Macdonald. However, the result was that 'In a clear indication of how inward-looking and self-obsessed the ALP had become, Rees' actions galvanised the resolve of right-wing leaders to bring him down.'[50]

Nothing became Nathan Rees's premiership like his leaving of it. At a media conference:

> Rees's rhetoric was laced with white-hot anger. There was no spin, no sugar-coating … Thin-lipped with fury, Rees took the knife to those who had given him the crown and were now snatching it away. He decried the 'malign and disloyal group well known to the NSW community [who] had made the business of government almost impossible'.[51]

He concluded, 'Should I not be Premier by the end of this day, let there be no doubt in the community's mind, no doubt, that any challenger will be a puppet of Eddie Obeid and Joe Tripodi. That is the reality.'[52]

The image coloured the early coverage of new Premier Kristina Keneally – 'Keneally pays back puppet masters'.[53] Inheriting a hopeless cause, Keneally did as well as anyone could have in the next few months. Then, incredibly, she and Treasurer Eric Roozendaal sought to renew the push to privatise electricity. When eight members of electricity organisations resigned in protest, concerned about their organisations' future viability, Keneally prorogued parliament to prevent any investigation.[54]

The Labor Government of 2007–11 is one of only two governments to have two leadership coups in one electoral cycle. The leadership instability was a symptom of a deep malaise, but the coups only added to the government's problems, without offering any hope of a new beginning. The party plunged to one of the worst election defeats in modern Australian history.

The most bizarre coup. The only other occasion in which a ruling government has had two successful leadership challenges in the one electoral cycle was the National Party Government in Queensland in the late 1980s. It is not included in the countdown above partly because the events are so bizarre, and partly because the first of the coups, the removal of Joh Bjelke-Petersen as Premier, was – unlike the other cases of long-serving governments above – necessary, and offered the government a glimmer of hope.

After his 1986 election triumph, Bjelke-Petersen devoted most of his energies to his 'Joh for Canberra' folly. By the time this collapsed, developments in Queensland were beyond his control. Triggered by investigative reporting of police corruption by the ABC's *Four Corners* and the *Courier-Mail*, the Fitzgerald Royal Commission had been established. It began substantive public hearings in July 1987.[55] Its daily exposure of corruption transformed the political environment.

John Wanna and Tracey Arklay described the last year of Bjelke-Petersen's tenure as 'grotesque to the point of parody and disbelief'.[56] In late 1987, the Premier belatedly tried to regain the political initiative by announcing that he would resign the following August, on the twentieth anniversary of his becoming Premier. But he had already lost the support of many key players. He refused to meet with his Ministers and discuss his leadership. Next he sought to sack five Ministers he considered disloyal, but the Governor, Sir Walter Campbell (later described by the Premier as the only appointment he regretted making), advised him to consult his Ministers. The dissident Ministers believed Bjelke-Petersen's plan was to create a new Cabinet, and to use it to close down the Fitzgerald Royal Commission. The parliamentary party met, and by a large majority removed him from the leadership. He refused to resign, and barricaded himself in the Premier's office, on the fifteenth floor of the Executive Building. Eventually, prompted by the threat that the party and government would refuse to pay his legal costs, he resigned on 1 December.[57]

Bjelke-Petersen's successor, Mike Ahern, continued to be embarrassed by the Fitzgerald Commission's revelations about the preceding regime's corruption. In Parliament he was under forensic attack by Wayne Goss and the Labor opposition, forced either to defend the indefensible or weakly distance himself from what had occurred. From the time of the publication of the Fitzgerald Report, in July 1989, many Nationals believed they could not win with Ahern. Russell Cooper defeated him at the second attempt, with a contradictory alliance of two groups – the Joh loyalists who never fully accepted Ahern, and the original Ahern backers, including Cooper himself, who increasingly doubted Ahern's ability to win, and thought that only another new leader could contain the accumulated damage of the previous few years.[58] Unlike Ahern, Cooper was not committed to introducing the Fitzgerald reforms immediately. He went on to a resounding defeat at the 1989 election, almost certainly performing worse than Ahern would have done, and ushered in the first Labor Government in Queensland in 32 years.

The bizarre end of the Bjelke-Petersen reign is strong testimony to the uniqueness of political events, and to the fact that they are rarely reducible to a few neat formulas. There are some recurring patterns in the overthrow of government leaders, but there are always important exceptions as well. In nearly all these challenges, worry about the government's electoral position was important. Even when not the dominant concern, it added to the levels of tension and insecurity in the party room. Personal conflicts were often important: sometimes because of clashing ambition, but sometimes because of worries over leaders' performance and judgment. And as conflict sharpened, personal tensions rose. Sometimes the leaders were centrally responsible for the government's problems, but even when this was not true, removing them became seen as the most feasible route to recovery, a hope which more often than not proved illusory.

CHAPTER 8

Media and Momentum

Party leadership is, first of all and inescapably, leadership of the party room, of a relatively small group of MPs, who share the wish to win elections, but will have different policy views, different views on strategy, and competing ambitions. They are a unique group, with the intensity of a sports team, but without the catharsis of frequent matches. They mix together regularly for long periods, with camaraderie, friendship and intimacy among some, but also rivalries and animosities with others.

Glyn Davis has captured the intensity of these internal relationships by likening party leadership to leadership of a street gang. The gang leader must embody the gang's values and culture, but must also be sensitive to the wishes of those he or she leads, and 'loyalty is always provisional'.[1] Similarly, in the eyes of Tony Abbott the personal relations inside the Howard Liberal Government overrode any rational political calculus: 'John Howard wasn't only our leader; he was like our father … You can't kill your father.'[2] Peter Costello bemoaned the fact that the members who had won their seats in 1996 felt a sense of gratitude to Howard for that victory and that Howard was the only party leader they had known: 'For many of them the Liberal Party was the Howard Party.'[3] Conspicuously, Rudd after 2007 and Abbott after 2013 failed to generate such sentiment among the first-term members who had won on their coat-tails.

Relationships inside the microcosm are crucial to the leader's survival, but these bear an uncertain and changing relationship to the public spectacle. In all political conflicts, there can be a disjunction between public appearances and private realities, but this is particularly marked in leadership struggles. Public statements are often calculated to conceal what is happening, so the media must rely on leaks and briefings, but their accuracy and their significance are often very difficult for the public to discern. Moreover, what appears in the media impacts directly on the relationships and personal attitudes inside the party room. Finally, the processes of a challenge are marked by uncertainty, so bringing them to a climax is often a fraught process, and what appears in the media is likely to have a different impact in the party room than it does among the public. These last issues are illustrated by looking at the misadventures of Andrew Peacock and Kim Beazley in party leadership struggles.

The minefield of public statements

I'll tell you why I should be leader of the Liberal Party – I'm the best – that's why I should be. I can give leadership to my team and they will all follow me. If I asked [them] to walk through the valley of death on hot coals, they'd do it. Every one of them trusts me. Everyone recognizes my political judgement and, if I say something must be this, it will be. That's why I'm leader.

Bill Snedden, November 1974[4]

News surveillance of party politics is so intense that participants must have strategies for dealing with it. Even when private relations are tense, they need ways to try to diminish that perception in the public. After the tensions between Bob Hawke and Paul Keating, following the Treasurer's 1986 'banana republic' statement on the economy, the Liberals sought to embarrass them in parliament. Keating returned fire, brazenly declaring that he and Hawke formed the 'greatest partnership of economic achievement in half a century' while Labor backbenchers cheered him on.[5] Even in 1988, when their personal relationship was on the brink of collapsing, they 'agreed to say publicly they had an ongoing working relationship – to keep the party happy and maintain a public front'.[6]

But declarations of confidence need to have some basis in reality. Snedden's proclamation of self-confidence (opposite) would have been bombastic at any time, but coming at a time when the whole press gallery knew his leadership was endangered made it more ridiculous.

Sometimes the determination to publicly agree leads to absurd formulations. In April 2012, when Gillard was overseas and the controversy over former Speaker Peter Slipper's wrongs was raging, Bill Shorten was interviewed on Sky. Not knowing what she had said, Shorten replied, 'My view is what the Prime Minister's view is … I support what she said', and 'I haven't seen what she's said, but let me say I support what it is she said', prompting the *Guardian* to ask, 'Is Bill Shorten the world's most loyal politician?'[7] Not quite as ridiculously, in February 2009, after reports about tensions in the party room between Costello and Turnbull, Turnbull told Melbourne radio, 'Peter and I have discussed it and we agreed that I would say, and the position would be, literally, that he had made it clear that he was not interested in a frontbench or leadership role.'[8] Neither Shorten's blind loyalty nor Turnbull's convoluted prose about an agreed public formulation were very convincing.

The Chaser comedy team on ABC TV made fun of the hypocrisies surrounding leadership challenges by having veteran Liberal backbench MP Alan Cadman read a statement unequivocally professing his loyalty to Howard and his lack of interest in challenging. As soon as he finished, the *The Chaser* panel all chorused, 'It's on', as if a challenge were imminent. In a later election special they made fun of the ritual phrase often used by politicians, namely that if the leader is run over by a bus, they might be interested in replacing them. They had a manic Costello driving a bus, trying to run over Howard as he went on his morning walk.

The Chaser's first item involving Cadman stems from the media's relentless search for wiggle room, or escape clauses, in politicians' statements; the weasel words and conditionals that make seemingly definite statements less than absolute commitments. Such humour arises partly because of the hypocrisies of politicians, but partly also because the media put them into a double bind. It is conventional wisdom that a leader who announces they will retire at some future date becomes a lame duck from the moment of the announcement. That then puts pressure on leaders to make unconditional statements saying that they will stay, so when sudden resignations then occur there is outrage. The news media relish sharp conflicts much more than expressions of agreement and mutual admiration.[9] Politicians know this, and become adept at trying to make statements that are at least inoffensive. This all too often leads them into the tired clichés (such as if the leader is run over by a bus) that most observers know can mask a much sharper and more problematic reality.

In an area ripe for hypocrisy and double talk, it is not surprising that the trend on all sides has been towards ever greater cynicism. In 1974–75, as Malcolm Fraser was stalking Snedden, he consistently denied all ambition to replace him. 'I support the Parliamentary Leader of the Liberal Party' was his mantra. After the November move against Snedden failed, Fraser issued a statement claiming:

> I took no part in what occurred this morning in the party
> room. I asked no one for support, nor would I do so. What
> occurred was initiated by other people without my knowledge
> or encouragement ... I support the parliamentary leader of the
> Liberal Party.[10]

After Fraser had indeed replaced Snedden, in a TV interview, his chief public backer, Tony Staley, claimed that when he raised the leadership with Fraser the latter's response, was, 'Oh my God, don't talk to me about it. I can't bear to think about it.' Appearing on the same program, John Gorton, still bitter about his own overthrow, made the simple but devastating riposte, 'I bet he did.'[11]

Fraser's absolute denials cost him considerable credibility. Years later, John Howard, who had in 1975 been a Fraser supporter, said he found Fraser's assault on Snedden while denying it distasteful; he himself 'was determined to avoid the accusations of hypocrisy [that had been] levelled against Fraser'.[12] At the time journalist Laurie Oakes wrote, 'Perhaps the most perplexing thing about Fraser is what a former Liberal Minister describes as "a pattern of contrast between what he says he's going to do and what he eventually does".'[13] Among Fraser's successors, such a perplexing pattern has become more, not less, common.

A generation later, after Keating lost his initial challenge to Hawke, he solemnly promised there would be no second round. His followers held a celebratory party, rejoicing at how well they had done, and 'the media, with justification, promptly declared the start of "round two"'.[14] No one expressed any outrage that Keating was publicly lying. This had become so much the norm that when Kerry Chikarovski was challenging Peter Collins a spin doctor prepared a dossier for her which included advice on what she should say. The remarks scripted for her included: 'Personally I like Peter but the party simply believed he allowed Bob Carr to get away with too much' and 'I have no intention of challenging.'[15]

Within just five years of the indignation at Fraser's hypocrisy, there was much less reaction to Hawke's lying. While still not a Member of Parliament, Hawke told a US audience in 1980, at which Australian journalists were present, that Bill Hayden would easily lose the 1980 election and that he, Hawke, would take over after the debacle. After this was reported in Australia, an embarrassed Hawke simply denied the stories, even though they were true.[16]

As politicians have become ever more brazen about lying, their public statements are a less and less useful guide to what is occurring; indeed they often give a deliberately misleading picture. Only the media's use of leaks and briefings can provide a more penetrating view.

Leaks and truth

Much of the action in leadership conflicts is subterranean, and public statements are often designed to camouflage what is actually happening. Leaks and a range of covert briefings and gossip more generally are necessary if one wants to have any idea of what is actually occurring. A reliance on covert news sources whose identity is not revealed publicly is indispensable in reporting the internal politics of parties. However, this poses risks for the journalists, the public and the politicians themselves.

A recurring risk for politicians amid such secrecy is that the private reality will become publicly exposed. Keating would have been politically damaged, perhaps to the extent of destroying his leadership ambitions, if an intercepted telephone conversation he had with Richardson in 1988 had been published. When Keating was angry with Hawke following the 1988 budget (see Chapter 4), Richardson tried to mediate. He got Hawke to appear on television extravagantly praising Keating, and then rang the latter urging him to make peace. Instead Keating let loose with a wave of invective full of four-letter words.[17]

Soon word spread that the mobile phone call had been intercepted and a transcript was being offered, for a price. Fortunately for Labor, no media outlet decided to purchase and publish it. However, Hawke soon had a copy, and read it on a plane from Canberra to Sydney. He then kept an audience of 200 at a Labor fundraiser waiting for 45 minutes while he rang Keating and 'blasted him unmercifully'. In his memoirs, he related with some pride that his press secretary, Barrie Cassidy, 'said afterwards that my language would have emptied the bar of the John Curtin Hotel in my drinking days'.[18] Hawke told Keating that if the transcript became public he would retaliate.

Perhaps it was an indicator of the relative good fortune Labor was having at the time and the bad luck that plagued the Liberals that while this mobile phone call was not published, an earlier one between Victorian Opposition Leader Jeff Kennett and Peacock, attacking Howard, was, and indeed resulted in Peacock being demoted by Howard. A call from Kennett late on a Saturday night woke up his friend Peacock. Kennett was angry that some public comments by Howard had undermined his campaigning in a state by-election. In the tirade that followed, Peacock was largely trying to calm the over-excited Kennett, who was pouring abundant scorn on Howard. Nevertheless, once the transcript of the call was published in the Melbourne *Sun*, Howard required Peacock's resignation because of his disloyalty.[19]

Howard himself faced a similar danger in an amusing episode in 1984. On the day after the election in which the Liberals, under Peacock, had done much better than anyone expected, the journalist Peter Rees rang Howard at home. At the time, Howard, 'shocked by the results, looked doomed to the role of loyal deputy … He had expected and did not fear a bad Liberal defeat; he would have relished the chance it gave him.'[20] Rees was startled first by the warm greeting he received from Howard, and then by the very frank, harsh criticisms Howard made of Peacock. Howard said he thought Peacock had 'fundamental weaknesses' and would 'never be Prime Minister', and likened the current situation to 1974, where Snedden had performed fairly well in the election but was still replaced by Fraser before the next election. Their talk was interrupted, and Howard suggested Rees call back. When he did, Howard was shocked and alarmed to find that he had been talking to journalist Peter Rees and not his colleague Peter Reith. Howard, who had problems with hearing, asked Rees not to publish his remarks because they were given on the basis of mistaken identity. Rees somewhat reluctantly agreed, but reserved the right to publish later, which he did, after Howard had replaced Peacock as leader.[21]

If the media had to rely solely on the public statements of the participants, the public would know much less, and much of it would be quite misleading. But the dependence on leaks also poses dangers for reporters and difficulties for the public.

Brian Dale, first a NSW state political reporter and then press secretary for Labor leader Neville Wran, was on both sides of this potential for manipulation. After Askin's 1973 election victory, Dale was one of four journalists to visit the Premier's house. Askin told them that the ageing Attorney-General, Ken McCaw, would have to go, because he was now almost blind. They all published it, but then Askin denied that McCaw would stand down, said he didn't know how the story had started, and denounced the reporters for their irresponsibility.[22] They were unable, of course, to respond. Dale later became press secretary to Opposition Leader Wran, and said in his memoirs that in presenting the ALP's private party polling, he 'always added a point or so to Wran and deducted it from [Liberal Premier] Willis'.[23]

Even when there is no deliberate misleading of journalists by sources, it is very difficult to know the balance of numbers or shifting sentiments, especially if access is to only one side. Normally it would be good for reporters to be close to the Premier's office, in order to know what a party is likely to do, but if the usual key sources are not in touch with what is happening elsewhere, this can be a trap. In the last months of Morris Iemma's and Michael Costa's tenures as Premier and Treasurer respectively, the ground was shifting in other parts of the party, and the journalists close to these two were thus misled. Former NSW Minister and political analyst Rodney Cavalier quotes four separate occasions in the period leading up to Iemma's forced resignation where the *Daily Telegraph*'s Simon Benson pronounced the Premier safe: 'The campaign to dump Morris Iemma is dead in the water. Fini. Kaput. Terminado … The plot is officially foiled.'[24]

Even when both sides are available to journalists, it may be impossible to decide between competing versions. In the history of the Hawke–Keating years, the two principals 'had entirely different viewpoints on what had happened within the Labor government'.[25] Keating 'resented to the point of fury', for example, stories saying he was reluctant to float the dollar.[26] Hawke thought that Keating's 'ambition became the prism through which all events of the past and present were viewed'[27] – a comment that others might also apply to him. One incident on which they gave directly contradictory accounts was an argument they had over Hawke vacating the leadership. Hawke charged that Keating said that if he didn't get his chance, he would not be sticking around: 'We won't be staying here – this is the arse-end of the world.'[28] Keating disputed vigorously that he ever said this. Only the two of them were present.

Sometimes the accounts given by participants, all apparently genuinely held, cannot be reconciled. In February 2009, after Julie Bishop was forced to resign from the shadow Treasury, journalist Michelle Grattan wrote that confusion 'reigned in the Opposition over whether Malcolm Turnbull [had] offered the shadow treasurer's post to Peter Costello … While well-placed sources insisted the offer had been made, others close to Mr Costello strongly denied this.'[29] She continued, three days later:

> Colleagues juggling both Turnbull's and Costello's versions of their Sunday conversation about Bishop's situation shake their heads; they decide who is telling the truth according to how they judge the two men. The net result of this madness was to diminish Turnbull's authority and remind everyone that Costello continues to sit there with undisclosed intent.[30]

Peter Hartcher observed, 'If Costello and Turnbull disliked each other last weekend, by this weekend they loathe each other. That's one point on which they can agree.'[31]

In many instances it is very hard for either the media or the public to know what occurred. In February 2002, at the height of the crisis concerning Governor-General Peter Hollingworth, who was being criticised for not having acted properly in response to child abuse accusations when he was Anglican Archbishop of Brisbane, Glenn Milne, in *The Australian*, cited an unnamed senior Cabinet Minister who suggested that Janette Howard, a High Anglican in the same faction as Hollingworth, had been instrumental in his appointment. She denied this and demanded an apology. She and Milne traded insults. Wayne Errington and Peter van Onselen doubt the accuracy of Milne's account, suggesting that the actions he described would have been uncharacteristic of Howard.[32] If the leak was accurate, it is interesting; if it was wrong, perhaps a fabrication, it is doubly interesting.

Sometimes even apparently straightforward leaks that are not publicly challenged also turn out to be problematic. On 17 July 2007, *The Australian* ran a front-page story under the headline 'PM asks Cabinet: Is it me?' This much-remarked-upon report suggested a moment of open-mindedness from Howard. But after the election, Costello told Hartcher (and other Ministers concurred with his account) that 'I sat next to Howard the whole time – it never happened.'[33]

And even stories that deserve to be true may not be. After former Liberal Minister and strong Gorton supporter Jim Killen died, Mungo MacCallum's obituary repeated a story from Canberra folklore: at a Liberal Party meeting after McMahon had displaced Gorton as leader, the Prime Minister said 'sometimes I think I'm my own worst enemy', and Killen, from the back of the room, had growled 'Not while I'm alive you're not.'[34] It may be that Killen said that, but the same quote is also attributed to two Ministers in Britain's Attlee Labour Government in the 1940s: it was sometimes said that the brilliant Minister for Health, Aneurin Bevan, was his own worst enemy. When told of this, his great rival, Ernest Bevin (they could not even agree on how to spell their name) replied, 'Not while I'm alive he's not.' My guess is that joking about such an interaction between Killen and McMahon became established in some minds as 'fact'.

Journalists are vulnerable to the risk that information may be wrong or partial, but if there is an established relationship of trust, and the information seems credible, the journalist may be willing to go public immediately. When Graham Richardson told Oakes about the Kirribilli agreement, he went to air with the news straight away, correctly making the judgment that he wouldn't be misled on such a major story. But even in an established relationship other factors may intervene. In 2004, Labor Opposition Leader Latham suspected Kevin Rudd of feeding material to Oakes, and decided to set him up, telling him about non-existent focus groups on Iraq. Immediately Oakes wrote a *Bulletin* article about the 'research'. 'Trapped him,' Latham boasted to his diary, and added that Rudd was 'a terrible piece of work', 'addicted to the media and leaking'.[35]

Even when there are no tricks being played, it is very difficult for the public to know what to think about a leak: is it true? What is the source? What is the motive? Sorting out the authoritativeness of a leak may be impossible. According to Costello staffer Niki Savva, when it looked as if Howard would stay forever, Costello would say, 'we're going to have to blast him out', 'And before you knew it, the junior woodchucks [her term for Costello supporters such as Christopher Pyne and George Brandis] were out there lobbing little hand grenades which often rolled back onto our doorstep.' When Costello was to visit Bruce Baird's electorate, it was leaked that Baird was Costello's preferred choice for deputy. Savva had to spend a couple of days cleaning up the subsequent mess: 'Pyne, who was the source for the story, protested that he was simply acting on instructions' from Costello.[36]

Sometimes both the likely source and the motive for a leak are impossible to fathom. On 6 August 2007, as the sense of despair among the Liberals at the prospect of electoral defeat was becoming increasingly profound, a front-page report by Malcolm Farr in the *Daily Telegraph* reported Liberal Party strategist Mark Textor's confidential report to the Liberal leadership, revealing just how dire their private polling showed the situation to be.[37] Who leaked Textor's report and why? Whose interest did it serve? It could have been meant as a further wake-up call to the party, but given their already profound pessimism it was more likely to result in reinforcing a sense of hopelessness and further feeding the impression that the political momentum rested with Labor. Perhaps the leaker wanted a switch to Costello, and thought this would help to prompt it. Perhaps people associated with Textor or the campaign team leaked it as insurance to protect their future credibility so that after the Liberals lost, the campaign team would not be blamed.

The content of what is leaked is only one reason why leaks can have such dramatic impacts. Often the central question – and one studiously avoided by the media reporting the leak – is who leaked and why. Occasionally it is the leaking itself rather than the content which is the principal point. In order to ensure a single, clear message, the practice of the leaders' offices giving MPs daily talking points – so that when, for example, they are entering Parliament and giving doorstop interviews they are giving consistent messages and sticking to the day's chosen themes – has grown.[38] Lenore Taylor obtained the Abbott Government's talking notes for one day in December 2014, and found them 'neither coherent nor convincing'.[39] The most spectacular such disclosure came in the latter days of the Gillard Government, when Rudd supporter Joel Fitzgibbon produced the papers on Channel Seven's *Sunrise* program. With the government going poorly in the polls, and amid much hilarity, he read from the notes that 'polls come and go and the only poll that matters is on election day'.[40] It was a deliberate stirring of the challenge against Gillard. Similarly, but anonymously, in the final month of the Abbott prime ministership, the talking points were leaked to Fairfax Media three days in a row, with the first two days, but not the third, including the claim that Cabinet was functioning 'exceptionally well'.[41]

An important sub-plot is the way secrecy lends drama and

intrigue to the politics. The case of Turnbull either offering or not offering the shadow Treasurer position to Costello (cited earlier) occurred when the Liberal Party decided that Julie Bishop was incapable of performing the role. A series of leaks against her appeared in *The Australian* in December 2008, prompting *Crikey* to ask, 'Who, we wonder, is out to get poor Julie Bishop? ... Someone is taking pot shots at Julie Bishop via *The Australian*' – is it one individual, or a 'carefully-orchestrated assault? Or is it just that once there's blood in the water, all the sharks come in for a bite?'[42] The continued leaking magnified her mistakes, and she stepped down from the shadow Treasurer position the following February, a move precipitated by yet another leak. Her problems in the portfolio:

> would have passed in time but for her detractors in her party.
> A group of fellow Liberals exaggerated her mistakes. And they
> crowed to reporters, on a non-attributable basis, that she was
> incompetent. Bishop grew frustrated that her public appearances
> had become a game of gaffe watch. She could not cut through.
> Then, on the front page of last Saturday's *Herald*, the paper's
> chief political correspondent, Phillip Coorey, broke the news
> that Bishop's support had collapsed. There was a near-universal
> view that she should leave the shadow treasury post.[43]

But who leaked what, and with what purpose?

Sometimes the purpose of a leak is fairly clear. For example, publicity can be used to lock in those who may be wavering. As WA Labor MPs felt that Peter Dowding was further embroiling the party in the WA Inc. scandals, state secretary Stephen Smith concluded that Dowding could not win another election, was no longer capable of taking advice and that they could not work together. When Dowding was overseas in early 1990, Rothwells' chief executive Tony Lloyd was convicted of fraud. This potentially implicated the government. After convening a meeting of MPs, Smith leaked that they had the numbers to make Dowding resign, and install Carmen Lawrence as his successor.[44] It was a classic use of predictive publicity to bring about the desired outcome.

A contrasting example may also have involved Smith. When the federal ALP was failing to make much progress against the Howard Government in 2006, Beazley's leadership was increasingly under threat. The Rudd–Gillard team were hoping that the transition could be smoothly executed without the open conflict of a challenge. But one of the 'roosters' (the name Latham gave to Beazley's top supporters: Smith, Wayne Swan and Stephen Conroy) leaked to the press that Rudd lacked the courage to challenge, in effect daring him to mount a frontal assault.[45] In response, Rudd did, and won. By that time there were already sufficient members of Caucus who saw Beazley as yesterday's man, and no publicity would change that. It only meant that there was an actual showdown, which the Rudd–Gillard team won 49–39.[46]

While the strategic element of leaks is often paramount, it would be a mistake to overestimate the rationality of all those involved. During the Hawke Government, Hayden sometimes indulged his special status as a former leader who had resigned to help the party. On one occasion, the Sydney afternoon tabloid, the *Daily Mirror*, published a story about a 'bitter brawl' in Cabinet in which Bill Hayden 'took a prominent role'. Actually, the Cabinet meeting had been postponed, so the *Mirror*'s leaked account preceded the actual meeting by some hours.[47] Hayden's games provoked retaliation. When Robert Ray suspected that Hayden was leaking to Niki Savva, he claimed to some Labor MPs that Hayden and Savva were having an affair. When Savva quizzed Ray about this, he said he did it to see how long it would take for the claim of the affair to get back to Hayden and Savva.[48]

Sometimes, especially in parties that are currently ineffectual and that are preoccupied with internal politics, politicians wanting to show their Machiavellian prowess end up engaging in silly games. In Frank Sartor's account, NSW Labor frontbencher Eric Roozendaal backgrounded two senior News Limited journalists that he would be announcing a challenge to Premier Nathan Rees's leadership. He wanted the story to run in *The Australian* and *Daily Telegraph* before the last Caucus meeting of the year. Both journalists filed their stories. Much later the same evening Roozendaal issued a media release denying any such challenge. One of the journalists said, 'At least you could have let the story appear before denying it.'[49]

Dysfunction feeds on itself. In the latter days of the Iemma Government, two hours before an ALP fundraising dinner at which Treasurer Costa was the main speaker, Costa withdrew, saying he would no longer attend any fundraising events held under the auspices of the NSW head office. According to Simon Benson, he faxed his letter criticising them to head office, 'and to the newsroom of two newspapers'. With the outbreak of a crisis following publication, Iemma summoned Costa, Eddie Obeid and Joe Tripodi to discuss it. Costa told them, 'Someone leaked it to the papers. I don't know how that happened.'[50] In this decaying NSW Labor Government, for Costa and Roozendaal, internal games had replaced any interest in external effectiveness.

The personal-cum-political impact of leaks

Because they are tools in a conflict, leaks create resentments and often involve a breach of trust. Even when they only slightly change the course of events, they can leave a residue of bitterness. When South Australian Premier Mike Rann was being pressured to bring forward his planned resignation by several months, his greatest anger was not about the content of the decision, but about its leaking: 'While a fellow from the Shop Assistants' Union was in my office it was leaked to the media, so it was an ambush, basically. I think this involves a lack of respect.' Rann thought that leaking what was supposed to be a confidential meeting while it was happening was 'contemptible'. The people involved in the leaking were, he thought, 'fairly low on the IQ food chain'.[51] Nor are these resentments always quick to disappear. In 2009 former WA Premier Dowding was launching a book by a colleague, but instead opened his speech with an attack on Smith. 'Relations between the two had been poisonous since Dowding lost the Labor leadership' in February 1990, when Smith orchestrated Dowding's removal, including the leak cited earlier.[52]

Those leaked against usually see the story as quite inaccurate, but may feel powerless to contest it. After Hayden resigned in favour of Hawke in 1983, he gave only one interview, to his local paper:

> I realise that in many important aspects I have been damaged by hostile leaks to the media. The media doesn't manufacture leaks – they were maliciously leaked and many of them were wrong, but very damaging. Some of them told only part of the story about things taking place in the party. And that was the part that was damaging to me.[53]

This rather restrained statement does not begin to capture the emotional battering Hayden had undergone while being stalked by Hawke, and his is perhaps the most dramatic case of a besieged leader's judgment and performance disintegrating under the pressure of destabilising media coverage. Leading journalist Anne Summers observed that 'the tension in Hayden over his rival was almost visible. In private the two men constantly denigrated each other, Hayden sarcastically questioning Hawke's competence and Hawke caustically comparing Hayden's electoral popularity with his own.'[54] It was exacerbated by Hayden's 'loner' personality and his distrust of others, which 'can occasionally verge on paranoia, especially when he becomes obsessive about those he regards as his opposition'.[55] Through 1982 Hayden made an increasing number of mistakes. His previous good relations with the press gallery deteriorated. Summers notes that 'His grip on political realities – and his party – was slipping visibly.'[56] Similarly, his colleague and friend John Button thought that 'the challenge by Hawke had a dam-

aging effect on Hayden's confidence and behaviour ... [He] vac-
illated between assertiveness and suspicion ... He and some of his
staff seemed foolishly vindictive towards people who'd voted for
Hawke.'[57] Like other leaders, Hayden's sense of being under siege
led him into counter-productive actions that further worsened his
position.

The sense of personal betrayal and the resentment at being undermined runs through many leadership conflicts. Bob Carr's biographer, Marilyn Dodkin, observed that 'whenever Carr was attacked by
a colleague he felt the wound more deeply than any criticism from
political opponents'.[58] Carr's own diary, from when he was at a low
ebb as Opposition Leader in 1990, reveals the personal toll wrought
by adverse publicity stemming from within his own ranks:

- 8 Sept 1990: 'All week I was being rubbished by [Peter]
  Anderson and another MP, Paul Gibson, moreover Pam Allan
  tells me of a lunch with Anderson, who devoted himself non-
  stop to assailing me. He and the Trogs [a sub-faction of the
  Right faction] get together and drink until late in the Whip's
  room, and the whingeing and whining comes out about me
  ...'
- 18 Sept 1990: 'I've been planning to get out myself, fed up by
  Anderson's undermining which keeps leaching into the press,
  and after a *Sun Herald* story I did my block. Only barely talked
  out of resigning.'
- 3 Oct 1990: 'Last week I told the Shadow Cabinet I would
  not put up with any more undermining. Quote: "No more
  articles of that sort or I will be responding publicly. If other
  people can pick over my alleged deficiencies in public, I will be
  highlighting theirs," I said.'[59]

An ironic end was in sight, though. The challenge from Anderson
was only possible because in 1989 Carr had intervened in a preselection wrangle and imposed him as the candidate. In his time as
an MP, Anderson failed to secure his preselection at local level. Carr

very quietly told the left to contest it, and discouraged the party machine from intervening. After the left candidate won preselection Anderson left politics. Carr boasted to his diary: 'They still haven't found my fingerprints on the axe handle.'[60]

The career stakes and the personal anxieties evoked by leadership conflicts extend beyond the contenders and their immediate supporters to the party room at large. Journalists are privy to gossip and rumour grapevines, and their reporting of party machinations is often more thoroughly grounded than the public may realise. Veteran Canberra correspondent Graeme Dobell observed to me:

> Coups do more than make and unmake leaders. These rare moments can make or destroy the careers of many of those in the caucus who decide the leader. Pick well and the ministry beckons. Go wrong and be marooned on the backbench. The MP agonising over scenarios and the shifting tide of party room numbers has to guard every word uttered to fellow politicians. One reason so many in caucus are prepared to confide in journalists (usually on background) during the build-up and the coup crisis is the psychological need to talk it through. This is not just sending signals via media to other members of caucus.

These comments point again to the volatile role played by the media in this most personal of political conflicts.

The misadventures of Andrew Peacock and Kim Beazley

Often in leadership challenges, there is a long, slow build-up, and then a fairly quick climax, but even these last steps – triggering a spill without alienating potential support – are surrounded by uncertainties. Peacock and Hawke were having a friendly discussion in 1981 about the progress of their challenges, to Fraser and

Hayden respectively, according to Peacock's biographer, Russell Schneider. Hawke said he had the numbers, but Peacock asked whether he had the numbers for the leadership or for a spill, and Hawke replied that he had the numbers for the leadership if there was a contest, but not the numbers to force the contest. Peacock replied that if you don't have the numbers for a spill, then you don't have the numbers.[61] Peacock's apparent sagacity about the difficulties of triggering a spill may have stemmed from his own bitter experience in early 1975.

Fraser's supporters were waging 'a war of attrition against Snedden'.[62] In parliament, Gough Whitlam was monstering him: 'this embattled pygmy has to show his failing followers that he is a big boy after all'.[63] Meanwhile, wrote Paul Kelly:

> a number of Fraser supporters established a solid and regular rapport with senior newspaper correspondents and the psychology of crisis or, as it came to be known, the 'siege mentality' afflicting the leadership was further exacerbated. The more it was written about, the more real it became.[64]

At the height of this tension, Peacock suddenly declared that the Liberals had to put an end to the uncertainty.[65] 'Peacock's comments hit the parliamentary Liberal Party like a bombshell,' wrote Kelly. Snedden was stunned and deeply depressed.[66] From the day of this statement by his closest public ally, Snedden had no choice but to call a party meeting,[67] and Fraser duly defeated him.

In their 1976 accounts, both Oakes and Kelly agree that Peacock acted after being urged to by a group of MPs who felt that the very public tensions had to be resolved.[68] Later, both Kelly and Fraser's biographer, Philip Ayres, thought there was also an element of self-interested positioning in his action.[69] Ayres notes that after the statement, Peacock told Snedden 'that it was because he [Peacock] supported him [Snedden] that he wanted the leadership crisis sorted out. As one of Snedden's closest supporters put it, "that was the ultimate treachery, when a man stabs you in the back in public but tells you to your face that he's trying to help".[70]

Whatever his motives, Peacock helped deliver the leadership to Fraser, facilitating the outcome he claimed to be trying to forestall, earning the opprobrium of Snedden's supporters, but no kudos from Fraser's. Fraser was facing the problem of translating his growing support inside the Liberal Party into a leadership challenge without heightening his reputation for disloyalty. Indeed Fraser's enemies used to quip that he 'was born with a silver spoon in his mouth – and a silver dagger in his hand'.[71] Peacock's intervention solved that problem for him.

At the time of his chat with Hawke, Peacock faced a much trickier situation. After he resigned from Cabinet in April 1981, he never had the numbers to challenge Fraser directly. Instead he sought to shape sentiment in the party and build up public support by highlighting government weaknesses and promoting himself as a more progressive alternative. He therefore had to achieve sufficient destabilisation to keep Fraser off balance, but not so much that it triggered a showdown he could not win.

There were several times when he and his supporters overstepped. In August, his chief supporter, Senator Reg Withers, released a list of six prominent Ministers Peacock would not keep in his Cabinet.[72] There was a peak of publicity in October, when Fraser was hosting the Commonwealth Heads of Government meeting in Melbourne. The summit meeting was overshadowed by page-one stories on a possible Peacock challenge, and a bizarre, false rumour that Fraser had cancer.[73] Ten days before the Victorian election, Grattan had a front-page story in *The Age* reporting that Peacock was poised to challenge Fraser once the Liberals lost in that state.[74] On the Sunday after the election, Fraser called a special meeting for the following Thursday to resolve the leadership, saying, 'Speculation about leadership challenges has continued for virtually a whole year, and it has obviously been promoted.'[75] Fraser won 54–27.

Sydney Morning Herald journalist Peter Bowers remembers that:

> Fraser perceived that his position could only weaken unless
> he met the challenge head on. [The Saturday of the Victorian
> election] I chanced my arm [and] did a paragraph which said,
> 'Look out Malcolm, here comes Andrew'. It should have said
> 'Look out Andrew, here comes Malcolm'. He pulled on the
> challenge and won two to one.

Peacock's misadventures in leadership challenges were not yet over. He became Liberal leader after the Fraser Government lost the 1983 election, and the Liberals performed much better in the 1984 election than most people expected. When he walked into the first party meeting after the election, he was given three cheers. However, from this time on, Howard, although still Peacock's deputy, began undermining him in preparation for a challenge. Even later that day, Howard infuriated Peacock by refusing to answer a question about a challenge on the grounds that his track record of loyalty to leaders meant it was not necessary for him to do so. In contrast, before the election he had unequivocally ruled out a challenge.[76]

When Oakes reported on TV that Howard had said that Jim Carlton would be Treasurer in a Howard Government, Peacock's patience finally snapped. However, he then 'elevated bad tactics into an art form'.[77] He decided to confront Howard, and to remove him as his deputy. Howard briefed journalists that if defeated he would retreat to the backbench, and lobbied his colleagues furiously to keep the deputy's job. Kelly reports, 'Peacock had the numbers against Howard as leader. But Howard was not challenging Peacock; Peacock was challenging Howard's right to stay as deputy.'[78] Peacock had decided that if his move against Howard failed, he would resign the leadership, but he told almost nobody this.

So when the party room voted to retain Howard as deputy leader, they were also, unknowingly, voting for Peacock to resign. Howard became party leader when he not only did not have sufficient support for a direct challenge, but because Peacock had moved against him rather than vice versa, he did not have the opprobrium a direct challenge would have brought. Again, Peacock had forgotten the political wisdom he had showed in his 1981 talk with Hawke about needing the numbers for a spill.

Peacock handled his next actions in leadership challenges much more skilfully. The coup that defeated Howard on 9 May 1989 was executed with ruthless efficiency. It was mounted quickly, and the numbers were well marshalled. Moreover it caught Howard completely by surprise. This was one of the most successful ambushes ever in federal politics, and Peacock won convincingly, 44–27.

Almost immediately, however, the triumph soured. Howard went to the backbench when Peacock offered him the Education Ministry rather than Defence, which was what he had wanted. Most importantly, the coup plotters went on ABC's *Four Corners*, boasting to Marian Wilkinson about their success in moving against Howard.[79] Their gloating tone rubbed salt into the wounds of Howard and his supporters. The day after the program, the recriminations in the Liberal Party became intense, with accusations of deception, claims that Peacock had been plotting much longer than he had publicly admitted, and a Howard supporter calling for all five of Peacock's main supporters who appeared on the program to be dismissed from the ministry. The righteous indignation of Howard and his supporters punctured any political momentum Peacock might have gained.

So on four occasions between 1975 and 1989 Peacock and/or his followers committed major missteps in the heat of a leadership challenge. This is particularly remarkable because Peacock was widely seen as a skilful and smooth political operator. Similarly, the equally prominent and experienced Beazley and his attempts to regain the Labor leadership in 2003 were thwarted by poor tactics and counter-productive media coverage. Peacock's problems centred on the difficulty of bringing challenges to a climax. In Beazley's case what seemed to be positive publicity in the media generally was counter-productive in the party room.

Beazley lost two elections to the Howard Government, although his supporters could claim that in both he had victory plucked from his grasp. In 1998, the GST election, Labor won a majority of the national 2PP vote, but the distribution of the vote delivered more seats to the government. After this very narrow loss, Labor surged ahead in the polls for the next few years. In early 2001, Beazley told his party room that 'a Labor Government is within our grasp'.[80] But a determined fightback by Howard, and then the *Tampa* asylum seeker crisis, followed by the 9/11 terrorist attacks, led to a dramatic turnaround.

After this loss, Simon Crean, Beazley's deputy, was elected leader unopposed, but he inherited a party that, according to journalist Annabel Crabb, who closely chronicled Labor's travails in that period, was by now overcome by 'exhaustion and hopelessness'.[81] Crean undertook some internal reforms, such as reducing trade union representation at Labor National Conference. He also promoted some young talent to the frontbench – Mark Latham, Craig Emerson, Kevin Rudd, Julia Gillard, Nicola Roxon. However, in that process he alienated several of those he demoted, especially because he did not communicate the news to them himself.

His key problem was that he was making no electoral impact: in March 2003 Howard was ahead of Crean as preferred Prime Minister 62 per cent:17 per cent,[82] with Crean's approval ratings trending down. The increasing sense of desperation about the party's electoral prospects revived Beazley's leadership ambitions.

In April came an incident that encapsulated the way in which public statements can inflame leadership tensions. Beazley gave an interview to *The Bulletin*, talking about some of the changes he would like to see in Australian politics. The magazine's cover ran the dramatic headline: 'If I were Prime Minister'. Beazley said there were no anti-Crean intentions behind his commentary on political trends, and from the words alone one could argue that the magazine had engaged in a fairly savage 'beat-up'. Crean saw it differently. According to Latham, Crean was 'stunned and bewildered' at Beazley's 'bastardry'.[83] At a media conference Crean said, 'I showed him total respect and total loyalty and I expect the same in return.'[84] According to Crabb, 'Crean's very public response, which seemed slightly excessive at the time, in fact hurried Beazley along the track to candidacy.'[85]

After Beazley and Crean eventually had a meeting, Crean said publicly that Beazley had ruled out a challenge. Beazley was incensed, feeling he had been verballed, as he had carefully refrained from ruling out a challenge. According to Crabb, 'The atmosphere between the two men by now was crackling with paranoia.'[86] One of Crean's problems was that so many in the leadership group were Beazley supporters. At a meeting where he asked them for a pledge of support, there followed two minutes of excruciating silence.[87]

Events now moved towards a Beazley challenge, but publicity interfered with his planning. First a secret meeting of Beazley supporters became public after Oakes reported it on Channel Nine. Then another group was headed for a secret meeting in Canberra, but was spotted by Fairfax reporters, and their photo appeared in *The Age*.[88] As public attention to the challenge was increasing, internally, according to Latham, a Crean supporter, 'the Beazley challenge [was] going nowhere'. He wrote in his diary about Beazley supporters Swan and Smith: 'Little Swannie and his mate Smith have rooted their reputation [sic] with a good part of Caucus.'[89]

As the tensions grew more visible, Crean called a special Caucus meeting for 16 June. Beazley publicly announced his candidacy, highlighting his capacity to 'connect' with the Australian public. Smith and Swan went further, forecasting a 'train wreck' for Labor and a huge Liberal win unless Beazley became leader. The Friday before the ballot, an opinion poll supported their view, with the public favouring Beazley over Crean 60–30. However, the Caucus voted for Crean 58–34.[90]

Beazley's numbers were better in the press gallery than in the Caucus. Two journalists wrote a song about Crean, based on the

Nat King Cole classic 'Unforgettable' but substituting the word 'Unelectable'. After Beazley's defeat, Alan Ramsey wrote a scathing column about 'Simon and the Lemmings Party', and quoted one anonymous Beazley supporter saying, 'When it came to it, the turkeys voted for Christmas.'[91] The Beazley tactics had worked quite well in generating media momentum, and he maintained by far the better public image, but inside the party there was considerable anger at how the public criticisms had given ammunition to the Coalition and made Labor's prospects worse.

Crean's poor performance in the polls meant he continued to be vulnerable. There was considerable resistance to Beazley, both because of his perceived disloyalty and among the younger members Crean had promoted, who saw Beazley as too conservative and insufficiently interested in party and policy renewal. So there was a mounting feeling that Crean's position was untenable, but many were unwilling to embrace the only alternative. The position was so grim that Senate Leader John Faulkner approached NSW Premier Bob Carr with a proposal to draft him into the federal leadership. Then, according to Crabb, Faulkner approached Beazley and offered him a smooth ride to the leadership if he promised to keep Latham as shadow Treasurer, but Beazley refused.[92]

The party's lack of internal discipline and cohesion was manifested in various ways. The NSW Labor Government of Carr and Treasurer Michael Egan had moved towards a new tax on the richest of the leagues clubs in the state. Latham took it upon himself to criticise them:

> I fired a warning shot across Carr's bow to stop him
> destabilizing Crean and the Federal Party. He's having a big blue
> with John Singleton about his Government's new clubs tax, so I
> took Singo's side, endorsing him as my kind of fella.[93]

Meanwhile, the NSW ALP state secretary, Eric Roozendaal, insisted that a right-wing faction candidate must head the Senate ticket for the 2004 election, so Labor's leader in the Senate, John Faulkner, was demoted to number two in what was a self-indulgent display of factional power. After Whitlam and Keating wrote letters endorsing Faulkner, Roozendaal had their photos in head office taken down.[94]

The latent discontent erupted into crisis in late November. While secret negotiations had been going on, Jim Middleton reported on the ABC evening news that a group of powerbrokers was about to move against Crean. Crean was at first dismissive, but later that night was informed that it was true. Latham then met with Faulkner, a central player, who told him that Bob McMullan had leaked it to Middleton and this had upset all their timing. Crean, meanwhile, was determined that if he could not win he would help one of his supporters win ahead of Beazley, and so he threw his support behind Latham.[95] Beazley supporters saw this as Crean in 'vengeful mode', but others were receptive to the argument that Beazley should not be rewarded for his 'disloyalty'.[96]

No journalist tipped Latham to win, and some predicted that he would lose in a landslide.[97] But he defeated Beazley 47–45. Coalition MPs cheered the news of Latham's election, believing him easier to beat than either Beazley or Crean.[98] Beazley, the contender seemingly best placed publicly, had lost, at least partly because positive media coverage had damaged him inside the party room.

These Peacock and Beazley misadventures are telling testament to how media coverage interacts with the momentum of leadership challenges. They highlight how, in these the most personal of all political conflicts, decided by the party room rather than the public at large, the impacts of media coverage can be hard to predict. Similarly for the public, in a field marked by self-serving public statements, and where so much reporting relies on leaks, it is hard to gauge the accuracy and significance of particular reports.

CHAPTER 9

Reporters and Players

Analysts or advocates

What sort of adjectives could describe the role of the media from June to December 1991? Craven? Blood lusting? Incompetent? Biased? Bigoted? None of them adequately describes the way Hawke was treated by the Gallery, nearly all the Gallery.

Senator Robert Ray[1]

It is clear from the preceding chapters how closely the media interact with unfolding leadership challenges. This raises the possibility of deliberate interventions by the media to aid or damage particular contenders, and politicians involved are not slow to make such accusations. As is clear in Robert Ray's quote above, feelings can run high. Ray was a Hawke supporter. In much less insulting language, Keating supporter Graham Richardson broadly agreed: 'The pro-Keating pack was led by Paul Kelly, now [1994] editor-in-chief of *The Australian*, Laurie Oakes and Michelle Grattan. As his subsequent writings on these events have shown, Paul Kelly was an unabashed Keating supporter.'[2] Kelly himself acknowledged Hawke's complaint that the leading journalists were pro Keating, and observed that in late 1991 Hawke's 'relations with the main print journalists virtually collapsed'.[3]

However, an important distinction should be made here. Politicians' interest is in the outcome, the bottom line, while journalists are more oriented towards disclosure, to securing a competitive advantage, pursuing what they judge most newsworthy. The political attitude is reflected in Liberal MP Peter Howson's 1968 diary entry: 'the press has been attacking me this morning, saying that I am bound to be dropped from the Ministry at the end of the week'.[4] That such reports proved to be accurate did not affect Howson's view of them as 'attacks'. Kelly, Oakes and Grattan – the most eminent political journalists of the last half century – were always interested in breaking stories; they were, and are, equally interested in accurately analysing developments. In their opinion columns they may have argued in favour of a change in the Labor leadership at critical moments, but their reporting went towards whatever newsworthy material they could uncover, no matter whose interests it served.

Interactions between journalists and politicians are many-sided, involving strong but sometimes ambiguous norms of professionalism, and weak enforcement mechanisms. Inevitably, though, personal relationships are coloured by evaluations of competence and character. Mark Latham, for example, thought that Oakes was always biased against him: 'I never get a break from Jabba the Hutt' (Latham's nickname for Oakes).[5]

There is also an element of self-interest in journalists' interactions with politicians. Former journalist and later Costello staffer Niki Savva wrote about this very frankly in her memoirs. She cited right-wing Washington columnist Robert Novak, who wrote, 'in this town you're either a source – or a target'. She then says that if she rang a Labor backbencher seeking information and they told her they never gave briefings about Caucus discussions, 'I never rang them again. And I never mentioned their name in a story either. Unless they had done something wrong, of course.'[6] After working for Costello she said her opinion of journalists had fallen much further than her opinion of politicians: 'When it comes to

scheming and lying, plain old hypocrisy, and dishonesty, journalists – apart from a few honourable exceptions – win hands
down.'[7]

While there is much talk about journalistic enterprise and
leaks, what are called 'drops' are at least as important in shaping
the news. A 'drop' is an act of patronage: giving one journalist
rather than another a story. In his interviews with media advisers,
David McKnight found that 'advisers from both the Howard and
Rudd governments gave similar descriptions of the conditions
they expected in return for exclusives. These were a guarantee
that a story would be run on a particular day and that no opposition comment would be sought before it appeared.' One said,
'If it's a good yarn … you don't really have to state it because the
journo may never get another drop. So they know the rules.' In a
few cases relationships between journalists and Ministers became
so strong that they were 'virtual alliances', and such cooperative
relationships could last many years and be 'very good for both
parties'.[8]

Key Rudd adviser Bruce Hawker described this patronage
at work in 2013. Rudd had decided to intervene in the NSW
branch; but he wanted to drop it to *The Australian* the night before
the scheduled public announcement. Hawker confides in his diary
his view that this would cause trouble:

> Sure enough, when [NSW ALP secretary] Sam Dastyari found
> out that [*Daily Telegraph* correspondent Simon] Benson was
> not getting an exclusive he became very worried and said
> that Benson would be cranky. Cranky was an understatement
> – Simon went ballistic. Anyway, I placated him and promised
> him a better story down the line.[9]

This is hardly Woodward and Bernstein.

Most of the time coincidences of interest and the complexities of personal relationships, rather than any desire to promote

one contender over another, explain journalists' behaviour. But as self-sustaining patterns develop, it is easy for motivations to become murkier. Over the years, News Corp's Glenn Milne was sometimes seen as a spruiker for Costello. In 2006 this led to an amusing clash between Milne and Howard loyalist Piers Akerman. Milne had scored a great scoop, which the rest of the media had had to madly follow up, when he revealed that former Liberal Party President and Howard Government Minister Ian McLachlan had witnessed a meeting in December 1994 where Howard had said he would hand over the leadership to Costello after one and a half terms (see Chapter 4). In the *Sunday Telegraph*, Akerman denigrated Milne as the 'little jockey', the 'Dwarf', Costello's 'mini-microphone' and the 'bantamweight columnist'. When Milne read it, he rang Akerman and there followed an abusive conversation in which Milne referred to Akerman's weight, and accused him of conspiring with the Prime Minister's 'dirt team'. *The Australian* media section recounted that these 'two pundits [were] at each other's throats'. Amazingly, however, it concluded, 'The consensus is that Akerman has had the better of Milne, principally because for now he [Milne] has landed on the losing side. In short, both Milne and Mr Costello needed better advice.'[10] Here a media section of a quality newspaper seems to think the essence of journalism is to be on the winning side. Through his enterprising reporting, Milne had produced a scoop and made an important public revelation, while Akerman had done no more than write a column with no important revelations, wholly predictable except for its level of invective against Milne. But according to *The Australian*, this constituted an Akerman victory.

This was Milne's greatest coup in his reporting of the Howard–Costello relationship. At other times, he had made many predictions that turned out to be incorrect. As early as 2002, he wrote, 'the Treasurer's supporters believe the party is already in transition from Howard'.[11] And in 2005, after a public falling out between Howard and Costello, he wrote, 'Both sides now accept the inevitability of one of two outcomes: Mr Howard will hand over the leadership to Mr Costello by April/May next year; or he will face a challenge from the Treasurer by the same deadline.'[12]

Milne made his final inaccurate prediction on the morning after the Coalition's 2007 election loss, when he wrote, 'Peter Costello will take over a defeated coalition unopposed ... And despite speculation [that] he might not want the job after almost 12 years as Treasurer, Mr Costello has already taken the decision to accept the challenge of the opposition leadership.'[13] Unfortunately for Milne, later that morning, Costello announced that he would not take up the leadership. Milne tried to retrieve the situation the next day by writing that Costello's decision 'late on Saturday night ... was as sudden as it was swift'.[14] Another News Corp journalist, Sue Dunlevy, reported the same day that 'He'd known what he would do for 16 months',[15] a view broadly confirmed by Costello in his memoirs.[16] Milne was often a news breaker, and his inaccuracies in the cases above did not seem to hurt his career at all.

The nature of journalistic self-interest has been changing: in the past, journalists' reputations were made primarily as news breakers, for the accuracy and reliability of their reporting, and for their insights as analysts. When Robert Ray was complaining about the biases of the gallery in 1991, the major political correspondents often had opinion/analysis columns, although they were reporters first and commentators second. Now not only do many gallery reporters write regular columns, but the injection of interpretation into what was once considered straight reporting has gone much further.

In the mid-1970s, US journalism scholar Bernard Roshco wrote that 'the history of the American press can be seen as an account of how it continually enlarged its conception of the information it could properly publish'.[17] Equally, it could be argued that in recent decades the Australian press has continually enlarged its conception of when and how opinions could be expressed. The line between fact and opinion has become increasingly blurred, in terms of both interpreting events and passing personal judgments.

Not only has opinion been increasingly injected into the presentation of news stories, but the trend has seen an increase in the number of columnists – in all newspapers, but especially in News Corp publications – who do minimal reporting and whose main stock in trade is commentary. The appeal of these columnists is their strength of opinion rather than their capacity to bring understanding or uncover new facts. For some readers these columnists' work will reinforce their opinions; for others it will provoke outrage. The greatest fear of these columnists is to be ignored; errors are only sometimes damaging.

A parallel trend in commercial talk radio has seen announcers who have a right-wing populist mix of resentments, and who appeal principally to older audiences. Again, their primary appeal is the strength of their opinions, and inaccuracies and false charges rarely seem to affect their audience's confidence in them. Indeed the most famous of the current 'shock jocks', Sydney's Alan Jones, survived a scandal, the cash for comment scandal, that would have ruined a more orthodox career.[18]

The extent to which the commentariat's ethics differ from traditional journalism was on display in two examples in early 2016, both involving fallout from the overthrow of Abbott. There were news reports that Channel Ten might not continue with *The Bolt Report*, featuring Andrew Bolt, whom the *Herald Sun* describes as the most read columnist in Australia. Bolt, an avid supporter of Abbott, commented, 'one liberating factor is that now I don't have a dog in the next election fight I can do other things without feeling I am deserting'.[19] In the second case, there was considerable tension over preselections in the NSW Liberal Party. Craig Kelly, the Member for Hughes and from the conservative wing of the party, was facing a possible challenger in moderate Kent Johns. Jones had Kelly on his program, and afterwards declared him 'a dyed-in-the-wool ordinary Australian', and added: 'You'd better pull your head in, Kent Johns, because … if you put [it] up, there'll be a hell of a story that'll be told about you.'[20] 'Having a dog in the fight', threatening to tell a story if a candidate nominates – these are the exact opposite of the traditional journalistic ideals of telling the truth without fear or favour.

One cannot imagine Oakes, Kelly or Grattan making such statements. But it is plausible that attitudes have changed in the press gallery as well. There were always some reporters, such as Alan Reid, who relished their role as activists, as shapers of events. But perhaps there are now more of them. Kelly thinks that 'journalists have always backed one candidate or another in leadership contests, often with strong advocacy. The difference now is they have moved from advocacy to active campaigning.'[21] Grattan has also talked about the rise of 'intriguers' in the gallery.

The growth of the soapboxers has transformed the amount and the nature of political commentary. Overwhelmingly they promote right-wing views. After the end of the Howard Government, Bob Carr commented on this change: 'No prime minister has had a Praetorian Guard like it, a body of opinion makers so fiercely and one-sidedly and resolutely in his camp. They were Howard's adulators.' For Carr, none of Howard's predecessors could 'count on such consistent support from a group of commentators'. But he thought that their impact was counter-productive: 'they fed and nurtured and consolidated his attachment to the orthodoxies that did him in ... Delicious.'[22]

Normally these commentators devote themselves to advancing the conservative cause against Labor, but sometimes – as with Jones, earlier – they get involved in favouring one Liberal figure over another. Costello's memoirs record with understandable disbelief a lunch at Kirribilli House just before the 2007 election, where Howard, having promised to stand down in the coming term, hosted News Corp journalists Dennis Shanahan, Terry McCrann, Andrew Bolt and Piers Akerman. According to Costello, one of the journalists (not named) said, 'If you win, all bets are off. If you win, people will say that you have to stay.' So even in the bunker, near the end, these Howard loyalists were engaging in wishful thinking, which included Howard going on indefinitely into the future.[23]

Sometimes, News Corp publications in particular are not just pro the Liberal Party but pro the conservative faction inside the party. The *Daily Telegraph* became very involved in an ongoing civil war between conservatives and moderates in the NSW branch, which resulted in perhaps the dirtiest and the most counter-productive leadership coup of all.

John Brogden had defeated Kerry Chikarovski for the leader-ship on 28 March 2002, but in the following election, in 2003, the Liberals had made little headway against the Carr Govern-ment. However, after that the polls had sometimes been promising. Brogden must have felt that his prospects lifted when Carr resigned after a decade as Premier, and was replaced by Morris Iemma, who had not had a high public profile. However, immediately afterwards Brogden's political career collapsed.

The *Sunday Telegraph* published a story by Milne, its Canberra correspondent, which described how at the end of the week Carr resigned, Brogden had been in high spirits, and fuelled by beer and euphoria, had behaved inappropriately at a function at the Hilton Hotel. His most important transgression was to refer to Helena Carr, Bob Carr's wife, as 'the mail order bride'. In addition, the story said he had propositioned two female journalists. After sat-uration coverage of the Carr insult, Brogden resigned at a media conference on the Monday morning.

But the *Daily Telegraph* was not finished with Brogden. Its Wednesday first edition had the headline 'Brogden's Sordid Past. Disgraced Liberal leader damned by secret shame file'. It included several new charges, which were soon denied. It said that Brogden had proposed having a threesome to two reporters and had said that they were so attractive they should be in a nunnery. ABC's *Media Watch* contacted the two, who both denied the *Telegraph*'s account and were angered by it. The paper also said he had had an affair with a former staff member, and that his father-in-law told him to get rid of her, but his father-in-law denied this.[24] Finally, the paper claimed that Brogden had resigned because of the allegations of sexual misconduct it was about to make.

After the paper's journalists contacted Brogden with these charges, he attempted suicide.[25] His deputy, Barry O'Farrell, went to the hospital, with some other colleagues, to support Brogden's wife. O'Farrell then withdrew from the coming leadership contest, and Peter Debnam became leader. Apart from the personal tragedy, the episode highlighted the internal divisions in the NSW Liberal Party, and the way the conservatives had been gaining at the expense of the moderates, despite claims of their dirty tactics.[26] *Daily Telegraph* executives revealed that its stories had come 'from the Liberal Party, including at very high levels of the Liberal Party'.[27]

The following day at two party functions, Health Minister Tony Abbott made jokes about Brogden and his condition. The next Sunday on ABC TV, he defended himself to Barrie Cassidy by saying, 'look, I have never claimed to be the world's most sensitive man'.[28] Labor's shadow Health Minister, Julia Gillard, said Abbott, the person responsible for Australia's mental health system, should resign, because his reaction was grossly inappropriate.[29] Liberal backbencher George Brandis thought Abbott's remarks were 'disgusting'.[30]

The Liberals lost the next election very badly, despite the many political scars accumulated by the 12-year-old Labor Government. It is possible that if Brogden had remained leader, the Liberals would have won. The Liberals' performance was dismal. Former NSW Labor Minister Rodney Cavalier thought that Peter Debnam was 'a gift to Labor' and that the Liberals lost 'courtesy of one of the most comprehensive forfeits ever offered in Australian political history'.[31] The *Telegraph* had brought down Brogden, but they had also inflicted great damage on the Liberals' prospects.

Tribal loyalties – Murdoch and Abbott

Rupert Murdoch's political views have been broadly constant since the mid-1970s.[32] The degree to which they are expressed in his papers, however, has varied according to immediate commercial interests, how the political tide is running, and his personal relationships with key players. As he has got older, however, Murdoch has lost his populist touch and seems more determined to make his papers embrace his political views. News Corp has employed, in senior positions, editors who are ever more conformist.

In the 2013 election, the various currents in Murdoch's world were all running in the same direction, and he gave wholehearted support to Abbott and the Liberal Party.[33] This continued into government. As Grattan observed, 'News Corp is seen as part of the tribe. Government announcements, big and small, are routinely made through its papers.' After the election, 'in a flaunting of tribalism, Abbott entertained a batch of conservative commentators at Kirribilli House'.[34]

This alliance remained until late 2014. By then, however, with the government consistently trailing in the polls, Murdoch and others thought that changes needed to be made. At Murdoch's suggestion, over the Christmas break Abbott overhauled his media team, including dumping his senior communications adviser.[35] Then as Abbott's summer worsened, culminating in the spill motion against him, Murdoch offered more public and much more unhelpful advice. In an unprecedented and attention-grabbing move, the media proprietor offered his thoughts on a Prime Minister's staffing arrangements. In late January, Murdoch posted three tweets:

Abbott again. Tough to write, but if he won't replace top aide Peta Credlin she must do her patriotic duty and resign

Forget fairness. This change only way to recover team work and achieve so much possible for Australia. Leading involves cruel choices

Credlin a good person. Just appealing to her proven patriotism[36]

Murdoch's call followed an earlier conflict between Savva, one of his columnists on *The Australian*, and Credlin. In October, after a critical column from Savva, Credlin sent an extraordinary text to the editor, Chris Mitchell: 'I've had enough, you have to sack her.' Mitchell was shocked, and said that in his 24 years as an editor, no political staffer had ever made such a request. Then Abbott contacted Mitchell, but to the editor's credit he again refused to act against Savva.[37] The incident, though, is testament to the government's expectations of the Murdoch press.

Murdoch's public intervention was counter-productive. As journalist Laura Tingle observed, it:

> only achieved two things. The first was to make it even more difficult for the prime minister to part with his long-serving staffer Peta Credlin. The second was to highlight how quickly the fortunes of the prime minister and the government have spiralled downwards.[38]

Grattan thought 'the Murdoch intervention is damaging because it escalates the issue and given its timing, it may feed the paranoia about leadership threats that already exists in the Prime Minister's Office'.[39] After Abbott's survival, Murdoch tweeted on 7 February 2015: 'Abbott, good guy, not perfect but no case for rebellion. Remember last one gave us Gillard disaster. Country still paying for it'.

After Abbott's near-death experience, life in the government returned to normal, which was that it was consistently trailing in the polls. In September Abbott consulted Murdoch on election timing and Murdoch tweeted that Abbott should call a double dissolution and go early.[40] This was poor advice in every way: it ran the very large risk – indeed the strong probability – that Abbott would lose; that an early rush to the polls would create a public backlash; and that an election for the whole Senate, rather than the normal half Senate, almost guaranteed that minority parties would again hold the balance of power. So even if re-elected, Abbott would still face what he saw as an obstructionist Senate. Paradoxically, Murdoch's tweet lent urgency to the Turnbull forces' planning. They thought that Murdoch and Abbott were close and feared that Abbott would call a snap election to pre-empt their challenge. One told Hartcher: 'He's bonkers enough to do it.'[41]

The suddenness of Abbott's fall left his supporters shocked and angry. The media fallout was unique. In much media coverage, the treatment of Turnbull was favourable, but the pro-Abbott outlets were more vociferously partisan than in any previous leadership coup. The *Herald-Sun* referred to the winner as 'Malcolm Turncoat' and the *Daily Telegraph* called him 'the smiling assassin'.[42]

The 2GB radio shock jocks Alan Jones and Ray Hadley were among Abbott's strongest supporters. Hadley even turned on Scott Morrison, a regular guest, demanding that he swear on a bible that he was telling the truth.[43] Back in June 2014, Jones had told Turnbull on air that he had 'no hope of ever being the leader, you have got to get that into your head'.[44] Jones had begun that 'interview' by asking Turnbull to repeat after him 'as a senior member of the Abbott Government I want to say here I am totally supportive of the Abbott–Hockey strategy for budget repair'. Turnbull indignantly replied that he was not going to take dictation from Jones,[45] before declaring, as a Cabinet Minister, his support for all aspects of the budget.[46] Perhaps Jones's most memorable outburst, among many on the morning after Turnbull's accession, was that 'As a caller just wrote to me, ... "People don't want to vote for Turnbull, and they don't want to vote for Shorten. We've got a shit sandwich." And I think that's most probably it.'[47]

Bolt wrote that the decision to oust Abbott broke his heart: 'That he has been betrayed and deposed doesn't just break my heart. It makes me fear for this country.'[48] Straight after the coup, he declared that 'Turnbull's plotters make [many Liberals'] skin crawl.

I've talked to MPs, even moderates, who are sickened.' He talked of 'the anger many conservative Liberals already feel for Turnbull – for a man of the Left they think has hijacked their party'.[49]

News Corp publications and journalists now had an uncomfortable choice between adjusting to the new reality or denouncing it; between their loyalty to the Liberal cause or their loyalty to the Abbott cause. Many solved this by not denouncing Turnbull but praising Abbott extravagantly. The *Telegraph*'s Benson thought that Abbott 'was potentially the best prime minister we had but never knew it'.[50] As Abbott gave his version of events, either openly or confidentially, to favoured outlets in the following days and weeks, the tensions in these outlets continued. Bolt and Mitchell clashed, with Bolt declaring that the Turnbull coup had 'set off a civil war within News Corp', and charged that Mitchell's *Australian* was losing $20 million a year, and he should therefore be less disparaging of the others in the group who subsidise him.[51]

Months later the Murdoch tabloids were still keen to do Abbott's bidding, declaring in a front-page story that 'in a move that is bound to further frustrate Prime Minister Malcolm Turnbull', Obama and Abbott had had a private dinner in Washington, evidence of the high regard in which the former Prime Minister was held. Most of the rest of the media took up the story, many including the invented reaction that Turnbull was meant to have had. Soon after, the ABC's *Media Watch* skewered the story, revealing that Abbott had actually been Murdoch's guest at a lunch hosted by leading civil rights activist Vernon Jordan. The President had shaken Abbott's hand there, as he had the hands of the 100 other guests, but there had been no private meeting and no initiative by the President to meet with Abbott.[52]

In the lead-up to the 2 July 2016 election, public criticism of Turnbull by disaffected Liberals and their media allies was muted as they concentrated on the fight against Labor. But once the election was over, with the result uncertain on election night and for some days after, and in the end much closer than some had forecast, Liberal conservative critics inside the government took the opportunity to hammer some of their favoured themes. The tribal supporters in the media were far less restrained. Bolt, on election night, called the result a 'disgrace', and said 'no one can seriously argue that Tony Abbott wouldn't have done better'. Turnbull's 'failed'. He had torn 'the Liberals apart and for this result? It's just unbelievable. Out you go!'[53] In contrast, Turnbull said during the campaign that the Coalition would have lost with Abbott. His comment was based on a Galaxy poll that showed that while the parties were currently 50–50 2PP, if Abbott were leader respondents said they favoured Labor 53–47.[54] Then Jones on Channel Seven and Credlin on Sky elevated Australian political discourse by referring to those Lib-erals who moved against Abbott as 'bed wetters'.[55] Credlin, now a commentator for Sky, also said, 'If they think that I've tried to settle scores, well they ain't seen anything yet.'[56]

The avid support of Abbott by News Corp and its proprietor was not able to save him. As Tingle commented:

> One of the more gob-smacking features of Abbott's departure
> statement on Tuesday was his suggestion that his downfall was
> due to internal white-anting and a hostile media. This was
> from a prime minister whose path to destruction was littered
> with more own goals than any other failed leader of recent
> times; whose prime ministership has been cosseted and egged
> on by the largest media organization in the country. Even the
> perpetual fawning of News Limited toadies, the manufacture
> of ludicrous stories about Abbott's opponents, the ignoring
> of unfortunate or embarrassing issues, couldn't save him from
> himself.[57]

The cases in this chapter are not encouraging for any media who desire to be kingmakers, at least in regard to leadership coups. The *Telegraph* managed to get Brogden deposed, but the key outcome was a boost to Labor. The pro-Abbott chorus then demonstrated its ineffectualness, showing how much it was out of touch with mainstream opinion not just in the electorate, but within the Liberal Party.

CHAPTER 10

Iatrogenic Spin Doctoring

The focus on spin in politics is now so ubiquitous that it is surprising that the term 'spin doctor' only made its public debut as recently as 1984. Under the headline 'The debate and the spin doctors', the *New York Times* reported on the second presidential debate between Ronald Reagan and his challenger, Walter Mondale:

> Tonight at about 9.30, seconds after the Reagan–Mondale
> debate ends, a bazaar will suddenly materialize in the press
> room of the Kansas City Municipal Auditorium. A dozen men
> in good suits and women in silk dresses will circulate smoothly
> among the reporters, spouting confident opinions. They won't
> be just press agents trying to impart a favourable spin to a
> routine press release. They'll be the Spin Doctors.[1]

During that era, the most successful TV political comedy was *Yes Minister* and its successor *Yes Prime Minister*, where the humour came from the machinations of the public servant Sir Humphrey Appleby, and how he triumphed over his hapless Minister, Jim Hacker. In recent years, the most successful political comedies have instead focused on spin doctors. There have been at least three — the Australian series *The Hollowmen*, set in Canberra and starring Rob Sitch as the Prime Minister's Principal Private Secretary; the British series *Absolute Power*, about a PR firm, starring Stephen Fry and John Bird; and *The Thick of It*, with its foul-mouthed central character, the Prime Minister's spin doctor Malcolm Tucker (actor Peter Capaldi). The common themes in these comedies are the disjunction between appearance and reality, the cynicism and brazenness of the practitioners, and the subjugation of principle and substance to image engineering.

The activities of spin doctors are also increasingly the subject of public commentary. Indeed, in the UK, one journalist pronounced 1997 the year of the spin doctor,[2] while the *Sydney Morning Herald*'s media critic, Jack Robertson, pronounced the spin doctor 'the most memorable person of 2003'.[3] The commentary is almost invariably adverse. 'This systematic attempt to fool most of the people most of the time is the work of some of the most intelligent, best-informed and highly paid men and women in Western societies,' according to Oxford historian Timothy Garton Ash.[4] Indeed the spin doctor has become one of the bogeymen of contemporary politics. Former British Prime Minister John Major was scathing about the state of spin under his successor, Tony Blair:

> Spin is the pornography of politics. It perverts. It is deceit licensed by the Government ... The daily line from No. 10 was ruthlessly disseminated. It was formidable propaganda. The press became the receptacle of Orwellian attempts to manage the news.[5]

Yet submerged within this chorus of criticism is a paean of praise. All the denunciations of spin's pernicious influence – how it is harmful to democracy, the public's right to know and the quality of journalism – are also testimonies to its effectiveness. So, over-whelmingly, the popular image of spin is of a negative, evil force that is also a powerful, effective force. This chapter looks at how and why efforts at spin control become counter-productive, and how they compound the tensions around leadership conflict.

The word 'iatrogenic' comes from two Greek words: 'genesis', meaning beginning, and 'iatros', meaning doctor. So iatrogenic sicknesses or iatrogenic medical problems are those that come as a result of medical treatment, such as the side effects of drugs, or post-operative complications. The idea was probably first popularised by Florence Nightingale during the Crimean War, when she said that the first duty of a hospital is not to make it more likely that a patient would die. In other words, British military hospitals at the time were so unhygienic and so prone to infectious diseases that a soldier could go in with a minor wound, it would become infected and he would die as a result. In the contemporary era there has been much more attention to how treatments can set up their own future problems, advanced most radically by social analyst Ivan Illich in his book *Medical Nemesis*.[6] So this chapter's title captures what happens when spin doctors' efforts go wrong and produce more damage for their cause than good.

Iatrogenic spin doctoring is intertwined with leadership instability. For spin doctors, selling the messenger, the leader, is the precondition for selling the message. The key spin doctors work for the leader rather than the party as a whole, and it is very easy for them to equate what is good for the leader with what is good for the party. Their preoccupation with the immediate, with rapid response and tactical manoeuvring, is another force for short-termism in Australian politics, and feeds into leader instability.

The scale and meaning of spin

Brian McNair has correctly observed that most of the individual elements of spin doctoring pre-date World War II by a considerable amount.[7] Public relations is often said to have begun in America in the period following World War I,[8] with one of its earliest practitioners, Edward Bernays, proclaiming its possibilities while social analyst Walter Lippmann observed that a new age of opinion management had arrived. Public opinion polling began in the US before World War II, and the parties gradually started to do their own. Politicians have always kept files on their opponents' statements, seeking ammunition with which to attack them. The evolution of the position of press secretary has been going on for a long time. All these individual activities substantially pre-date the coining of the phrase 'spin doctor'.

Nevertheless, to emphasise the antiquity of the individual antecedents of spin indicates nothing about the scale of change. In the contemporary spin doctoring industry, the whole is greater than the sum of its parts. What is new is the intensity of the enterprise, the huge resources devoted to it, the integrated and professional approach and the capacity for speedy action and response. What used to be done casually and sporadically and slowly is now done professionally and systematically and immediately. There has never in history been anything to parallel this effort. It is now at the heart of how political leaders conduct their work and make decisions.

In the early 1960s, there were 500 public relations practitioners in Australia, but by 2007 this had grown to around 10,000, according to researcher Bob Burton.[9] That growth is continuing. Political scientist Ian Ward estimated that there are over 4000 media and communications staff working for state and federal government departments.[10] It has prompted discussion of a public relations state,[11] and public relations democracy.[12] Others have argued that we have entered a third age of political communication[13] and of election campaigning,[14] one characteristic of which is the 'thoroughgoing professionalisation of political advocacy'.[15]

As important as its growing size is spin's growing scope. Harold Burson summarised the history of public relations thus: at first clients 'told us "here's the message, go deliver it"; then it became "what should our message be?"; now it's "what should we do?"'[16] Few, however, have gone as far as Kevin Rudd, who, according to Wayne Swan, once 'asked the ALP national secretariat to conduct a comprehensive poll and advise him what his "one core belief" was'.[17]

All branches of the persuasion industry have grown. The number of registered lobbyists in Canberra in 2009 outnumbered MPs and

Senators four to one,[18] and this number does not include those employed by corporations to directly lobby on their behalf. Advertising in general has grown, and political and government-sponsored advertising have grown proportionately.[19] Magazine content is very much intertwined with the celebrity industry and therefore with professional publicists,[20] while in terms of general news content, the Australian Centre for Independent Journalism found in late 2009 that nearly 55 per cent of published stories were driven by some form of public relations.[21] Part of the reason for the growth is the massively increased presence of the media, and the recognition that media can make or break careers and campaigns. This has led to an increasingly calculating approach, not only in political campaigns but by all major institutions – from the Vatican to football clubs – especially when saturation coverage is expected.

Journalists' views of spin have become progressively more pessimistic. In the late 1990s, the Sky News UK reporter Adam Boulton said of Tony Blair's New Labour Government that 'on a good day, you can see an intelligent, honest administration at work. On a bad day I feel soiled, when we end up seeing the press conniving in our own manipulation.'[22] A few years later he thought that 'top figures in New Labour increasingly regard journalists as "scum". Now they are treating them as such.'[23] By the time he retired, in 2014, he thought the Cameron Government was worse than Blair's, and contrasted today's 'cautious pre-prepared approach to politics' with Thatcher, who 'would tell you exactly what she thought'.[24]

On the other hand, political scientist Joe Atkinson commented on 'a growing tendency in Western news discourse to mix extreme cynicism about politicians and public officials with a contrastingly utopian and fantasized view of the media'.[25] This false moral polarisation serves a strategic purpose and perhaps also a psychological one. As media scholar Raymond Kuhn observed, 'by first demonising the power of spin, journalists can hope to create a positive image of themselves'.[26]

In denunciations of spin, it is sometimes talked of as an almost mesmeric force. So it is important to explore what it means, to specify how it works as a flesh and blood activity. The contemporary spin enterprise – as it affects political news reporting – is a combination of four central activities:

1. Catering to media demands, and in particular the orchestration of photo ops and sound bites

Most basically, spin doctors know how the news media work and how they can enhance or reduce news coverage. The media are such a massive presence in contemporary democratic politics that all governments and other institutions under constant media scrutiny need machinery for dealing with their demands. Spin is not just a matter of shaping the content, but the prominence and intensity of reporting, to maximise the good news and to contain and minimise the impact of bad news. Many media advisers are former journalists. They know news cycles and routines, they understand news values, and so have a strong sense of what will become a headline, and what will be the key phrase used in a sound bite. Some spin doctors are very good at orchestrating photogenic occasions which will show their candidate in a good light, and just as importantly save him or her from embarrassments. This includes gaining coverage in 'soft news' outlets where the leader can appear sympathetic, without irritating interrogation.

2. Use of public opinion polling and focus groups as a tool to shape the presentation – and, increasingly, the substance – of policy

All political parties use private polling to assess their prospects and guide their strategies. This polling data is used to map not just the shape of public opinion, but also the degree to which different themes resonate, which face of an issue to highlight, and which parts of public opinion are hard and immovable and which are soft and ambivalent. As with most aspects of spin, this is most intense in the US. The famous Clinton 'war room' in his successful 1992 presidential campaign was getting new public opinion data every day, and using it to fine-tune their phrasings and emphases. Tracking voter sentiment and targeting potential swing voters are central parts of all contemporary campaign planning. Similarly, focus groups can help guide how parties phrase their messages. In 2007, Labor strategists used words such as 'tricky' and 'trust' because they had found that these themes resonated with uncommitted voters,[27] and described Howard as 'a very clever politician'.[28] Instead of saying Howard was out of touch, it was better to say he had 'lost' touch, to win back those who had voted for him in the past.[29]

3. Media monitoring and rapid rebuttal

The term 'rapid rebuttal' was first used by Tony Blair's New Labour in Britain during their rise to power. Their aim was to contest damaging charges as soon as possible, to not let accusations run uncontested. The practice keeps evolving, so that the other side's criticisms are anticipated and attempts can be made to circumvent them even before they are made – 'prebuttal'. However, media monitoring is used not just to inform defensive spin operations, but also to provide the ammunition for offensive actions.

4. Background briefings to shape the interpretation of public events

Originally, the term 'spin' referred to giving anonymous guidance about the 'real meaning' of public events, shaping the interpretation of success and failure, to give ambiguous moments the desired shape and political definition in subsequent news reports. Before the event it can be to shape expectations about what a good performance would be or what the opponents' weaknesses are, or about traps to look out for. Such briefings succeed most fully when they are inserted into journalists' reports without any attribution, when the spin doctor has successfully helped to frame the story the journalist writes.[30]

Spin doctors picture themselves as simply increasing the professionalism and efficiency with which messages are communicated to the public.[31] What could be more harmless than a government arranging its diary so that major announcements do not interfere with each other? Surely it is good to be responsive to public opinion. All their activities can be made to sound anodyne, simply a neutral, commonsense pursuit, but each also has the potential for manipulation.

A spin doctor's effort to secure the best coverage for their side is not like an advocate or debater preparing the best case. To stretch the analogy, spin doctors' efforts go into deciding which case will be heard. All recent federal governments – it is likely that this also happens with all state governments but in a less intense way – begin the day planning how they will 'feed the beast'. The Rudd Government took this to a new peak with its Command and Control approach. David McKnight's study of these processes revealed that Rudd's media advisers thought that such disciplined communication was essential. The purpose of planned media advice, they said, was to deny 'your opposition any space to move ... you are keeping the journalists fed and happy with material so they're busily working away on [your] stuff ... it's your agenda'.[32] It is also necessary defensively: 'Any display of inconsistency by members of a government meant "you'll be eaten alive by every journalist in the cycle".'[33]

The effort is made not just to influence the content of news coverage, but to affect its prominence and duration, and the number of people who see it. All major news makers have strategies for 'putting out the trash', getting rid of negative stories in a way that means they will have minimal impact. The Gillard Government was in the habit of releasing freedom of information documents on a Friday afternoon,[34] in the hope that the media would not scrutinise them properly in time for the Saturday papers, and that pre-weekend TV news audiences were lower.

The saga of Scott Morrison and Save the Children illustrates the contest over determining news priorities. In October 2014, Immigration Minister Morrison launched a ferocious attack on Save the Children staff working with detainees in Nauru. He ordered ten staff members of the charity off the island because, he said, they were organising protest activities and coaching detainees in self-harm and to allege abuses. Morrison no doubt wanted to deflect attention from any sympathetic consideration of the detainees' plight. The government commissioned a report by former integrity commissioner Philip Moss. The Moss Review was embarrassing for the government because it failed to validate these incendiary claims. The government sat on the review for a month, then released it mid-afternoon Friday. Moreover, on this particular Friday the national focus was on Malcolm Fraser's sudden death. However, the government denied managing the timing of the report's release in this way.[35] Then the news that the government had reached a confidential agreement, including financial compensation, with Save the Children was released the same day as a flurry of other last-minute announcements, as Parliament was rising before the 2016 election.[36] Overall, the original false allegations received far more prominent and prolonged coverage than both the refutations and the compensation.

There was no subtlety about the Iemma Government's timing in November 2005. Under attack about Sydney's cross-city tunnel – there were claims that it was a white elephant – the government released 30,000 pages of documents on the afternoon of the Melbourne Cup. Although the opposition criticised this blatant ploy,[37] it still probably reduced the government's embarrassment. But the most shocking example of spin doctors' cynicism came after the September 11 terrorist attacks in New York. Within minutes of the planes hitting the World Trade Center, Jo Moore, a minder for the British Transport Minister, sent an email to other staff saying that today is 'a very good day to get out anything we want to bury'.[38]

Counter-productive spin doctoring

Spin does not transcend and trump all other political resources. No Orwellian dystopia of all-powerful spin doctors is imminent. Like most black magic, its power is much reduced when it is subjected to close scrutiny. The relationship between politicians and the media should be seen as three interacting sets of games: politicians versus politicians (both between and within parties); journalists competing with each other; and politicians and journalists relating to each for their own advantage.[39] The dangers of spin are most pronounced when these relationships become unbalanced. The dominant tone of public commentary on spin is misleading in that it fails to consider the limits on its effectiveness – the fact that one side's spin is countered by that of its opponents, that there are often great variations in competence among spin doctors, and that the precepts of image enhancement are more easily stated than achieved.

The attempt to look like a strong leader, for example, often leads to hollow and unconvincing posturing. When Gillard visited Queensland during some terrible floods in early 2011, she used the word 'I' more than 50 times in the text of her flood-package speech, including twice in the title – '"I see what needs to be done and I will do it". For good measure, there were more than a dozen uses of "my".'[40] Some leaders are aiming for an ever bigger bang, so when Rudd's speechwriter, Tim Dixon, wrote in a speech about a 'significant increase' in hospital funding, the Prime Minister's response was: 'Significant? Significant? I don't do significant. I only do first time or biggest ever.' Then he stormed out of the room.[41]

Constant spin quickly degenerates into a cliché machine. Mike Rann, before he was South Australian Premier, was chief spin doctor to an earlier Labor Premier, John Bannon. In retirement,

Rann proudly recalled how in 1985, when Bannon launched:

> [his campaign] to have the Collins class submarine project
> located in SA, he didn't follow other states who announced
> their bids in a speech or news conference. He did it in a
> submarine … John Bannon was lowered by winch from a navy
> helicopter off the NSW coast into a surfacing submarine with
> media helicopters filming and reporting.[42]

Having a Premier lowered by winch into a submarine would still
be a pretty stunning visual ploy, but the norm is much more pedestrian. Laurie Oakes remembered how in his efforts to dominate
the news cycle, 'Rudd would dash hither and yon, dressed in a hard
hat here or a surgical gown there, providing picture opportunities, holding doorstop news conferences and making all manner of
announcements.'[43] Similarly, Barrie Cassidy recalled:

> [Tony Abbott's] interminable doorstops at a factory within easy
> driving distance from Parliament House that usually involved
> the prime minister putting on a hard hat and mouthing vacuous
> slogans. They happened almost every day and rarely did they
> advance the national interest one inch. Instead, they simply
> served as fodder to the meaningless, mindless political argument
> du jour.[44]

Spin gives rise to verbal as well as visual clichés. Gillard used 'moving
forward' 20 times in her opening election speech in 2010.[45] Then
she and her Ministers were determined to slip it into every verbal
exchange, and very quickly it became a standing joke.[46] Rudd listed
several quite different issues as his 'Number One Priority'.[47] The
attempt to seem on the same wavelength as the public can lead to
a false folksiness, with Kevin Rudd's 'fair squirt of the sauce bottle'
and Tony Abbott's 'Team Australia' more dissonant than resonant.
Nor did it help Rudd's cause when in an unfriendly encounter

with shock jock Ray Hadley, Rudd called him 'mate' 12 times in the interview.[48] Politicians' determination to stay on message can also backfire. Political analyst Lindy Edwards thought that in the Gillard Government 'the rigid discipline with which key players have "stayed on message" has made them appear wooden, arrogant and dishonest'.[49]

So efforts at spinning the news are more often pedestrian than inspired. The argument of this chapter goes still further, however: namely, that the practice of spin doctoring has inherent vulner-abilities and dominant tendencies which create their own pathol-ogies, and these have been important in the fates of recent leaders.

The triumph of tactics over strategy

What sorts of people become successful spin doctors? One char-acteristic is an unquestioning allegiance to their own side – 'The notion that [President] Clinton might deserve whatever criticism the paper was dishing out seemed not to have crossed [his press secretary Mike] McCurry's mind.'[50] Another is believing that the end justifies the means. They then apply themselves to those means with determination and skill and flair. They know news formats and news cycles intimately and have a great feel for exploiting them – 'Alastair Campbell [Blair's closest political confidant and strategist] is a tabloid journalist to his fingertips.' Their focus is very much on the immediate. This combination of tactical sense and combative-ness, of a complete absorption in the immediate and a huge will to win, is what makes them so successful. But strengths can also be weaknesses, and these normally effective traits can instead become counter-productive. A concentration on tactics can set up longer-term strategic problems, and combativeness can unnecessarily esca-late minor problems into more major conflicts.

Rudd's office staff, they told researcher Pat Weller, was 'focussed on winning the 24 hour cycle'.[51] As one media adviser told

McKnight, 'If you win the TV news one night, and then five out of the seven [nights] and 25 out of the 31 days of the month and eight of the 12 months of the year, then you're probably going to win the next election.'[52] This has a seductive, but flawed, simplicity. Most importantly, the tactician's mentality runs the risk of sacrificing a consistent narrative to the exigencies of the moment, of sacrificing a strong sense of self in order to provide 'a persona for every demographic'.[53]

If any policy needed stability of direction and a steadiness of nerve, it was mitigating climate change. Ross Garnaut described it as a 'diabolical' policy problem.[54] By this he meant that effective action required concerted international agreement on a very large and difficult-to-achieve scale, and that in order to obtain a future benefit (or a reduced future cost), immediate costs had to be borne.

The early omens were not good. Opposition Leader Brendan Nelson questioned the costs of the policy, especially increases in the cost of living and consequences for affected industries, claiming it would be economic suicide if Australia acted alone. Rudd, intent on winning each news cycle, thought the best tactic was not to talk about costs with any specificity. The longer-term result of this deliberate vagueness, however, was that the government could not counter their opponents' outrageous scare campaigns.[55]

Nothing, however, compared with the revelation that the Rudd Government had abandoned for the foreseeable future their ETS (see also Chapter 2). Just a few weeks before the reversal, he had told Cassidy, 'There is no way, Barrie, that when you are really dealing with the big challenges of the future … you can walk away from emissions trading.'[56]

After he did walk away, the commentariat's response, not surprisingly, was almost uniformly critical. Bernard Keane thought that the decision to indefinitely delay any action on an ETS revealed Rudd as a leader not only unwilling to stand by his most important values but, even more dangerously, 'lacking core principles'.[57] Economics editor Tim Colebatch thought the dumping of the ETS was 'an act of breathtaking cynicism … It told Australians that what this Government cares about is keeping power, and anything else is expendable to that end.'[58] Peter Hartcher thought 'Every policy will now be seen as just another piece of clever politics. What's the point of Kevin Rudd? Australians don't know any more.'[59] Lenore Taylor judged it 'the decision that appeared to snap voters' faith in the government and in Kevin Rudd'.[60] This was immediately manifested in the polls. For the first time since the 2007 election, the Coalition moved ahead of Labor, whose primary vote dropped to 35 per cent. In one month, Rudd's approval rating dropped from 59 to 45 per cent.[61] No amount of winning days compensates for a loss of credibility of that magnitude.

Rudd's surrender is perhaps also indicative of the cynical view that public perceptions are endlessly malleable. One of the sillier political clichés equates perception with reality. President George W Bush's chief spin doctor, Karl Rove, once told a journalist that he, the journalist, was part of 'the reality-based community' who 'believe that solutions emerge from your judicious study of discernible reality'. But, said Rove:

> we're an empire now and when we act, we create our own reality. And while you're studying that reality – judiciously as you will – we'll act again, creating other new realities, which you can study too, and that's how things will sort out. We're history's actors … and you, all of you, will be left to just study what we do.[62]

Rove's hubris soon collided with reality. He orchestrated a seemingly triumphant Bush in May 2003 on the aircraft carrier USS *Lincoln*, in front of cheering troops and under a large banner proclaiming 'Mission Accomplished', declaring that in Iraq the US and its allies had prevailed. It was wonderful television, and looked as if it could become the basis for an advertisement in the 2004 election … before subsequent developments in Iraq destroyed that possibility.

As in that case, the tactical successes, despite their ability to influence short-term appearances, can set up longer-term targets. They set up a record of claims and promises against which later developments will be measured. As a probably apocryphal journalist asked at a US military briefing in Vietnam, 'Yes General, but aren't your victories getting closer to Saigon?'

Over-promising and under-delivering is one of the chief means by which long-serving governments exhaust the public's goodwill. Journalist Joe Hildebrand noted that 'ten years after unveiling its bold transport plan for Sydney, the State [Labor] Government has failed to build a single one of the five major rail projects it promised'.[63] It was, thought former Labor Minister Rodney Cavalier, 'a fatal problem' for the government that 'people stopped believing [its] grand announcements … One tally of major rail projects announced over 15 years counted 12 that had been cancelled – including revivals being cancelled again.'[64] According to leading journalist Ross Gittins, 'The government's chronic problems with the trains are a direct result of preferring the flashy over the important-but-boring.'[65]

So, in the long term, spin is not a substitute for performance, but it is easy for political leaders to get caught up in their own realities. As one of the architects of British Labour's 1997 victory, Peter Mandelson, observed, 'communications is not an after-thought to our policy. It's central to the whole mission of New Labour.'[66] But instead of communication being simply an integral part of policy-making, its own imperatives soon dominated. According to Blair spin doctor Lance Price, 'new policies were plucked out of thin air because the Prime Minister had an interview to give'.[67] Some public service chiefs lamented that No. 10 was 'asking for announcements before we have a policy'.[68] According to another government adviser, Geoff Mulgan, 'New Labour often confused announcement for reality, believing that if they were getting a success in the newspaper you were getting a success on the ground.' That, said Mulgan, is 'a very dangerous habit to get into'.[69] In

Australia also, the preoccupation with spin encroaches ever more on the process of policy formation. Lindsay Tanner, Finance Minister in the Rudd Government, thought that 'reliance on market research is now so absolute that the policy formation occurs in reverse'.[70]

When an unwelcome issue is running in the news there is pressure to respond immediately. But sometimes a rapid response leads to the wrong response being locked in. In October 2009, Australian authorities received a distress call regarding a boat carrying 78 Sri Lankan asylum seekers in Indonesian waters. The Australian vessel *Oceanic Viking* picked them up. Then, without consulting anyone, including Immigration Minister Chris Evans, Rudd despatched them to Indonesia, saying he had made a deal with President Susilo Bambang Yudhoyono for Indonesia to take them. Andrew Metcalfe, the head of the Immigration Department, said immediately, 'They won't get off the boat.'[71] And so it proved. The acutely embarrassing affair went on for four weeks.[72] Rudd's attempt at a tough and immediate solution instead got the government into a quagmire, one which dramatised its difficulties on the asylum seeker issue. Until then there had been no sustained outcry over the increasing number of asylum seekers; Evans thought that this was a political disaster that dramatically indicated that the government could not manage its borders.[73]

The West Wing delusion

For a time I was attracted to a TV series, *The West Wing*, which centres on the staff of President Jed Bartlet, a US President who had earlier won a Nobel Prize for Economics. The show was very good at drawing out the relationships of the main characters as they sought to juggle competing political considerations. For some reason, the program then palled with me. Inside the West Wing were competent, conscientious people, working for a wise and beneficent president, while many outsiders – the elected members of Congress, bureaucrats and so on – were portrayed unsympathetically. Now when I want political drama I think I will go for something more realistic, such as King Arthur and the Knights of the Round Table.

The West Wing does point to a new and important political reality. There is a large group of political appointees who are close to the exercise of power, but who are neither elected representatives nor public servants. Some are policy advisers; others are spin doctors.

The contemporary spin enterprise is inextricably intertwined with a centralisation of control within parties and governments.[74] The closeness of the spin doctors to the leaders cuts across other important relationships. Laura Tingle, reviewing Gareth Evans' diaries as a Minister in the mid–1980s, says:

> you can almost see the beginnings of the more modern politics peeking out of the diary as Evans and Paul Keating lament the increasing time Hawke spends with his advisers instead of his cabinet colleagues and the isolation they believe he suffers from as a result.[75]

Since then, the trend towards Prime Ministers becoming all-powerful within government has been a persistent one. Thus, Tingle notes:

> the mindset of collective responsibility, of ministers being sworn in to run their portfolios, started to fade somewhere along the way and, some would argue, all but totally disappeared in the Rudd and Gillard years. Think of all those complaints about how nothing could get done because the prime minister was the road block, or wouldn't turn up for a meeting, or of the terror of ministers saying anything before it was cleared by the PMO.[76]

So ministerial staff, including spin doctors, have an access and closeness to the leader that many elected politicians lack. Inevitably this creates resentments, especially if the staff are perceived to be exercising power beyond their remit, or if they start acting towards others as if their authority were the same as the leader's.

It was an issue that contributed to the end of Rudd's prime ministership. Gary Gray, a Minister, formerly the party's national secretary and so an expert on electoral matters, thought Howard's changes to electoral registration were wrong in principle and were costing Labor votes. He was trying to get Rudd to change it. Eventually, in September 2009 there was a meeting of some Ministers, parliamentary secretaries and Rudd's staff. At one stage Gray asked staff to leave so they could have a political discussion. The staff refused, and ten minutes later he got a text message from Rudd's Chief of Staff, Alister Jordan, saying he was excluded from any further meetings.[77] Cassidy cites another example. Rudd's press secretary, Lachlan Harris, phoned Agriculture Minister Tony Burke, who was in Darwin, and told him he was assigned to do five radio interviews that day. But Burke was sick, and losing his voice. After he told Harris this, Harris shouted at him that he was not pulling his weight, and then circulated an email making the same point.[78] Cassidy concluded: 'It was inconceivable before the Rudd prime ministership that any press secretary could treat a minister in that way. But authority had shifted away from elected officials to staffers given obscene powers by the leader himself.'[79]

A leader's quest for control easily becomes obsessive, a reason for always narrowing the range of people immediately involved in decision-making. The interaction of spin processes and decision processes then impacts on the quality of policy. Robert Reich argued that 'no White House in modern history has been as adept at politics and as ham-fisted at governing' as George W Bush's. But he sees a link in the orchestration of all levels of government to stay on message. He argues that the 'same discipline and organisation that's made the White House into a hugely effective political machine has hobbled its capacity to govern'.[80] 'The squelching of troublesome information', Reich thought, is effective in the short term in keeping the media and opposition parties at bay, but prevents top policy-makers getting the data and perspectives they need to make effective policy. So the closing of decision-making processes is prone to producing groupthink: a failure to acknowledge other considerations.

This was an important element of the Rudd Government's failure on climate change. In Paul Kelly's summation, Rudd took to 'dizzy and unsustainable heights what is best called the cult of prime ministerial governance. He gave priority to his personal office over cabinet.'[81] At the first meeting of the climate change committee in early 2008, Rudd arrived late and in a frightful mood. He then threw out all the department heads except the Head of the Department of Climate Change and all Ministers except Swan and Penny Wong. So such central agencies as Prime Minister and Cabinet and Finance were kept out of the loop. Part of Rudd's thinking was the fear of leaks.[82] But the result, as researcher Philip Chubb wrote, was that he 'killed at birth the normal processes of debate among departments and ministers', resulting in a 'lack of depth and variety in the advice he received'. This radical narrowing of the decision-making group gave Rudd greater control and latitude, but it was the 'catalyst for the long slide towards a policy fiasco'.[83]

Climate change was one case of a wider attitude. An experienced bureaucrat told Chubb that there was 'more of a chasm between the senior levels of the public service generally and the Rudd government than has been the case previously in Canberra'. Moreover, by late 2009 some believed that 'Rudd was really only talking to his chief of staff, Alister Jordan, and economic adviser Andrew Charlton.'[84]

This narrowing of decision-making groups inevitably creates its own frictions, increasing resentments among those excluded. It also complicates the tensions and stakes in leadership struggles because there is a large group of people who tend to not only identify the government's interests with the leader's, but also tie their own prospects and commitments to one contender rather than another. So, as Keating's direct challenge was getting underway in 1991, his 'press secretary Mark Ryan and political adviser Stephen Smith spent all day on the phone or in the corridors. They longed for battle.'[85] This was even more pronounced in Britain, where the tensions between Tony Blair and Gordon Brown were played out among their staffs. Thus Campbell 'derived immense satisfaction when [Brown's press officer Charlie] Wheeler was forced to resign at the start of 1999 over his role in leaking information'.[86]

Leaders' personal staff have been implicated in leadership upheavals from as early as 1970. When John Gorton dropped Dudley Erwin from the ministry, Erwin gave as the reason: 'It wiggles, it's shapely, it's cold-blooded and its name is Ainsley Gotto [Gorton's 21-year-old private secretary].'[87] The complaints became more frequent over the years as the number and power of staff increased.

Nothing, however, had come close to the public spotlight and ferocity of the conflicts surrounding Tony Abbott's Chief of Staff, Peta Credlin. Even while the Liberals were still in opposition, journalist Matthew Knott noted that:

> Peta Credlin, Tony Abbott's chief of staff, is the biggest control
> freak in Canberra – with the notable exception of Kevin Rudd.
> She travels everywhere with the opposition leader, pulls Liberal
> MPs into line when they veer off message, and is driving the
> Coalition's relentlessly negative agenda.[88]

Soon after the election of the Abbott Government there were complaints, especially about her vetoing of ministerial staff appointments. Credlin set up a panel that had to approve all 420 appointments, and there were complaints that 'if Credlin doesn't like someone, they don't get the job'.[89] Senator Ian Macdonald publicly charged that the Prime Minister's office, led by Credlin, had instilled a culture of 'obsessive centralised control'.[90]

Amazingly, after Abbott's fall the titles of two books (by Patrick and Savva) gave the Chief of Staff equal billing with the Prime Minister. Journalists relished the tales of bitchiness and bullying; of tantrums, pettiness and dysfunctionality; of personal feuds and of critical or independently minded people being frozen out. Whether or not they were all true, their sheer volume showed how this relationship cut across and damaged other relationships in the government. Backbench and frontbench Liberals expressed dismay to journalists:

> that they keep hearing about major policy announcements for
> the first time via leaks from the [PMO] to the media. Some
> ministers are even finding out about major developments in their
> own portfolios this way. There is also a strong suspicion that the
> PMO has been briefing the media against other ministers.[91]

In the lead-up to the February spill motion, conservative standard-bearer Miranda Devine offered the most biting comment:

> anyone who has objected has been sidelined, demoted, pushed
> out by Credlin. She has centralised control in Stalinist fashion,
> determining all staff appointments, and pay, vetoing the wishes
> of even senior ministers to hire a chief of staff or adviser of
> their choice. Some of the tactics used to get rid of contrary
> people are so petty as to be unbelievable. Crucial staff are
> undermined by being left off email lists so they miss meetings,
> for instance.[92]

But it was easier to blame Credlin than to confront the harder truth: that the problem was not so much 'her pernicious influence' as 'his fundamental incapacity'.[93] Abbott remained unflinchingly loyal to her. In his farewell speech after being defeated, he singled her out as having been 'unfairly maligned by people who should have known better'.[94] In an ironic epilogue, the week after Abbott was deposed, Credlin was scheduled to speak at an *Australian*

Women's Weekly function, after the magazine had named her (ahead of, for example, deputy Liberal leader Julie Bishop) the most powerful woman in Australia.[95]

Faux professionalism

Spin doctors learn on the job. Many of them are well steeped in political and media folklore. However, their apparently hard-headed professionalism, based on craft knowledge, can sometimes mislead. Moreover, there is always considerable scope for subjective judgments and personal considerations to intervene. After the success of the Kevin07 campaign, advertising executive Neil Lawrence was given great credit for his strategic and creative work. However, after Karl Bitar became national secretary, Lawrence was not reappointed. Mark Arbib told Lawrence, 'Karl just didn't think he could control you.'[96]

Two aspects are particularly pertinent. The first is that for spin doctors, politicking takes precedence over governing. Their skills at political persuasion have grown much more than their skills at policy development. Too often, for them, gaining partisan advantage becomes the whole of politics. The second is that despite the increasing use of polls and focus groups, their findings are sometimes accorded a hardness and solidity that they do not warrant. The movement from poll results to political decision is often much more complicated than the quick fix that seems obvious.

Harris, Rudd's press secretary, told the ABC documentary *The Killing Season*: 'There is only one speed in politics when it comes to your opponents, and that is you take every gun you've got and you fire every bullet at them and you don't stop shooting till they're gone.'[97] This is not a passage you are likely to find in Sun Tzu's *The Art of War*. Without any larger consideration of strategy, this will waste many bullets. But perhaps more importantly, it represents the dominance of politicking over governing.

This was clearly, and fatefully, the case with the Rudd Government's actions on climate change. Their priority was always seeking advantage over the Liberals rather than securing the policy. Criticising the Liberals was more prominent in their rhetoric than persuading the public of the necessity and wisdom of an ETS. Transcripts from seven ABC interviews given by Climate Change Minister Penny Wong show that in six she focused on the opposition. In one, ten of her 13 answers were about the opposition.[98] This lack of positive purpose was paralleled by falling polls.

Rudd's strategy was to pass the ETS with support from the Liberals, for good reason (to lock the alternative government in) and bad (to lock the Greens out). Contradicting this, however, was his wish to use the issue to destabilise his main policy ally and chief political opponent, Turnbull. According to Swan's account, in July 2009 Wong advised that the deal should be locked in as quickly as possible, to reduce the scope for business dissent. Rudd, however, told Wong and Greg Combet to 'drag out the process as long as possible. His objective was to extract as much political advantage as possible from a divided Opposition.'[99] Chubb judged that Rudd was 'fixated on the quick thrill of wedge politics'.[100] Swan thought: 'Whenever Turnbull seemed to be bringing the issue back under control, Kevin would' send in his spear-throwers, with 'strategically placed leaks about how much the Coalition, under [Turnbull's] leadership, was conceding to the government on climate change'.[101] Rudd staffer Sean Kelly reflected that in late 2009, he 'spent every afternoon in the press gallery, spruiking division within the Coalition. The aim was to stoke discontent on their side, leading to troublesome media stories for them and a victory in the nightly news skirmish for us. As a media strategy it succeeded brilliantly.' It climaxed in Abbott's victory over Turnbull and the defeat of the ETS in the Senate. Never, concluded Kelly, 'has there been a clearer case of winning the battle and losing the war'.[102]

Having forsaken the possibility of establishing an ETS in July

2009, Rudd forfeited the political opportunity of a double dissolution election on the issue in early 2010. Then after months of drift, frustrating all the other major actors in the government, he renounced the scheme altogether in April 2010. Feeding into the disastrous decision, perhaps, was the knowledge that support for the policy was ebbing in the polls, a major issue for such a poll-sensitive government, but of course that decision made the polling much worse. As Harris commented, what polling can't tell you is how someone will judge a leader who changes the policy.[103]

Key players in the government, such as Arbib and Bitar, were hyper-sensitive to movements in the polls. Some called Arbib the 'red cordial man' because he was too excitable, his judgments too short-term.[104] Bitar wrote a private email to Rudd Chief of Staff Jordan demanding that 'every policy and announcement must pass the Lindsay test' (see Chapter 2).[105] There were two basic problems with the Lindsay test. The first is that no single electorate, no matter how marginal – and this Western Sydney seat is very marginal – encapsulates all the regional variations across the country. The second, and much more fundamental, problem is that basing policy decisions on public opinion is like building on quicksand.

The movement from poll to policy is often complicated; not only in terms of policy substance, but also in relation to electoral pragmatism. According to Cavalier,[106] when Arbib was NSW Labor Party secretary 'he trespassed into matters of policy detail not ordinarily of concern to a party official'. Labor Premier Iemma particularly resented Arbib's demand that the government announce mandatory sentencing because the polling supported that announcement: 'By refusing to enter the customary race to the bottom on law and order that generally characterizes NSW elections, Iemma achieved a critical differentiation with the Coalition parties.'[107]

Somewhat later, the new NSW state secretary, Bitar, concluded from the party's polling that the results were so bad that they all (Iemma, Costa, Roozendaal, Sartor, Meagher, Tripodi, John Della Bosca) should be dumped.[108] Because Iemma and any of his circle would 'take the party to annihilation', the only option, they thought, 'was a cleanskin'.[109] They promoted Nathan Rees. Bitar briefed Cabinet Minister Frank Sartor on the polling; Bitar reasoned 'that the Cabinet was too "on the nose" and that there were too many "wogs". Rees, he said, was a break from that – an Aussie Westie. What a way to choose a Premier!'[110]

It is notable that the party's private polling was different from the publicly available polls. Leading expert Murray Goot concluded that 'Labor entered the second year of its term looking electable under Iemma.'[111] He also noted that under Rees, Labor never again achieved the 2PP vote it had had in the last poll under Iemma.[112] It may not emerge in polling, but the idea that a 12-year-old government could credibly leap to a 'cleanskin' is an illusion that only a hardened spin doctor could embrace.

Labor had not learned from an earlier electorally disastrous leadership change that had been justified by polling – one by their opponents. A central player in overthrowing Peter Collins as Liberal leader and replacing him with Kerry Chikarovski was state director, Remo Nogarotto. Collins resented the intervention of a party official in the parliamentary party: 'By setting out to remove me as Leader, Nogarotto broke every rule.'[113] When Collins was overthrown his colleagues, all parroted to him the line, pushed by Nogarotto, that 'the polls say you cannot win'.[114] Their polling deteriorated after the change.

Like generals perfectly prepared to fight the last war, the spin mentality often misses, or is late catching, the newest waves. Peter Brent pointed out how fear of the social conservatism of the electorate and being wedged by the Liberals had led Labor astray in its stances on marriage equality:

In 2004 the Howard government introduced the Marriage Amendment Act to specifically outlaw same-sex marriage, and the Labor Party, led by Mark Latham, voted in favour. Rather than seeing an opportunity for differentiation, Labor viewed it as yet another trap by the evil genius [Howard], a 'wedge' to be avoided.

When the issue arose again, this time under Labor, Gillard opposed any change to the Marriage Act to allow same-sex marriage, apparently oblivious to how quickly public sentiment was changing. According to Brent, 'this is how a political party ties itself in knots ... If Kevin Rudd's flaw as prime minister was lack of courage, Gillard's was far worse: a total capitulation to the nostrums of apparatchiks like Bitar.'[115]

A self-diminishing resource

Spin doctors are typically the private bad cop who allows the leader to be the public good cop. Beneath the statesmanlike surface may be a much more manipulative, even threatening, set of private dealings. *Guardian* journalist Kevin Maguire said of Campbell, Blair's right-hand man, that you knew when you'd been 'Campbelled': Alastair Campbell 'operated by menace, he'd heave his 6ft 2in frame into your room and stand over you. Stare at you and try and put you down with either a well-chosen swearword ... or a long stare, or a tirade of abuse.'[116]

When Campbell's colleague, John McTernan, came from the UK to work for Gillard, he was widely credited with bringing a new peak of verbal aggression to Canberra. His Scottish accent and flow of obscenities made many compare him with the fictional, foul-mouthed spin doctor Malcolm Tucker. Journalist Ross Greenwood said that in one 12-minute phone conversation, McTernan dropped 'the F-bomb at least 30 times'.[117] Later a series of McTernan's emails was leaked. They showed a similar flow of invective and said that an ABC journalist who had reported criticisms of him was to get nothing, not even the most basic information, from the PM's office.[118] *Financial Review* columnist Joe Aston wondered if these 'juvenile, confected tirades' had any effect.[119] Labor Party figures were divided. Talking to journalist Andrew Crook, one was scathing, saying the 'Scottish experiment has failed'. McTernan's 'aggressive style has alienated the whole gallery. He's tried to placate the *Daily Telegraph* with disastrous consequences.' But another close observer thought him 'more interesting than the entire Labor senior team put together'.[120]

The journalist–spin doctor relationship, while often allowing for cooperation, is also marked by constant petty irritants, such as trying to manage the timing or extent of revelations or to avoid particular words and admissions. Journalists and spin doctors have overlapping interests but conflicting purposes. A politician's trading mentality, a carrot and stick approach, may produce resentment among journalists, and perhaps a brittle relationship. Michelle Grattan recalled that 'Keating's spin came with the classic techniques: promises and threats. Buy it and you would be "on the drip"; reject it and no drip, and probably a lot of abuse.'[121] A *Sun-Herald* journalist taped Keating abusing him in 1991, including Keating's statement: 'I am a simple fellow. You have hurt me and I will hurt you. You can count on it.'[122]

It is an open question how much effect such threats have. One that proved counter-productive involved Rudd as Opposition Leader and his press secretary, Harris. Rudd had made much of the trauma of his family after his father, a tenant farmer, was killed in a car accident, and how the family had then had to move. The *Sun-Herald*'s Kerry-Anne Walsh spoke to a member of the farming family who thought that Rudd's version unfairly impugned the man's father, and the care he had shown for the Rudds. When Walsh approached Rudd's office, according to Alan Ramsey's account, Harris rang her back 'ranting like a lunatic'. Her 'insulting' questions were 'disgusting' and 'impugned Kevin's integrity'. He then refused to discuss it further. Later he rang back in the 'same feral, belligerent mood'. On 'deep background' he went through the timeline in detail, and then said if you still publish 'we will regard it as a deliberate malicious assault' on Rudd, and if that happened, 'we'll have 100 people ready to roll tomorrow morning to trash you and your paper'. Later Rudd himself became involved, calling the story a 'disgrace', 'the wrong thing for yourself, and you're kicking my dead mother in the guts'. The paper ran the story.[123] Afterwards, Rudd arranged a peace meeting with editor Simon Dulhunty. Dulhunty told staff 'he was struck by Rudd's constant and inappropriate use of the f-word … He wasn't swearing in context. It just didn't seem to work for him.'[124]

Labor's Liberal successors had their own such incidents. Journalist Peter van Onselen witnessed Abbott staffer Dr Mark Roberts threaten the head of an Indigenous body with the loss of federal funding, telling him we will 'cut your throat' once we are in government. Roberts then approached van Onselen and promised to be a source for him in Abbott's office if he stayed quiet about the incident. Van Onselen refused and immediately sent several tweets expressing his total disgust. Roberts was subsequently 'counselled' by Abbott, and demoted within the office.[125]

So behind the public facades there is often a much less attractive private reality, one that is in constant danger of being exposed. Also, the attempts at coercion or manipulation may become less effective over time, which is one of the basic limitations of spin. The last word ought perhaps be from former President Nixon, who wrote in his memoirs: Presidents 'must try to master the art of manipulating the media … to win in politics but … at the same time they must avoid at all costs the charge of trying to manipulate the media.'[126]

The rise of spin is perverse testimony to the strength of democracy and the political demands of the media. It is evidence that more coercive means of political control will not suffice. The core democratic problem with spin, however, is the rise of cynicism and the mix of dishonesty and noise that makes it harder for the public to gain perspective. Spin is not likely to disappear or become less important. It is not a realistic solution for professionals to become amateur again, for political heavies to become more gentlemanly, or for governments to pretend that they will devote fewer resources to these efforts. As long as it remains politically rewarding, spin will continue to grow. But, perhaps thankfully, it is far from fool-proof and is prone to its own counter-productive pathologies. Rudd's leadership, which early on was such a testament to the success of spin, was fatally undermined by his myopic concern with tactics, and both his and Abbott's leaderships were compromised by the way their relationships with personal staff cut across other relationships. The preoccupation with spin is one reason for leadership instability having increased so drastically over the decades; and the presence and activities of spin doctors add greatly to the many-sided dramas of leadership struggles.

CHAPTER 11

The Doctrine of the Disposable Leader

Seventy-three leaders forcibly deposed in the major parties since 1970; just under half of all major party leaderships in recent decades terminated by the leaders' colleagues. Australian politics has entered an era marked by the doctrine of the disposable leader. What has driven this instability? And what factors determine the likelihood of success in individual cases?

Australian exceptionalism

This forced turnover of leaders is not the norm in any other country. No other parliamentary democracy has had anything resembling Australia's leadership instability. The total of 73, of course, combines seven different governments, but even if we confine the figure to the national level, it is still 16. No other country has had more than a handful. Although some countries have had dramatic leadership conflicts – such as between Tony Blair and Gordon Brown, or the fall of Margaret Thatcher in the UK, or the feud between Jean Chrétien and Paul Martin in Canada – Australia has had at least five times as many leadership coups at national level as any other country.

What has made Australia so different? This is especially puzzling when you consider that the three main factors driving the insta-bility – the perceived importance of leaders in electoral success;

the focus on leaders in the news; and the rise of leader-centred parties and governments – also broadly apply to the other democracies.

The international differences are dramatic, but perhaps the reasons are fairly prosaic. The frequency of elections is a stimulus to greater leader turnover. Australia has a distinctive electoral system. Most notably, the three-year federal election cycle means that the political temperature is high much of the time. Although some states now have a four-year cycle, few years pass without an election somewhere, state or federal (or local), so the American phrase, 'the permanent campaign', applies more to Australia than most countries. Other unique aspects of the electoral system, such as compulsory voting and preferential voting, whereby disenchanted voters can go to a minor party or independent on their favoured side of politics without crossing the major partisan divide, perhaps add to the volatility of the polls, which itself further heightens the focus on leadership. The clichéd formula for reporting the seemingly ever-more-frequent polls is to say that it means one or other leader is in trouble.

In Australia, the leader's fate is in the hands of the parliamentary party. If the leadership is decided by the wider party membership, for example, it is more difficult to effect a change and the process will be, at the very least, more protracted and more public. Federal Labor in 2013 did decide its leadership by a vote that included party members, but so far, all leadership coups have been decided in the party room. Sometimes, in some states, the size of the opposition party room can be quite small, so a very few people shifting allegiance can bring about a change of leaders.

Like other countries with two-sided party competitions, such as the US and UK, the zero-sum, winner-take-all logic has been pursued more and more ruthlessly over recent decades. The negativity of campaigning has increased, creating a self-sustaining gladiatorial tone, and discrediting – even, if possible, tearing down – the opposing leader has become a central element. The psychological assaults by one party sometimes feed into the internal machinations of the other.

Finally, it could also be that coups have become part of the routine repertoire for dealing with problems. Individually, none of these seems sufficient to account for the difference, but together they may provide part of the reason why Australia has been so different from other democracies.

In the discussion of individual challenges in earlier chapters, and in considering their general drivers below, two factors play a surprisingly minor role. The first is ideology and factions. The conflicts are much more over clashing ambitions and electoral prospects than over conflicting policy prescriptions. Very occasionally, a policy difference has been central, such as the environmental issues in the Tasmanian ALP in the early 1980s and attitudes to climate change in the fall of Malcolm Turnbull in 2009. However, Turnbull had already alienated many with his arrogance, his poor judgment in supporting Godwin Grech's false accusations, and his low poll numbers.

Factional battles and affiliations animate and dominate much party activity. When Malcolm Turnbull told a NSW Liberal conference, after his re-election as leader, that their party was not run by factions, delegates laughed at him.[1] Indeed, in a pattern that has been bemoaned by elder statesmen in both parties, factions are central in preselections and candidate recruitment. After his prime ministership, John Howard carried out an internal review for the Liberals and concluded:

> Some Liberal Party factions are nothing more than pre-selection cooperatives. As a result, far too many MPs, especially at a state level, have had no working-life experience outside a political or union office. It is becoming increasingly difficult for the talented outsider to win party favour.[2]

Howard was echoing a view that John Button had put on the Labor side when he deplored the 'new class of labour movement professionals who rely on factions and unions affiliated to the party for their career advancement ... Collectively they are destroying the diversity and appeal of the ALP.' He contrasted the mix of backgrounds and outside achievements in Gough Whitlam's ministry with contemporary recruitment: 'The trend points to the absence of a truly competitive selection process.' He felt that 'community stature and talent' are now less important.[3]

Factions have sometimes been pertinent in leadership challenges, although less so than their importance elsewhere might suggest. Button observed that 'after the 2001 election the leadership positions were decided by a straight Left/Right factional deal to install Simon Crean and Jenny Macklin, without any vote of the parliamentary party. This is unprecedented in the recent history of the ALP.'[4] But when Crean failed to cut through electorally, the deal quickly came unstuck. Kevin Rudd blamed his 2010 fall on the factions but the mood for change in his government crossed factional lines. Several leadership struggles have involved contenders from within the same faction. So while faction is not irrelevant, in most cases it is the combination of dynamics in the party room and electoral prospects that are most pertinent.

If faction is less relevant in leadership struggles than might be expected, a second absence is even more marked: the lack of relationship to the wider parties. Leadership instability is occurring in the context of a crisis in democratic participation. Party membership has declined radically over a long period. One estimate thought the Labor Party's membership in the 1930s of 370,000 had now fallen to 44,000.[5] The long-term decline seems to be accelerating. Rodney Cavalier has noted that in the life of the NSW Labor Government (1995–2011), 'some 130 ALP branches folded. Most of the rest are phantoms.'[6] Similar trends are at work in the Liberal Party.

The hollowing out of political parties signifies a crisis of identity: their mass membership gave them a base in civil society, and their responsiveness to their grass roots gave them democratic legitimacy and a sense of a shared larger purpose.[7] Debates about party reform – almost invariably conducted by the parties when in opposition – very often focus on how to increase membership and give members a more meaningful role. For Button, 'local branch members are the foot soldiers of the ALP, but … they are starved of weapons, imaginative leadership and good communications'.[8]

The lip service given to the members is in conflict with some contemporary realities. In practice, some leaders view the membership as an obstacle as much as a benefit. Blair, in his memoirs, referred with disdain to his party branches and rejoiced that he was able to 'construct an alliance between myself and the public' in order 'to circumvent' his party.[9] On the other side, in May 2013 David Cameron described Conservative Party activists as 'mad, swivel-eyed loons'.[10]

It is not necessary to have such a jaundiced view of party members to think that increased participation is not a cure-all. Greater say for the membership could well mean a sharpening of internal conflicts. Barry O'Farrell, referring to the factional conflicts besetting the NSW Liberals, described the situation as being like a 'writhing snake pit'.[11] Similarly, the weight of opinion inside the party membership would take the party further from the middle ground than electoral strategists would wish. After the Napthine Liberal Government lost in Victoria, one prominent member, John Roskam, said the party needed to become more conservative to differentiate itself from Labor. Robert Doyle, a former leader, and current Melbourne Lord Mayor, responded that lurching to the right would be a disaster: 'Some of those loonies on the right of the party have brought us into terrible disrepute.'[12] The parallel of Doyle's lament has often been heard also on the Labor side. The conservative element in both the NSW and SA Liberals has at times destabilised moderate leaders to the detriment of the party's electoral prospects.

The larger issue, however, is that election campaigning has moved from being labour-intensive to capital-intensive, and from mobilising the efforts of amateurs to adopting the strategies of professionals. Full-time party officials – the Liberals may have about 100[13] – and parliamentarians' staffs now provide a lot of the campaigning grunt. It is among these people, far more than among the wider membership, that leaderships are made and unmade.

Leader-centred electioneering

'I won three general elections,' declared former British Prime Minister Tony Blair, without a hint of false modesty. He thought that 'political analysts and practising politicians love to speculate on this or that voting trend ... but there is always a tendency to underplay the importance of the leader'.[14] British political scientists Ivor Crewe and John Bartle found the opposite: 'We have experienced at first hand the stunned disbelief, bordering on hostility, of a non-academic audience on being told that the impact of Blair's and Major's personalities on the 1997 election was negligible.'[15] Crewe and Bartle thought the electorate, faced with a government beset by scandal and division, after 18 years of Tory rule, was ripe to change to a Labour government.

How central is leadership in winning elections? While the media often present elections as a personal duel between leaders, much broader forces are also at work. There have been several cases of the less popular leader's party winning the election. At the least, then, the relevance of the leaders will vary between elections.

However, election outcomes are the most decisive determinant of whether or not a leader survives. In these electorally ruthless parties, leadership is seen as a key – by some as *the* key – to success, and changing the leader as the solution when a party is struggling. Moreover, as polling expert Ian McAllister has argued, the 'large group of undecided voters has fundamentally altered party campaign strategies and placed the leader at centre stage ... Leaders are a more important resource in elections than ever before.'[16] This is compounded by the increasing personalisation of politics, itself part of the battery of political changes wrought by the centrality of the media.

In the overwhelming majority of the 73 coups discussed in this book, the party's performance in the polls was an important factor. It was not always the critical factor, and the specifics of polls and subsequent leadership upheaval would not show a strong correlation. It should be added that only in a minority of cases did the change dramatically improve a party's electoral prospects, and in at least as many it made them worse.

Leader-centred news

For television and radio in particular, the leader is much more than the first among equals.[17] Much political news is conveyed to the audience by party leaders, and so they loom larger in the public imagination. Beyond personalisation, the impact of the media on politics is profound and many-sided. Thomas Meyer has even made the somewhat melodramatic claim that the media have 'colonised' politics.[18] Certainly, the presence of the media has accelerated the pace of political developments and complicated and changed many political relationships.

The news media's apparent preoccupation with leadership is sometimes criticised as a symptom of its shallowness, or as evidence that it is 'beating up' stories. Often it seems that the media presents politics as a game without substance, focusing on the latest spectacle without any sense of broader context or institutional memory. Moreover, as we have seen, there is often misreporting. To adapt a saying from business forecasters, the media have predicted 20 of the last four coups. On the other hand, the media cannot sustain reporting of a leadership challenge on their own. It is only when there is substance to the stories that there is continuing attention to leadership tensions in the news.

There is some truth in the charge that the news media find it easier to cover personalities and their conflicts than to cover policy. Equally, though, the politicians themselves are more often than not animated by personal ambitions and clashes rather than policy matters. In 1952, John Douglas Pringle, brought from the UK to edit the *Sydney Morning Herald*, met the 90-year-old former Prime Minister Billy Hughes, and found 'the old man … still one of the raciest and wittiest talkers in the world, full of amusing stories about the past. Like most old politicians he has lost all interest in causes and principles but preserved an immense interest in what I might call "the game".'[19] When Robert Menzies was awarded the Order of the Thistle on his retirement, its motto was 'Nemo Me Impune Lacessit' (No one wounds me with impunity).[20] It is a motto that would serve most politicians.

So journalists get at least some of their impetus for delving into personal conflicts from the importance which politicians themselves accord them. Equally, it can be argued that the public too is more interested in personalities than in policies. That sense of newsworthiness goes back a century, to one of the pioneers of tabloid journalism, Lord Northcliffe, who told his journalists, 'Never attack an institution, attack the man at the top.' This is good journalistic advice, but it presents an essentially misleading view of the world. It means there is far more attention to leaders' performances than to institutional functioning. In social science jargon, it means the explanations are all agency and no structure.

The news media are implicated in leadership instability in that they, like the spin doctors and politicians themselves, have an all-consuming focus on the immediate, without much sense of structural or historical context. It is a simple diagnosis and prescription to argue that the problem is the leader and the solution a change of leader.

Leader-centric parties and governments

It might seem to follow from the fact of 73 leadership coups that the key problem is that leaders are too vulnerable. Rudd thought so: when he returned to the leadership after defeating Gillard, he insisted that from then on a leadership spill would need a 60 per cent vote in the party room to succeed. (The change was purely symbolic, as any leader suffering even a 50 per cent vote against them would immediately become an easy target for attacks from all sides.)

However, in a perverse way, the opposite is also true. The problem is not that leaders have too little power; it is that they have too much. Over recent decades several trends have given leaders more power in relation to their parties, but that weakening of checks and balances has meant that often the only means of changing a leader's behaviour is to change the leader. When reform is impossible, regime change becomes more likely.

The leader's internal power has been buttressed by several trends. As noted, the media, especially television, made leaders much more visible to the public and greatly expanded their public persona relative to other Ministers and MPs. Similarly, with increased electoral volatility and the fraying of partisan loyalties, there is a strong belief among political professionals that leaders are the key to winning elections. This gives all MPs an interest in enhancing the leader's image. An ethic of 'follow the leader' that emphasises unity as a prerequisite for success is a force for conformity and affords the leader greater latitude in shaping the party's agenda and public stances.

Such recipes for electoral success, as well as the intensity of demands from the media, lead to politicians' preoccupations with influencing news coverage, and hence the growth of spin doctors. These staff often owe their primary loyalty to the leader rather than the party. At the least, spin doctors equate favourable coverage of the leader with good publicity for the party.

All these factors apply equally to both government and opposition. Indeed the Opposition Leader more often personifies the party to the public than the government leader does. In most states, perhaps a majority of the public could name the Opposition Leader, but far fewer could name any other opposition frontbencher. For many, the opposition is its leader. When the opposition is failing – and there are few sure markers of success in opposition, as morale rises and falls with the vagaries of opinion polls and parliamentary skirmishes – the leader is more vulnerable.

In government, three additional factors have furthered leaders' power in relation to that of their colleagues:
- within the public service, line departments have lost power to central agencies;
- senior public servants have lost power to political advisers; and
- increases in political resources have gone disproportionately to leaders.

Public stereotypes about the public service have lagged behind the rapidly changing reality. While public service heads used to be permanent, now the senior echelons are under contract, serving at the government's pleasure. Moreover, both the Howard and Abbott governments axed several serving heads on coming to office, an early, emphatic demonstration of where power lay. Sir Humphrey Appleby has been replaced by 'can-do' heads keen to please their Ministers. The result, according to leading journalist Laura Tingle, is that 'the bureaucracy has been cowed both by the prospect of being sacked and by a reward system which punishes risk taking'.[21]

A couple of generations ago, the public service often had close to a monopoly of expertise in many policy areas. Now, internal weakening and the strengthening of external resources mean this is far from true. In the departments that deliver services and regulate areas of policy, there has been a much higher turnover of staff, and some areas have been outsourced to private contractors, resulting in reduced institutional memory. As these line departments have been to some extent hollowed out, the central agencies, especially Prime Ministers' and Premiers' departments, have tended to grow in resources and role. As James Walter and Paul Strangio argue, 'policy coordination became policy control and PMC (Prime Minister and Cabinet) an instrument of the Prime Minister's power over other ministers'.[22]

The other major trend has been the growth of political advisers. They began increasing in numbers under Gough Whitlam and Malcolm Fraser. The aim was to provide perspectives other than those being provided by the public service, to ensure that the process of policy-making was responsive to the government's priorities and aims. Over time, advisers with policy expertise have been replaced by party activists 'with clear political ambitions, recruited from party or electorate office backgrounds'.[23]

All these factors have made the functioning of governments much more leader-centric than in the past. Both Walter and Strangio, who describe decisions as being characterised by 'oversimplification, isolationism and haste'[24] and Tingle, who uses the term 'political amnesia',[25] are concerned by the implications of this trend for the quality of policy-making. It also increases leader instability, as one of the recurring themes among MPs who support challenges is their sense of exclusion, their sense that they have been frozen out.[26] One way this expresses itself is frustration at the logjam in the leader's office, and a belief that central control results in decisions just not being made. The other is that they feel they are expected to support the leader's policies and stances despite the fact that they have had no input into them. They are thus hostages to the leader's judgment, and if that trust snaps, the relationship becomes much more brittle.

Another possible long-term effect of these short-term added advantages in immediate control and cohesion is that perhaps they make leaders more inclined to believe in their own indispensability. Former UK Minister David Owen called it the 'hubris syndrome' – long-term leaders become more high-handed and confident in their own judgment. Political leaders have rarely been good at realising the best moment to retire, and with colleagues becoming less tolerant of the possibility of failure, they are more likely to have the decision taken out of their hands.

Moreover, it seems that when a challenge starts to develop, it has become more difficult to reverse its momentum. Bynander and 't Hart found 'once the cat of speculation was out of the bag, leadership consolidation proved to be elusive'.[27] It was easy for a 'downward spiral' to develop, with recriminations and disunity, sliding polls and bad publicity, and so more speculation. Perhaps because challengers have become more skilful and numerate, once challenges become public, they more often than not seem to succeed. Change can occur almost immediately, or – and this can be one of the most interesting but politically disabling periods – the leader can be under prolonged attack from the other party and internally.

In sum, the underside of the aura of the indispensable leader has been the doctrine of the disposable leader. Several political forces have simultaneously given leaders an undesirable degree of power and a greater vulnerability. On top of that there is another driving force for instability: unrealistic expectations about what a change of leader can achieve.

Changing leader as a cure-all

The cry for new leadership is often an intellectual abdication. The analysis of deeper or more challenging problems is abandoned by putting all the blame for current problems on the leader, and seeing a new leader as the 'solution'. Sometimes this masks a somewhat authoritarian yearning for certainty and order, reflecting the old saying that what this country needs is a benevolent dictator. South America has a long tradition of yearning for the man on the white horse, the dictator who will sweep away the corruption, chaos and inefficiency of democracy. Of course in a strong, stable democracy such as Australia this is not a risk, but too often the concentration on leadership distracts from analysing difficult issues.

This analytical laziness is compounded by confused views of what 'strong' leadership is. Archie Brown begins his book *Strong Leaders* by criticising the misconception that strong leaders are ones 'who get their way, dominate their colleagues, and concentrate decision-making in their hands'. Rather, 'huge power amassed by an individual leader paves the way for important errors at best and disaster and massive bloodshed at worst'. It is a dangerous illusion that:

> the more a leader dominates his or her political party and Cabinet, the greater the leader. A more collegial style of leadership is too often characterised as a weakness, the advantages of a more collective political leadership too commonly overlooked.[28]

The media are often quick to applaud examples of 'strong' leadership. When Rudd declared, in the lead-up to the 2007 election, that he would appoint the ministry, rather than let Caucus elect it, it was seen as a sign of strength. No Labor member wanted to endanger the party's electoral prospects by being seen as undermining the leader's authority. Rudd's justification was that the current system gave too much power to the factions. This is a little like King John saying the Magna Carta gave too much power to the barons, and to stop the abuse of baronial power he was again claiming absolute power for the monarch.

Similarly, the media's demand for instant answers and the gladiatorial tenor of party politics means it is impossible for any leader to admit that he or she is uncertain. To consult is not seen as strong. Nor is postponing a decision while gathering more information or exploring more options.

By camouflaging the need for more honest discussions of strengths and weaknesses, the push for leadership change can often lead to inflated expectations – which are always likely to be followed by disappointments. Business analysts Mariano Heyden and

Dimitrios Georgakakis have traced a similar dynamic in business, where a struggling company appoints an outsider CEO rather than fully analysing its problems. The new appointee feels pressure to effect a quick turnaround and so makes a grandiose move, which sometimes makes the situation worse.[29]

The turnover of party leaders in Australia has been remarkable. Its primary driver has been a ruthless electoral pragmatism, even though overthrowing the leader only rarely leads to electoral success. Media preoccupations and practices have accentuated the power of leaders and the pressures on them, and often play a pivotal role as leadership tensions develop. Moreover, no matter how frequent they become, leadership coups are almost always disruptive, and often lead to lasting enmities. In any particular case the forcible leadership change might be justified and necessary, but the overall pattern suggests a pathology that is not contributing to better democratic government.

APPENDIX A

73 Leadership Coups

Appendix B Table 1 lists the 73 successful leadership challenges since 1970. This Appendix describes rules for determining whether or not a particular episode is a coup, and situations where a simple binary description does not capture the complexities of what occurred between the incumbent, the successor and their colleagues.

Did he jump or was he pushed?

The most common image of a leadership coup is of a determined challenger stalking and ultimately displacing an incumbent after a party room showdown. That is quite frequently how it occurs, but there are many variants. Often the incumbent bows to the inevitable and resigns before a party room vote, but the resignation occurred under duress. In our counting, wherever a resignation follows the announcement of a challenge, it is defined as a coup. However, there are grey areas, and sometimes there is limited access to key interactions and motives.

There were just two occasions when a successful challenge was launched in the immediate post-election period, when party leadership positions are normally up for re-election. Neville Wran displaced Pat Hills as NSW Labor leader after the 1973 election, and Barry O'Farrell replaced Peter Debnam as leader of the NSW Liberals after their 2007 election loss. Immediately after O'Farrell announced his candidacy, Debnam resigned. (This is perhaps the most borderline case included in the 73.) Hills and Wran had a closely fought contest, with Wran winning by a single vote. These are both included as successful leadership challenges, but given that they occurred at the institutionally designated moment, it is in some ways a stretch to call them 'coups'. The other 71 successful challenges occurred during the parliamentary term, which is one reason for their often being so disruptive.

So the first question is whether a particular leadership change should be included as a coup. Six cases illustrate the difficulty of drawing boundaries.

Frank Walsh. In 1965, when Walsh became South Australia's first Labor Premier in more than a generation, he was already aged 67. According to Labor Party rules at the time, that meant he had to retire at the next election. However, he was enjoying being Premier, and sought to have an exception made for himself. His colleagues resisted. In a neat manoeuvre at the state conference, a motion proclaiming his three great achievements – leading Labor back into government, bringing natural gas to Adelaide, and 'selflessly stepping down so that a new leader could establish himself before the next election' – was moved.[1] After a rousing acclamation, Walsh had little choice but to bow gracefully to the inevitable.

Verdict: Not a coup. It involved following party rules at the time, even though the leader wanted the rules changed. (There was a somewhat similar case, also judged not to be a coup, when Tasmanian Labor Premier Eric Reece was forced to retire by the party introducing an age restriction. The debate made no explicit reference to Reece, who had been leader for over 16 years.)[2]

Dale Baker. In the wake of Labor's Bank of South Australia scandal, the Liberals' prospects looked bright. According to his press secretary, Liberal leader Baker had offered a penetrating dissection of the disaster, but his political 'lean to the right' meant he was 'at odds with a handful of Liberals'.[3] Others, wrote political scientist Andrew Parkin, thought that the 'Liberals appeared to be reaping less of an advantage in terms of popular support than might have been anticipated, a situation widely attributed to Mr Baker's somewhat blunt and unsophisticated media image'.[4] Baker announced that he would stand down, and that former leader, John Olsen, then a Senator, would contest a by-election for a vacancy left by the deputy Roger Goldsworthy. But another veteran, Ted Chapman, father of future deputy leader Vickie Chapman, stood down to make way for Dean Brown. Olsen and Brown won their respective by-elections, held on the same day, and then contested the leadership. Olsen had defeated Brown for the leadership in 1982, but this time Brown defeated Olsen, 'to widespread astonishment – not least of Mr Olsen, who had sacrificed a Senate career to return to the State Parliament'. Brown easily won the 1993 election.

Verdict: Coup. Amid mounting dissatisfaction, Baker was persuaded to stand down, but he and his allies lost control of events, and the succession went to their factional opponents.

Nick Greiner. Greiner won government for the NSW Liberals in 1988, and just survived with a hung parliament in 1991. He resigned as Premier in 1992, following a ruling by the Independent Commission Against Corruption (ICAC) that within the meaning of the Act he had acted corruptly in the way that Terry Metherell had been appointed to a senior position in the Department of Environment. The case is full of ironies. Greiner was found guilty by an agency that his government had set up for breaking regulations he had instituted, all for a politician, Metherell, who had caused him more grief than any other. A controversial Education Minister, Metherell had had to resign from the ministry over a tax breach. After the 1991 election, he quit the Liberal Party to become an independent, and eight months later was appointed to a senior public service position with Greiner's blessing.[5]

After the ICAC finding, Greiner wanted to stay on pending an appeal (which eventually he won). The National Party solidly supported him, but there was some disquiet among the Liberals. Labor and the independents, however, who together formed a majority, made it clear that he had to resign. Greiner endorsed John Fahey as his successor, privately accusing the other leading contenders, Peter Collins and Bruce Baird, of disloyalty.[6]

Verdict: Not a coup. Greiner was angry with what he saw as a lack of support from some of his colleagues, but it was the combination of ICAC and Parliament that sealed his fate.

Richard Court. Court decisively lost the 2001 WA election to Geoff Gallop's Labor, with a swing of around 7 per cent. Having completed two terms as Premier, Court was expected to stand down, but he defied predictions of his imminent resignation by saying he would stay on for another eight years, and refused to endorse Colin Barnett as his successor. Some commentary thought Court's main reason was to thwart Barnett, his 'barely tolerated deputy'. On the morning of the leadership ballot, *The Australian* published a front-page story claiming that Court had secretly offered the leadership to federal MP Julie Bishop, and that the two of them would swap seats. Barnett said he choked on his Weet-bix as he read the details of the plan, and described it as an act of treachery. Nevertheless Court won the vote that day and retained the leadership. The offer to Bishop attracted considerable criticism. Former powerbroker Noel Crichton-Browne said WA Liberal voters 'must be wondering why it is the Liberal Party has to bring somebody back from Canberra … to find someone half respectable to run what's left of the opposition',[7] while a Barnett supporter called Bishop the wicked witch of the west.[8]

After Bishop rejected the offer, Court was in an untenable position. He resigned, and Barnett was elected. Barnett told Peter

Kennedy that he felt bitter about the events of 2001, and that since then he had had no relationship with Richard Court. He said that there was 'a lot of deceit, and untruths told'. 'It left me with a hopelessly divided Liberal Party. People had lied to each other. They were my hardest years in politics, leading a divided opposition.'[9]

Verdict: Coup. Developments did not follow Court's plan, and in the end he had no choice but to leave and have Barnett succeed him.

Mark Latham. According to Latham, he had defeated Kim Beazley for the leadership in December 2003 despite being 'opposed by almost every union and factional powerbroker in the Party'. However, once he lost the 2004 federal election to Howard, 'the powerbrokers quickly settled the score and marked me for the political scrapheap'.[10] He was re-elected leader, but there was some tension and manoeuvring in the months following the October 2004 loss. From Christmas, Latham went on holiday, but a few days later, he had a severe attack of pancreatitis – not his first. On New Year's Day he recorded in his diary 'the good news' that he could 'retire from Labor politics'. He kept this largely secret for a couple of weeks, maintaining a determined silence, even refusing to make any public comment on the devastation caused by the Asian tsunami. On Tuesday 18 January, he publicly resigned, citing his health, his family and media intrusion as his three reasons, but not mentioning his fourth, 'disillusionment with the ALP'.[11]

Beazley was elected unopposed, in a process that concealed the strong conflicts swirling around the leadership. ALP national secretary Tim Gartrell told Paul Kelly that 'from 2002, a number of senior organisational figures were alarmed about the growth of personal hatreds in the caucus. Our fear was that caucus animosities might reach beyond the point of no return.'[12] The way the factions manoeuvred to ensure that Beazley would succeed Latham incensed Kevin Rudd and Julia Gillard, and laid the foundation for their later alliance in challenging Beazley.

Verdict: Coup. Because of his severe health problems, and his feelings of personal dissatisfaction, Latham was ready to leave. But he no longer had the option to stay. Before his decision became public, active efforts to unseat him in favour of Beazley were underway. By the end, the plotters may have been pushing at an open door, but they were certainly pushing.

Paul Lennon. In 2004, Jim Bacon had to retire as Labor Premier of Tasmania because of cancer – it killed him some months later. His successor was his deputy and close friend Paul Lennon. However, Lennon's role in the government had been much more as the head-kicker, and almost from the moment he took over political conflicts intensified. Under both Bacon and Lennon, the Labor Government's style was described as 'brokerist', intent on deal-making to further developments it favoured, but criticism of this style increased, to the extent of charges of corruption.[13] Lennon was a very strong supporter of the plan by Gunns to build a pulp mill in northern Tasmania, a plan equally strongly opposed by environmentalists. In 2006, allegations of corruption against Lennon and criticisms of his closeness to Gunns reached fever pitch: 'Disquiet with the Premier's approach to politics lay at the heart of all these developments and fuelled conspiracy theories, which, in turn, contributed strongly to his eventual withdrawal from politics.'[14]

To the surprise of some, Labor won the 2006 election. But disapproval of the Premier continued to increase. In early 2008 he recorded his lowest approval rating, 30 per cent, and in May 2008 an even worse poll showed only 17 per cent approval. On 26 May Lennon confirmed that he was stepping down and quitting politics. Lennon said he expected the newly elected deputy leader, David Bartlett, to take over, and had full confidence in him. Two years later, after a close election, Bartlett survived by forming a coalition with the Greens.

Verdict. Not a coup. It is likely that by this time a majority of his colleagues wanted Lennon gone and thought they could not win another election with him as leader. It is also likely, however, that in any direct party room confrontation he would have survived. Lennon was the author of his own departure, including its timing and his succession.

Misleading binaries

Appendix B Table 1's list of incumbents and successors can be misleading where the successor was not the initiator or even supporter of the coup, but succeeded as one of the incumbent's allies, where the rebels had enough power to dispose of the old, but not to themselves win the succession. In 1978, the younger WA Labor MPs were pushing for a more energetic and effective opposition, discontented with the way Colin Jamieson was behaving. Their discontent was sufficient to dispose of Jamieson, but the successor was his ally and age-mate Ron Davies, who had been best man at Jamieson's wedding in 1960. In another example, the younger members of the Hamer Victorian Liberal Government in 1981 managed to destabilise the Premier, but his successor was his loyal deputy, Lindsay Thompson. A third case occurred as the Beazley forces gathered to take over from Simon Crean. Crean grasped that his own leadership was doomed, and instead threw his weight behind his ally, Latham, who went on to win a narrow victory.

Another scenario where a binary presentation is incomplete is where there is widespread discontent with the incumbent, but no consensus on who the replacement should be. Multiple contenders are jostling for pre-eminence before any move is made against the existing leader. Occasionally, the picture is more complex still. As noted in Chapter 3, the politics of the opposition's leadership after the 2007 federal election was complicated by the presence of Peter Costello, who had publicly renounced leadership ambitions.

Costello's presence on the backbench complicated first Malcolm Turnbull's stalking of Brendan Nelson, and then the set of conflicts which eventually resulted in Tony Abbott replacing Turnbull.

One of the longest-running leadership rivalries was between John Howard and Andrew Peacock, and it ran from 1983 until the early 1990s. In 1987, it was complicated by two further leadership pretenders. First came the Canberra crusade of Queensland Premier Joh Bjelke-Petersen. Bjelke-Petersen achieved his political zenith with the 1986 National Party state election victory. His victory speech proclaimed, 'our assault on Canberra begins right now'.[15] In Paul Kelly's words, 'Watching Joh on television, John Howard said to [his wife] Janette: "We'll have trouble with this lunatic now."' In February 1987, Joh declared 'I am determined to turn politics upside down in Australia.'[16]

Joh was promised financial support by what was dubbed the 'white shoe brigade', developers who had had friendly dealings with his Queensland government. He was supported by the muscle of the Queensland National Party, which forced its state and federal MPs to support him, and by the enthusiastic support of *The Australian* newspaper and some of its columnists.[17] Howard later wrote that '*The Australian* newspaper became a prominent vehicle for the propagation of the Joh cause … [It] gave huge coverage to anything that Bjelke-Petersen said or did.'[18]

No doubt motivated by personal ambition, Peacock flirted with the insanity: 'Sir Joh is a great Australian, a great patriot who always … puts his country first,' he proclaimed, much to Howard's displeasure.[19] Faced with the coming of the federal election in July, the Joh phenomenon collapsed in ignominy, but not before it had put Howard's leadership under further strain.

After Howard's loss in that election, Melbourne businessman John Elliott became Liberal Party President. Elliott's reputation as a businessman was then at its peak. Before the election, he had tried to enter Parliament by persuading the member for Higgins, Roger Shipton, to step aside, but Shipton refused. Elliott's commentary on the political scene was always newsworthy, and often created problems for Howard, such as when Elliott proclaimed that Australia needed a leader like Margaret Thatcher, as well as more vision and an indirect tax. Kelly judged: 'The Liberals were faced with the worst clash between a federal leader and federal president in the party's history.' Indeed 'Howard identified Elliott as the real threat to his position, both as a potential challenger and an agent for destabilisation.'[20]

The Elliott phenomenon came and went, but it was further evidence that many Liberals longed for a more dynamic leader than Howard. The 1989 coup is tabulated as Peacock supplanting Howard, but the Bjelke-Petersen and Elliott precursors had greatly weakened Howard's standing.

APPENDIX B

Tables

Table 1 Successful Leadership Challenges

Year	No	Incumbent	Successor	Party	Govt?	Sphere
1971	1	Gorton	McMahon	Lib	Govt	Fed
1972	2	Hall	Eastick	Lib	Oppn	SA
1973	3	Hills	Wran	ALP	Oppn	NSW
1974	4	Houston	Tucker	ALP	Oppn	Qld
1975	5	Snedden	Fraser	Lib	Oppn	Fed
1975	6	Eastick	Tonkin	Lib	Oppn	SA
1976	7	Lewis	Willis	Lib	Govt	NSW
1977	8	Willis	Coleman	Lib	Oppn	NSW
1978	9	Knox	Edwards	Lib	Govt★	Qld
1978	10	Jamieson	Davies	ALP	Oppn	WA
1981	11	Mason	McDonald	Lib	Oppn	NSW
1981	12	Lowe	Holgate	ALP	Govt	Tas
1981	13	Wilkes	Cain	ALP	Oppn	Vic
1981	14	Hamer	Thompson	Lib	Govt	Vic
1981	15	Davies	Burke	ALP	Oppn	WA
1982	16	Casey	Wright	ALP	Oppn	Qld
1983	17	Hayden	Hawke	ALP	Oppn	Fed
1983	18	Dowd	Greiner	Lib	Oppn	NSW
1983	19	Edwards	White	Lib	Govt★	Qld
1984	20	O'Connor	Hassell	Lib	Oppn	WA
1985	21	Peacock	Howard	Lib	Oppn	Fed

★ Junior Party in Coalition Government

Tables

Year	No	Incumbent	Successor	Party	Govt?	Sphere
1986	22	Hassell	MacKinnon	Lib	Oppn	WA
1987	23	Bjelke-Petersen	Ahern	Nat	Govt	Qld
1988	24	Warburton	Goss	ALP	Oppn	Qld
1988	25	Batt	Field	ALP	Oppn	Tas
1989	26	Howard	Peacock	Lib	Oppn	Fed
1989	27	Ahern	Cooper	Nat	Govt	Qld
1989	28	Kennett	Brown	Lib	Oppn	Vic
1990	29	Cain	Kirner	ALP	Govt	Vic
1990	30	Dowding	Lawrence	ALP	Govt	WA
1991	31	Hawke	Keating	ALP	Govt	Fed
1991	32	Beanland	Sheldon	Lib	Oppn	Qld
1991	33	Gray	Groom	Lib	Oppn	Tas
1991	34	Brown	Kennett	Lib	Oppn	Vic
1992	35	Baker	Brown	Lib	Oppn	SA
1992	36	MacKinnon	Court	Lib	Oppn	WA
1994	37	Hewson	Downer	Lib	Oppn	Fed
1995	38	Downer	Howard	Lib	Oppn	Fed
1996	39	Brown	Olsen	Lib	Govt	SA
1998	40	Collins	Chikarovski	Lib	Oppn	NSW
1999	41	Brumby	Bracks	ALP	Oppn	Vic
2001	42	Napier	Cheek	Lib	Oppn	Tas
2001	43	Court	Barnett	Lib	Oppn	WA
2002	44	Chikarovski	Brogden	Lib	Oppn	NSW
2002	45	Napthine	Doyle	Lib	Oppn	Vic
2003	46	Crean	Latham	ALP	Oppn	Fed
2003	47	Horan	Springborg	Nat	Oppn	Qld
2005	48	Latham	Beazley	ALP	Oppn	Fed
2005	49	Brogden	Debnam	Lib	Oppn	NSW
2006	50	Beazley	Rudd	ALP	Oppn	Fed
2006	51	Quinn	Flegg	Lib	Oppn	Qld
2006	52	Doyle	Baillieu	Lib	Oppn	Vic

Year	No	Incumbent	Successor	Party	Govt?	Sphere
2006	53	Birney	Omodei	Lib	Oppn	WA
2007	54	Debnam	O'Farrell	Lib	Oppn	NSW
2007	55	Flegg	McCardle	Lib	Oppn	Qld
2007	56	Evans	Hamilton-Smith	Lib	Oppn	SA
2008	57	Nelson	Turnbull	Lib	Oppn	Fed
2008	58	Iemma	Rees	ALP	Govt	NSW
2008	59	Seeney	Springborg	Nat	Oppn	Qld
2008	60	Omodei	Buswell	Lib	Oppn	WA
2008	61	Buswell	Barnett	Lib	Oppn	WA
2009	62	Turnbull	Abbott	Lib	Oppn	Fed
2009	63	Hamilton-Smith	Redmond	Lib	Oppn	SA
2009	64	Rees	Kenneally	ALP	Govt	NSW
2010	65	Rudd	Gillard	ALP	Govt	Fed
2011	66	Langbroek	Newman	Lib	Oppn	Qld
2011	67	Rann	Weatherill	ALP	Govt	SA
2012	68	Redmond	Marshall	Lib	Oppn	SA
2013	69	Gillard	Rudd	ALP	Govt	Fed
2013	70	Baillieu	Napthine	Lib	Govt	Vic
2014	71	Robertson	Foley	ALP	Oppn	NSW
2015	72	Abbott	Turnbull	Lib	Govt	Fed
2016	73	Springborg	Nicholls	LNP	Oppn	Qld

Table 2 Longest–Serving Party Leaders

Leaders who led their party continuously for 12 or more years
(post World War II)

Name	Year Began	Party	Length of Leadership (Years.Months)
Thomas Playford	1938	SA Lib	27.08
Frank Nicklin	1941	Qld Nat	26.07
Joh Bjelke-Petersen	1968	Qld Nat	21.04
Robert Menzies	1945	Fed Lib	21.00
John Cain Snr	1937	Vic ALP	19.10
Henry Bolte	1953	Vic Lib	19.03
Robert Cosgrove	1939	Tas ALP	18.06
Bob Carr	1988	NSW ALP	17.04
Mike Rann	1994	SA ALP	17.01
Eric Reece	1958	Tas ALP	16.09
Robert Askin	1959	NSW Lib	16.00
Albert Hawke	1951	WA ALP	15.05
David Brand	1957	WA Lib	15.03
John Bannon	1979	SA ALP	13.00
John Howard	1995	Fed Lib	12.09
Neville Wran	1973	NSW ALP	12.07
Angus Bethune	1960	Tas Lib	12.02

There are 17 politicians who since World War II have led their party continuously for 12 or more years. (Robert Cosgrove [Tas ALP] stood down for some months while he was on trial, but resumed after being acquitted.)

Table 3 Leadership Coups and Government Survival

Incumbent	Successor	Year	Sphere	Party	Term of Govt	Party in Govt Since	Next Election
Gorton	McMahon	1971	Fed	Lib	9	1949	Lost govt
Lewis	Willis	1976	NSW	Lib	4	1965	Lost govt
Lowe	Holgate	1981	Tas	ALP	14	1934	Lost govt
Hamer	Thompson	1981	Vic	Lib	9	1955	Lost govt
Bjelke-Petersen	Ahern	1987	Qld	Nat	11	1957	Lost govt
Ahern	Cooper	1989	Qld	Nat	11	1957	Lost govt
Cain	Kirner	1990	Vic	ALP	3	1982	Lost govt
Dowding	Lawrence	1990	WA	ALP	3	1983	Lost govt
Hawke	Keating	1991	Fed	ALP	4	1983	Won
Brown	Olsen	1996	SA	Lib	1	1993	Minority govt
Iemma	Rees	2008	NSW	ALP	4	1995	Lost govt
Rees	Kenneally	2009	NSW	ALP	4	1995	Lost govt
Rudd	Gillard	2010	Fed	ALP	1	2007	Minority govt
Rann	Weatherill	2011	SA	ALP	4	2002	Minority govt
Gillard	Rudd	2013	Fed	ALP	2	2007	Lost govt
Baillieu	Napthine	2013	Vic	Lib	1	2010	Lost govt
Abbott	Turnbull	2015	Fed	Lib	1	2013	Won

Notes

Chapter 1: Leadership Challenges from Menzies to Abbott

1   Martin and Hardy p. 143.
2   Brown, Wallace, 2002 p. 35.
3   Kennedy p. 6.
4   Kennedy p. 53.
5   Kennedy pp. 51–2.
6   Cassidy p. 187.
7   Kelly 1992, p. 399.
8   Mills 1993, pp. 133–4.
9   Costello p. 223.
10   Kelly 1992, p. 629.
11   Mike Steketee 'Now the brawls begin' *SMH* 13 July 1987.
12   Stanyer, p. 73.
13   Hawke p. 553.
14   Errington and van Onselen 2007, p. 101.
15   Latika Bourke 'Liberal leadership spill: emotional Julie bishop says "tears were shed" after Tony Abbott was dumped' *SMH* 15 September 2015.
16   Latika Bourke 'Tony Abbott staffer welcomes new Prime Minister Malcolm Turnbull with a four letter expletive' *Age* 18 September 2015.
17   Edwards 1996, p. 390.
18   *Labor in Power.*
19   Richardson p. 338.
20   Hawke p. 559.
21   Kelly 1992, p. 457.
22   John Lyons 'Great survivor goes down, alone' *SMH* 8 August 1990.
23   Daniel Meers 'How Bishop betrayed her king' *DT* 19 September 2015.
24   Peter Reith 'Liberal leadership: Why Tony Abbott remained under pressure' *SMH* 15 September 2015.
25   Matthew Knott 'Arthur Sinodinos: How John Howard's man helped undo Abbott' *SMH* 16 September 2015.
26   Manning, Paddy, 2015, p. 367; Patrick p. 152.
27   Mark Kenny 'Is Malcolm Turnbull's appearance on *Q&A* an early sign of impatience?' *SMH* 18 February 2015.
28   Kelly 1992, p. 650.
29   Kelly 2014, p. 322.
30   Latika Bourke 'Tony Abbott pleads the Fifth Amendment when asked if he's forgiven Malcolm Turnbull' *SMH* 1 October 2015.
31   Michelle Grattan 'Abbott's post-coup stress on display' *Conv* 29 September 2015.

Chapter 2: Rudd vs Gillard vs Rudd

1   Kelly 2014, p. 133.
2   Weller pp. 253, 256.
3   Stuart 2010, pp. 133–6.
4   Joseph Stiglitz 'Australia, you don't know how good you've got it' *SMH* 2 September 2013.
5   Wayne Swan 'GFC anniversary: political courage as urgent as ever' ABC *The Drum* 9 October 2013.
6   Cassidy pp. 62–3.
7   John Lyons 'Captain Chaos' *Aust* 21 June 2008.
8   Kelly 2014, p. 197.
9   Rodney Tiffen 'You wouldn't read about it: climate scientists right' *SMH* 26 July 2010.
10   Cassidy p. 75.
11   Ferguson pp. 96–7.
12   Kelly 2014, p. 276.
13   Kelly 2014, p. 350.
14   Kelly 2014, p. 257.
15   Kelly 2014, p. 28.
16   Cassidy p. 78.
17   Hawker p. 15.
18   Kelly 2014, p. 279.
19   Kelly 2014, pp. 279–80.
20   Kelly 2014, p. 281.
21   Shaun Carney 'Labor confused itself, and thus confused us' *Age* 22 August 2010.
22   Stuart 2010, pp. 171–2.
23   Cassidy p. 182.
24   Weller pp. 270–4.
25   Swan p. 195.
26   Cassidy p. 70.
27   Weller p. 276.
28   Chubb p. 68.
29   Howard 2010, p. 548.
30   Chubb p. 117.
31   Chubb p. 23.
32   Chubb pp. 77, 50, 26, 56.
33   Chubb p. 84.
34   Chubb pp. 32–3.
35   Lenore Taylor 'How Rudd's ETS was killed from within Labor ranks' *Age* 5 April 2011.
36   Chubb pp. 111, 112.
37   Swan pp. 203ff.
38   Kelly 2014, pp. 298ff.
39   McKnight and Hobbs.
40   Cassidy pp. 55–6.
41   Cassidy p. 94.
42   Swan p. 222.
43   Cassidy p. 53.

Notes

44 Megalogenis p. 29.
45 Swan p. 235.
46 Kelly 2014, p. 3.
47 Swan pp. 230–1.
48 Kelly 2014, p. 139.
49 Stuart 2010, p. viii.
50 Kelly 2014, p. 141.
51 Kelly 2014, p. 146; Swan pp. 230–1.
52 Stuart 2010, p. 70.
53 Kelly 2014, p. 206.
54 Swan p. 225.
55 Cassidy p. 85.
56 Hawker p. 9.
57 Kelly 2014, p. 5.
58 Cassidy p. 121.
59 Swan p. 237.
60 Swan p. 237.
61 Cassidy p. 102.
62 Hawker p. 14.
63 Mungo MacCallum 'Timor solution a stuffed-up version of whatever it takes' *Crikey* 12 July 2010.
64 Cassidy p. 112.
65 Chubb pp. 140–3.
66 Annabel Crabb 'Campaign madness breeds government regrets' ABC *The Drum* 6 May 2014.
67 Kelly 2014, p. 343.
68 Cassidy p. 111.
69 Peter Ker 'Mining tax revenue slumps' *SMH* 14 May 2013.
70 Lindy Edwards 'Strategically, Labor lost sight of simple heart of matter' *Age* 23 August 2010.
71 Megalogenis p. 1.
72 Cassidy p. 143.
73 Megalogenis p. 1.
74 Cassidy pp. 147, 157.
75 Cassidy p. 141.
76 Kelly 2014, p. 353.
77 Cassidy pp. 167, 163.
78 Shaun Carney 'Labor confused itself, and thus confused us' *Age* 22 August 2010.
79 Shaun Carney 'Labor confused itself, and thus confused us' *Age* 22 August 2010.
80 Cassidy p. 168.
81 Kelly 2014, p. 354.
82 Swan p. 253.
83 Kelly 2014, p. 353.
84 Cassidy p. 188.
85 Cassidy p. 195.
86 Rodney Tiffen 'Labor's six (almost) fatal mistakes' *IS* 22 September 2010.
87 Cassidy p. 237.

88 Gordon, Gordon and Grattan 'Many to blame – but only one to protect' *Age* 23 August 2010.
89 Stuart 2010, p. 230.
90 Cassidy p. 247.
91 Margot Saville 'McKew: I don't regret a minute of it' *Crikey* 23 August 2010.
92 Kent p. 353.
93 Swan p. 260.
94 Kent pp. 361–3.
95 Kent p. 364.
96 Kelly 2014, pp. 362–6.
97 Ferguson p. 252.
98 Chubb p. 222.
99 Chubb p. 233.
100 Philip Dorling 'US critical of Rudd's handling of asylum seekers' *SMH* 16 December 2010.
101 Kelly 2014, pp. 387–95.
102 Summers 2013 p. 121.
103 Summers 2013 pp. 124–5.
104 Hawker p. 45.
105 Summers p. 141.
106 Summers p. 141.
107 Summers pp. 141ff.
108 Ferguson p. 277.
109 Swan p. 287.
110 Kelly 2014, p. 470.
111 Kent, p. 401.
112 Weller p. 343.
113 Walsh pp. 297ff.
114 Weller p. 345.
115 Ferguson p. 268.
116 Weller pp. 345–6.
117 Swan p. 281.
118 Ferguson p. 280.
119 Weller p. 347.
120 Kelly 2014, p. 380.
121 Weller pp. 348–9.
122 Kelly 2014, p. 375.
123 Kelly 2014, p. 456.
124 Ferguson p. 284.
125 Kelly 2014, p. 460.
126 Swan pp. 290–3.
127 Kent p. 414.
128 Hawker p. 25.
129 Hawker p. 28.
130 Swan p. 300.
131 Kelly 2014, p. 470.
132 Kelly 2014, p. 455.
133 Weller p. 356.

134 Hawker p. 112.
135 Hawker p. 69.
136 Weller p. 359.
137 Weller pp. 360–3.
138 Kelly 2014, p. 490.
139 Hawker p. 176.
140 Kelly 2014, p. 493.
141 Weller p. 370.
142 Kelly 2014, p. 484.
143 Weller p. 365; Hawker pp. 135, 170; McKnight and Hobbs.
144 Kelly 2014, p. 138.

Chapter 3: Turnbull vs Abbott vs Turnbull

1   Kelly 2014, p. 239.
2   Marr, p. 74.
3   Marr, p. 67.
4   Manning, Paddy, 2015, p. 281.
5   Abbott pp. 157–9.
6   Crabb 2009, p. 75.
7   Manning, Paddy, 2015, p. 310.
8   Crabb 2009, p. 76.
9   Crabb 2009, p. 76.
10   Manning, Paddy, 2015, p. 310.
11   Stuart 2007, p. 52.
12   Crabb 2009, p. 76.
13   Manning, Paddy, 2015, p. 311.
14   Tony Wright 'How bombshell blew up in Nelson's face' Age 17 September 2008.
15   Manning, Paddy, 2015, p. 314.
16   Crabb 2009, p. 51.
17   Crabb 2009, p. 93.
18   Crabb 2009, p. 63.
19   Swan p. 86.
20   Swan p. 90.
21   Manning, Paddy, 2015, p. 321.
22   Cassidy p. 11.
23   Swan pp. 146, 152.
24   Cassidy p. 17.
25   Manning, Paddy, 2015, p. 326.
26   Kelly 2014, p. 243.
27   Cassidy p. 19.
28   Ferguson 2016, p. 67.
29   Michelle Grattan 'Georgiou attacks Liberal infighting' SMH 25 February 2009.
30   Manning, Paddy, 2015, p. 75.
31   Crabb 2009, p. 41.
32   Michelle Grattan 'Libs' IR stance in rivalry's shadow' Age 12 March 2009.
33   Savva 2010, pp. 278–9.
34   Kelly 2014, p. 248.
35   Cassidy p. 22.

36 Marr p. 73.
37 Marr p. 74.
38 'Malcolm and the Malcontents' ABC TV *Four Corners* 9 November 2009 (Sarah Ferguson).
39 Cassidy p. 25.
40 Manning, Paddy, 2015, p. 340.
41 Kelly 2014, p. 243.
42 Kelly 2014, pp. 26–7.
43 Kelly 2014, p. 27.
44 Marr p. 2.
45 Manning, Paddy, 2015, p. 338.
46 Kelly 2014, p. 29.
47 Kelly 2014, pp. 28–9.
48 Marr pp. 81, 80.
49 Kelly 2014, pp. 19, 22.
50 Stuart 2010, p. 203.
51 Savva 2016, p. 14.
52 Marr p. 42.
53 Savva 2016, p. 5.
54 Errington and van Onselen 2015, p. 175.
55 Marr pp. 16–17.
56 Manning, Paddy, 2015, p. 239.
57 Manning, Paddy, 2015, p. 239.
58 Marr p. 54.
59 Phillip Coorey and Tom Arup 'Garrett accused of industrial manslaughter by Abbott' *SMH* 12 February 2010.
60 Marr pp. 86, 47.
61 Michelle Grattan 'Woe betide those who fail the Abbott government's tribal test' *Conv* 14 March 2014.
62 Patrick pp. 95ff.
63 Errington and van Onselen 2015, p. 144.
64 Errington and van Onselen 2015, pp. 172–3.
65 Patrick p. 229.
66 Errington and van Onselen 2015, p. 176.
67 Michelle Grattan 'Abbott deploys 600 Australians to Middle East' *Conv* 14 September 2014.
68 Matthew Doran 'Islamic State: Australia declines United States request to increase military commitment in Middle East' *ABC News* 13 January 2016.
69 Peter Terlato 'Here's Tony Abbott's full statement' *Business Insider* 3 March 2015.
70 Savva 2016, p. 176.
71 Savva 2016, p. 97.
72 Patrick pp. 171–2.
73 Errington and van Onselen 2015, p. 173.
74 Laura Tingle 'Tony Abbott: determined to lead the Whitlam government of our time?' *AFR* 13 August 2015.
75 Lenore Taylor 'Tony Abbott: Labor wants to "roll out the red carpet" for terrorists' *G* 18 June 2015.
76 Peter Browne 'Gap Year' *IS* 28 November 2014.

77 Savva 2016, p. 139.
78 Errington and van Onselen 2015, p. 100; Savva 2016, p. 56.
79 Patrick p. 67.
80 Savva 2016, p. 69.
81 Savva 2016, pp. 144–5.
82 Patrick p. 111.
83 Errington and van Onselen 2015, p. 84.
84 Errington and van Onselen 2015, p. 136.
85 Patrick p. 152.
86 Savva 2016, p. 161.
87 Patrick p. 230.
88 Manning, Paddy, 2015, p. 368.
89 Errington and van Onselen 2015, p. 152.
90 Savva 2016, p. 196.
91 Savva 2016, pp. 207ff.
92 Lenore Taylor 'Tony Abbott's outburst: how the PM "dumped" on Andrew Robb over the China free trade deal' G 11 September 2015.
93 Phillip Coorey 'If you listen to Tony Abbott's frontbench, his leadership is back in danger' AFR 11 September 2015.
94 Manning 2013, p. 376.
95 Peter Hartcher 'Inside the coup' SMH 19 September 2015.
96 Myriam Robin 'Is it on? Press gallery in agreement spill is almost definitely maybe on' Crikey 14 September 2015; Myriam Robin 'Journos as fortune-tellers: who predicted the spill?' Crikey 17 September 2015.
97 James Massola and Tom Allard 'How it happened – the Abbott-Turnbull leadership change' Age 15 September 2015
98 Savva 2016, p. 265.
99 Axel Bruns '#returnbull: How Twitter Reacted to the Latest Leadership Spill' Conv 16 September 2015.
100 Errington and van Onselen 2015, p. 199.
101 Savva 2016, pp. 279–82.
102 Errington and van Onselen 2015, p. 3.
103 Savva 2016, p. 9.
104 Peter Hartcher 'Inside the coup' SMH 19 September 2015.
105 Savva 2016, p. 32.
106 Savva 2016, p. 28.

Chapter 4: Hawke vs Keating versus Howard vs Costello

1 Errington and van Onselen 2007, p. 91.
2 Kelly 1992, p. 230.
3 Errington and van Onselen 2007, p. 194.
4 Errington and van Onselen 2007, p. 196.
5 Kelly 2009, p. 227.
6 Edwards 1996, p. 362.
7 Hawke p. 560.
8 Hawke p. 554.
9 Kelly 1992, p. 226.
10 Shaun Carney 'A party of one' Age 15 September 2007.

11   Hartcher p. 133.
12   Costello p. 248.
13   Carney p. 312.
14   *Labor in Power.*
15   Richardson pp. 338–9.
16   *Labor in Power.*
17   Hartcher p. 23.
18   John Hewson 'Disloyal, lazy, no balls: it's time to move on, Peter' *Age* 22 February 2009.
19   Kelly 1992, p. 173.
20   Hartcher p. 106.
21   Kelly 1992, p. 627.
22   Carney p. 220.
23   Parker p. 131.
24   Carney p. 220.
25   Arthur Sinodinos 'Peter was not robbed' *Aust* 25 June 2009.
26   Kelly 1992, p. 639.
27   Kelly 1992, p. 434.
28   Edwards 1996, p. 436.
29   Kelly 1992, p. 70.
30   Hawke p. 447.
31   Edwards 1996, pp. 389, 392.
32   Mills 1993, p. 210.
33   Edwards 1996, p. 432.
34   Carney p. 284.
35   Aubin p. 214.
36   Errington and van Onselen 2007, p. 317.
37   Michelle Grattan 'Howard and Costello in TV love fest' *Age* 20 November 2007.
38   Carney p. 305.
39   Costello pp. 229, 248, 250.
40   Sid Marris 'Unkind will question Costello's nerve' *Aust* 26 November 2007.
41   Kelly 1992, p. 136.
42   Kelly 1992, p. 196.
43   Kelly 1992, pp. 213–14.
44   Kelly 1992, pp. 215–16.
45   Kelly 1992, p. 216.
46   Edwards 1996, p. 390.
47   Kelly 1992, pp. 435ff.
48   Mills 1993, p. 216.
49   Mills 1993, p. 216.
50   Hawke p. 449.
51   Hawke p. 449.
52   Mills 1993, p. 216.
53   Kelly 1992, p. 443.
54   Hawke p. 448.
55   Kelly 1992, pp. 444–5.
56   Kelly 1992, p. 637.
57   Kelly 1992, pp. 636–7.

Notes

58   Kelly 1992, p. 621.
59   Kelly 1992, p. 617.
60   Hawke pp. 490–1.
61   Kelly 1992, p. 617.
62   Hawke p. 497.
63   *Labor in Power*.
64   Edwards 1996, pp. 388–9.
65   Edwards 1996, p. 389.
66   Edwards 1996, p. 389.
67   Kelly 1992, p. 616.
68   Kelly 1992, p. 623.
69   Richardson p. 303.
70   *Labor in Power*.
71   Kelly 1992, p. 632.
72   Edwards 1996, p. 425.
73   Kelly 1992, p. 632.
74   Mills 1993, p. 241.
75   Hawke p. 452.
76   Kelly 1992, pp. 633–4.
77   Hawke p. 504.
78   Edwards 1996, pp. 438–40.
79   Edwards 1996, p. 440.
80   Hawke p. 544.
81   Hawke p. 553.
82   Edwards 1996, p. 433.
83   Hawke p. 538.
84   Hawke p. 544.
85   Kelly 1992, pp. 646–7.
86   Mills 1993, p. 261.
87   Kelly 1992, p. 648.
88   Kelly 1992, p. 649.
89   Hawke p. 552.
90   Kelly 1992, p. 650.
91   Mills 1993, p. 266.
92   Kelly 1992, p. 650.
93   Kelly 1992, p. 651.
94   Hawke pp. 550, 548.
95   Kelly 1992, pp. 652, 656.
96   Hawke p. 555.
97   Hartcher p. 123.
98   Michelle Grattan 'Costello bides his time as his supporters stir the pot' *Sun Herald* 6 March 2005.
99   Howard 2010, p. 603.
100 Antoun Issa 'I will decide who leads the Liberal party and under what terms I lead it' *Crikey* 12 September 2007.
101 Brett p. 2.
102 Aubin; Carney.
103 Carney p. 321.

104 Carney p. 321.

105 Costello pp. 156–7.

106 Errington and van Onselen 2007, p. 297.

107 Carney p. 321.

108 Errington and van Onselen 2007, p. 368.

109 Costello p. 233.

110 Hartcher pp. 123–4.

111 Glenn Milne 'Howard's phone call to heal rift' *Sunday Telegraph* 4 September 2005.

112 Hartcher p. 125.

113 Errington and van Onselen 2007, p. 204.

114 Costello p. 226.

115 Errington and van Onselen 2007, p. 201.

116 Costello p. 240.

117 *Howard Years*.

118 Hartcher p. 125.

119 Hartcher p. 126.

120 Hartcher p. 129.

121 Costello p. 239.

122 Hartcher p. 130.

123 Costello p. 241.

124 Hartcher p. 130.

125 Errington and van Onselen 2007, p. 385.

126 Peter Hartcher 'Awaiting his master's pleasure' *SMH* 1 August 2006; Peter Hartcher 'It's Peter, Peter, the word eater' *SMH* 1 August 2006.

127 Errington and van Onselen 2007, p. 386.

128 Glenn Milne '"Tired" PM neutered cabinet' *Aust* 10 December 2007.

129 Jason Koutsoukis 'Behave yourself and you'll win: Howard to Libs' *Age* 9 December 2007.

130 Hartcher pp. 129–30.

131 Costello p. 244.

132 Hartcher p. 136.

133 Michelle Grattan 'It matters who hears the alarm' *Age* 25 May 2007.

134 Errington and van Onselen 2007, pp. 387, 385.

135 Stuart 2007, p. 167.

136 Hartcher p. 29.

137 Hartcher pp. 7, 33.

138 Hartcher p. 5.

139 Costello p. 252.

140 Hartcher pp. 11–12.

141 Hartcher pp. 20–1.

142 Hartcher pp. 22, 25.

143 Hartcher p. 24.

144 Hartcher p. 25.

145 Hartcher p. 10.

146 Costello pp. 254–5.

147 Hartcher p. 30.

148 Costello pp. 253–4.

149 Michelle Grattan 'It matters who hears the alarm' *Age* 25 May 2007.

150 David MacCormack 'The life and death of Peter Costello' *Crikey* 26 November 2007.
151 *Labor in Power.*
152 Hawke p. 558.
153 Kelly 1992, p. 450.
154 Edwards 1996, pp. 395–6.
155 Hartcher p. 131.
156 Hartcher p. 11.

Chapter 5: Duelling Amateurs – Gorton vs McMahon

1   Mills 2014.
2   Peter Hartcher 'If in doubt, throw another leader on the barbie' *SMH* 25 June 2010.
3   Patrick p. 146.
4   Freudenberg p. 133.
5   Oakes 1973, p. 181.
6   Strangio pp. 327–8.
7   Wanna and Arklay.
8   Wanna and Arklay, Ch 13.
9   Coaldrake p. 172.
10   Wanna and Arklay.
11   Wear pp. 91–5.
12   Howard 2014, p. 511.
13   Hancock p. 143.
14   Hasluck p. 154.
15   Howard 2014, p. 494.
16   Freudenberg pp. 142, 119.
17   Brown, Wallace, 2002, p. 78.
18   Hancock p. 400.
19   Howard 2014, p. 494.
20   Bruce Juddery 'He led but they did not follow him' *CT* 21 May 2002.
21   Hancock p. 178; Hasluck p. 174.
22   Hancock p. 207.
23   Hancock p. 225.
24   Henderson p. 302.
25   Henderson p. 309.
26   Hancock p. 170.
27   Griffen-Foley p. 146.
28   Tiffen 2014, pp. 107–8.
29   Fitzgerald and Holt p. 218.
30   Tiffen 1988, p. 27.
31   Hancock p. 328; Fitzgerald and Holt pp. 229ff; Griffen-Foley pp. 163ff.
32   Griffen-Foley pp. 164–5.
33   Griffen-Foley pp. 166–7.
34   Hancock p. 322.
35   Hancock p. 327.
36   Howard 2014, p. 546.
37   Hasluck p. 133.

38   Hancock p. 327.
39   Griffen-Foley p. 167.
40   Ramsey 2009, p. 264.
41   Brown, Wallace, 2002, p. 103.
42   Brown, Wallace, 2002, p. 101.
43   Hasluck pp. 185, 191.
44   Hasluck p. 147.
45   Oakes 2008, p. 259.
46   Brown, Wallace, 2002, pp. 103–6.
47   Hancock p. 345.
48   Griffen-Foley p. 172.
49   Freudenberg pp. 215ff.
50   Hancock p. 365.

Chapter 6: Leadership Coups and Desperate Oppositions

1   Kelly 1984, p. 218.
2   Collins p. 263.
3   Nicole Butler 'Mark McArdle leader of Qld Liberal Party' *PM* ABC Radio
      6 December 2007.
4   Antony Green 'Tasmanian election', *ABC Election Blog*, 2006.
5   Latham p. 48.
6   Errington and van Onselen 2007, p. 109.
7   Latham p. 49.
8   Latham p. 6.
9   Anon 'We're facing oblivion: Doyle' *Age* 16 August 2002.
10   Leser p. 103.
11   Leser p. 142.
12   Leser pp. 156, 161.
13   Kennedy pp. 202–3.
14   Dale.
15   Howard 2010, p. 78.
16   Fraser and Simons p. 604.
17   Tanner.
18   Parkinson p. 56.
19   Economou 2006, p. 367.
20   Economou 2006, pp. 367, 363.
21   Parkinson p. 74.
22   Parkinson p. 99.
23   Parkinson pp. 104, 116–17, 120–2.
24   McAllister 2003, p. 270.
25   Economou 2006, p. 376.
26   Hayward p. 386.
27   Stuart 2010, p. 229.
28   Kennedy p. 288.

Chapter 7: Leadership Coups and Disintegrating Governments

1   Wear pp. 154ff.
2   Phillip Coorey 'Carr slams "impatience" to kick out Rann' *SMH* 2 August 2011.

Notes

3   Julia Baird 'Outgoing South Australian Premier Mike Rann' *Sunday Profile*, ABC Radio, 16 October 2011.

4   Abjorensen pp. 377, 379.

5   Mackerras p. 394.

6   Mackerras p. 394.

7   Abjorensen p. 382.

8   Kennedy p. 166.

9   Tiffen 1999, p. 25.

10   Kelly 1992, p. 560.

11   Anon 'The unluckiest politician in Australia' *Crikey* 21 October 2001.

12   Manning p. 198.

13   Richard Willingham 'Baillieu falls on sword' *Age* 7 March 2013.

14   Josh Gordon and Richard Willingham 'Baillieu "one stuff-up" from leadership fight' *Age* 6 March 2013.

15   Jared Lynch 'Abbott backs state Liberal director' *Age* 9 March 2013.

16   Melissa Fyfe and Royce Millar "Bombshell that ended Ted's rule' *Age* 8 March 2013.

17   Melissa Fyfe and Royce Millar 'Gift or poison chalice? *Age* 9 March 2013.

18   Josh Gordon 'Boost for Napthine' *Age* 11 March 2013.

19   Rodan p. 308.

20   Colebatch pp. 394ff.

21   Foley pp. 34–5.

22   Rodan p. 310.

23   Parkinson pp. 52–3.

24   Lowe pp. 40–1.

25   Lowe pp. 144–54.

26   G.S. 'Tasmania' *Australian Journal of Politics and History* 1982 p. 109.

27   Kelly 1992, pp. 528, 543.

28   Strangio p. 325.

29   Cain pp. 40, 242.

30   Cain p. 258.

31   Strangio p. 343.

32   Clune 2012a, p. 221.

33   Clune 2012b, p. 256.

34   McClymont and Besser p. 232.

35   Goot p. 274.

36   Cavalier 2010, p. 127.

37   *SMH* 8 September 2008, editorial.

38   Sartor p. 71.

39   Benson p. 64.

40   McClymont and Besser p. 8.

41   Sartor p. 71.

42   Cavalier 2010, p. 79.

43   Benson p. 95.

44   Benson p. 84.

45   Cavalier 2010, p. 79.

46   Benson p. 63.

47   Cavalier 2010, p. 110.

48   Andrew West 'Mistake to lock horns with dinosaurs' *SMH* 9 September 2008.
49   Benson p. 94.
50   Clune 2012a, p. 229.
51   McClymont and Besser p. 269.
52   Cavalier 2010, p. 179.
53   Andrew Clennell, Louise Hall and Brian Robins 'Keneally pays back the puppet masters' *SMH* 5 December 2009.
54   Clune 2012b, p. 248.
55   Tiffen 1999, pp. 94ff.
56   Wanna and Arklay Ch 13.
57   Wear pp. 123–5.
58   Wanna and Arklay Ch 16.

Chapter 8: Media and Momentum
1   Davis, Glyn, 2011.
2   Hartcher p. 262.
3   Costello p. 236.
4   Hancock p. 373.
5   Kelly 1992, p. 216.
6   Kelly 1992, p. 448.
7   Jon Henley 'Is Bill Shorten the world's most loyal politician?' *G* 27 April 2012.
8   Sabra Lane 'Turnbull reminds party that disloyalty is death' *PM*, ABC Radio, 20 February 2009.
9   Stanyer p. 76.
10   Edwards 1977, pp. 84–5.
11   Hancock pp. 374–5.
12   Kelly 1992, p. 179.
13   Oakes 1976, p. 49.
14   Kelly 1992, p. 636.
15   Collins p. 312.
16   Kelly 1984, p. 118.
17   *Labor in Power.*
18   Hawke p. 450.
19   Tiffen 1989, p. 168.
20   Kelly 1992, p. 150.
21   Tiffen 1989, p. 168.
22   Dale p. 5.
23   Dale p. 102.
24   Cavalier 2012, p. 125; also pp. 127, 131, 132.
25   Edwards 1996, p. 364.
26   Edwards 1996, p. 363.
27   Hawke p. 437.
28   Hawke p. 501.
29   Michelle Grattan 'Costello camp denies shadow offer' *SMH* 17 February 2009.
30   Michelle Grattan 'Turnbull's authority takes a beating after a week from hell' *SMH* 20 February 2009.
31   Peter Hartcher 'Daggers are drawn between Costello and Turnbull' *SMH* 21 February 2009.

32 Errington and van Onselen 2007, pp. 328–9.
33 Hartcher p. 225.
34 Mungo MacCallum 'Reluctant noble of politics' *Aust* 13 January 2007.
35 Latham p. 280.
36 Savva 2010, p. 147.
37 Hartcher p. 220.
38 Bernard Keane 'By turns incompetent and dangerous, Abbott's time as PM is up' *Crikey* 14 September 2015.
39 Lenore Taylor 'The Coalition's own messages are neither coherent nor convincing' *G* 5 December 2014.
40 Tony Wright 'Labor MP goes rogue on Gillard, down to the letter' *SMH* 5 June 2013.
41 James Massola 'Leaked talking points tell ministers to say "our cabinet is functioning exceptionally well"' *SMH* 19 August 2015.
42 Bernard Keane 'Who, we wonder, is out to get poor Julie Bishop?' *Crikey* 1 December 2008.
43 Peter Hartcher 'Daggers are drawn between Costello and Turnbull' *SMH* 21 February 2009.
44 Kelly 1992, pp. 559–60; Kennedy pp. 168ff.
45 Hartcher p. 165.
46 Kelly 2014, p. 107.
47 Tiffen 1989, p. 111.
48 Savva 2010, p. 72.
49 Sartor p. 82.
50 Benson p. 193.
51 Julia Baird 'Outgoing South Australian Premier Mike Rann' *Sunday Profile*, ABC Radio, 16 October 2011.
52 Kennedy p. 149.
53 Haupt p. xiv.
54 Summers 1983, p. 29.
55 Summers 1983, p. 27.
56 Summers 1983, p. 28.
57 Button 1998, p. 188.
58 Dodkin p. 33.
59 Carr pp. 8–9.
60 Clune 2005, p. 38.
61 Schneider p. 135.
62 Oakes 1976, p. 42.
63 Freudenberg p. 312.
64 Kelly 1976, p. 109.
65 Oakes 1976, p. 43.
66 Kelly 1976, pp. 117–18.
67 Freudenberg p. 313.
68 Oakes 1976, p. 43; Kelly 1976, p. 117.
69 Kelly 1984, p. 125.
70 Ayres 1987, p. 246.
71 Oakes 1976, p. 33.
72 Kelly 1984, p. 159.

73   Fraser and Simons pp. 519–20.
74   Kelly 1984, p. 164.
75   Ayres p. 424.
76   Kelly 1992, p. 179.
77   Kelly 1992, p. 189.
78   Kelly 1992, p. 186.
79   Kelly 1992, pp. 509–11.
80   Crabb 2005, p. 64.
81   Crabb 2005, p. 90.
82   Crabb 2005, p. 120.
83   Latham pp. 218–19.
84   Crabb 2005, p. 123.
85   Crabb 2005, p. 124.
86   Crabb 2005, p. 128.
87   Crabb 2005, pp. 130–1.
88   Crabb 2005, pp. 134, 139.
89   Latham p. 224.
90   Crabb 2005, pp. 139–44.
91   Alan Ramsey 'Withering lines give lemmings a song to remember' *SMH* 18 June 2003.
92   Crabb 2005, pp. 155, 165.
93   Latham pp. 236–7.
94   Latham pp. 237–9.
95   Latham pp. 246–7.
96   Crabb 2005, pp. 167–8.
97   Latham p. 249.
98   Dennis Shanahan 'Coalition not tuned to sound of alarms – Labor under Latham' *Aust* 3 December 2003.

Chapter 9: Reporters and Players

1   *Labor in Power* Episode 5.
2   Richardson p. 310.
3   Kelly 1992, p. 449.
4   Tiffen 1988, p. 27.
5   Latham p. 274.
6   Savva 2010, p. 55.
7   Savva 2010, p. 97.
8   McKnight 2015, pp. 24–6.
9   Hawker pp. 75–6.
10   Helen McCabe 'Colleagues, but no love as political heavyweights slug it out' *Aust* 20 July 2006.
11   Glenn Milne 'Succession in the air' *Aust* 8 April 2002.
12   Glenn Milne 'Howard's phone call to heal rift' *STele* 4 September 2005.
13   Glenn Milne 'Costello to take over coalition "unopposed"' *STele* 25 November 2007.
14   Glenn Milne 'PM's hubris leaves the Liberal Party in ruins' *Aust* 26 November 2007.
15   Sue Dunlevy 'Costello quietly plotted revenge' *DT blog* 25 November 2007.

16   Costello p. 6.
17   Roshco p. 23.
18   Tiffen 2002, pp. 146–8.
19   Myriam Robin 'Bolt Report might be canned, but Bolt's not going anywhere' *Crikey* 18 January 2016.
20   Sean Nicholls and James Robertson 'Alan Jones attack threat to potential Craig Kelly challengers' *Age* 4 February 2016.
21   Paul Kelly 'Negative politics the biggest enemy of reform' *Aust* 23 September 2015.
22   Bob Carr 'Paddy lost the plot' *Aust* 30 January 2008.
23   Costello p. 256.
24   Rodney Tiffen 'The Daily Telegraph, John Brogden and hyena journalism' *Online Opinion* 14 September 2005.
25   Robert Wainwright and Jonathan Pearlman 'Shattered Brogden's suicide bid' *SMH* 31 August 2005.
26   Andrew Clennell and Robert Wainwright 'Leadership fight to be cliffhanger' *SMH* 31 August 2005; Anne Davies, Andrew Clennell and James Button 'Wipeout: party brawls begin' *SMH* 28 November 2005.
27   Rodney Tiffen 'The Daily Telegraph, John Brogden and hyena journalism' *Online Opinion* 14 September 2005.
28   *Insiders* 'Abbott admits to insensitive Brogden comments' ABC TV 4 September 2005.
29   AAP 'Abbott "should resign" for mocking Brogden' *SMH* 5 September 2005.
30   AAP 'Abbott's Brogden antics slammed by Brandis' *SMH* 5 September 2005.
31   Cavalier 2010, pp. xii, 67.
32   Tiffen 2014, pp. 145ff.
33   Hobbs and McKnight pp. 8ff.
34   Michelle Grattan 'Woe betide those who fail the Abbott government's tribal test' *Conv* 14 March 2014.
35   Phillip Coorey 'Prime Minister Tony Abbott takes Rupert Murdoch's advice' *AFR* 29 January 2015.
36   Latika Bourke 'Rupert Murdoch calls on Tony Abbott to make "cruel choice" and sack Peta Credlin' *Age* 28 January 2015.
37   Peter Hartcher 'Shirtfronted. The story of the Abbott government', Five part series, *SMH* 29 November 2015 to 3 December 2015.
38   Laura Tingle 'Bad week ends with no love lost for Tony Abbott' *AFR* 30 January 2015.
39   Michelle Grattan 'What's wrong with Team Abbott is a lot bigger than the Credlin problem' *Conv* 28 January 2015.
40   Bernard Keane 'By turns incompetent and dangerous, Abbott's time as PM is up' *Crikey* 14 September 2015.
41   Peter Hartcher 'Shirtfronted. The story of the Abbott government', Five part series, *SMH* 29 November 2015 to 3 December 2015.
42   Anne Davies 'Prime Minister Malcolm Turnbull's troubles with the powerful' *Age* 20 September 2015.
43   Phillip Coorey 'Tony Abbott says Scott Morrison has "blotted his copybook" over Hockey claims' *AFR* 18 September 2015.
44   Katharine Murphy 'A painful morning for Alan Jones, who told Malcolm Turnbull he'd never be PM' *G* 15 September 2015.

45   *Media Watch* 'The Turnbull takeover' ABC TV 21 September 2015.
46   Lisa Cox '"You are the bomb thrower": Malcolm Turnbull accuses Alan Jones of doing Labor's work for it' *SMH* 6 June 2014.
47   Megan Levy '"We've got a shit sandwich": Alan Jones defends Tony Abbott after leadership spill' *SMH* 15 September 2015.
48   Anthony Colangelo 'Andrew Bolt's love letter to Abbott draws scorn' *New Daily* 28 September 2015.
49   Andrew Bolt 'Turnbull creates a right old problem' *DT* 17 September 2015; Cassidy Knowlton and Sunny Liu 'Andrew Bolt's Five states of grief' *Crikey* 13 October 2015.
50   *Media Watch* 'Beating up the banquet' ABC TV 8 February 2016.
51   Dominic White 'Liberal leadership spill sparks News Corp "civil war"' *SMH* 22 September 2015.
52   *Media Watch* 'Beating up the banquet' ABC TV 8 February 2016.
53   *Media Watch* 'Marathon with no winner' ABC TV 3 July 2016.
54   Michelle Grattan 'Abbott would have lost "resoundingly"' *Conv* 27 June 2016.
55   Media Watch 'Marathon with no winner' ABC TV 3 July 2016.
56   Latika Bourke 'Vindicated Peta Credlin unleashes ferocious attack on Turnbull's "hapless bedwetters"' *SMH* 5 July 2016.
57   Laura Tingle 'Leadership spill: Turnbull coup resets a government that had stopped working' *AFR* 17 September 2015.

Chapter 10: Iatrogenic Spin Doctoring
1   Jack Rosenthal 'The Debate and the Spin Doctors' *NYT* 21 October 1984.
2   Stephen Castle 'The things that shaped our year – the triumph of the spin doctor' *Independent on Sunday* 28 December 1997.
3   Jack Robertson 'The most memorable person in 2003: the spin doctor' *SMH* 18 November 2003.
4   Timothy Garton Ash 'Fight the Matrix' *G* 5 June 2003.
5   Major pp. 12–13.
6   Illich 1975.
7   McNair 2000, p. 123.
8   Tumber.
9   Burton.
10   Ward p. 17.
11   Deacon and Golding, Ward.
12   Davis 2002.
13   Blumler and Kavanagh p. 209.
14   Esser et al. 2001.
15   Blumler and Gurevitch p. 207.
16   Palluszek 2002.
17   Swan p. 228.
18   Bernard Keane 'Four to one: our lobbyist to MP ratio' *Crikey* 8 September 2009; also Fitzgerald.
19   Young 2007a; Young 2007b; Barns.
20   Turner et al.
21   Matthew Knott 'The Power Index: the world of spinners and advisers' *Crikey* 6 February 2012.

22   Franklin 2003, p. 46.
23   Claire Cozens 'GQ mostly PR-driven, says editor' G 15 March 2005.
24   Jason Deans and John Plunkett 'Cameron's spin doctors more obsessive than Tony Blair's, says Adam Boulton' G 3 February 2014.
25   Atkinson.
26   Kuhn 2002, p. 66.
27   McKnight 2015, p. 28.
28   Ferguson p. 34.
29   Kelly 2014, p. 122.
30   Hobbs p. 11.
31   McNair 2004, p. 327.
32   McKnight 2015, p. 22.
33   McKnight 2016, p. 3.
34   Tom Cowie 'Friday arvo document dumps subvert FOI reform: editors' Crikey 8 April 2011.
35   Mark Kenny 'Taking out the trash but too clever by half' Age 20 March 2015.
36   Nicole Hasham 'Taxpayers billed for government mistake over Save the Children workers on Nauru' SMH 6 May 2016.
37   Anon 'NSW Govt releases secret tunnel documents during Cup' ABC Online 1 November 2005.
38   Kuhn 2005, p. 106.
39   Tiffen 2012, pp. 17–18.
40   Michelle Grattan 'Gillard now in the I of a storm' Age 28 January 2011.
41   Ferguson p. 110.
42   Mike Rann 'Politics, the media and public policy' School of Social and Policy Studies, Flinders University, 2 April 2012.
43   Laurie Oakes 'A media cyclone has us all in a spin' DT 16 October 2010.
44   Barrie Cassidy 'Tony Abbott's self-indulgent and damaging farewell radio tour' ABC The Drum 2 October 2015.
45   Lindy Edwards 'Strategically, Labor lost sight of simple heart of matter' Age 23 August 2010.
46   Peter Brent 'A little bit of Turnbull honesty might need to go a long way' IS 15 September 2015.
47   Stuart 2010, p. 173.
48   Cassidy p. 65.
49   Lindy Edwards 'Strategically, Labor lost sight of simple heart of matter' Age 23 August 2010.
50   Kurtz p. 46.
51   Weller p. 317.
52   McKnight 2016, p. 4.
53   Megalogenis p. 8.
54   Chubb p. 5.
55   Chubb pp. 69, 74, 77.
56   Cassidy p. 42.
57   Bernard Keane 'How Rudd blew it: finding ways to upset everyone at the same time' Crikey 18 May 2010.
58   Tim Colebatch 'Control fetish stifles ALP' Age 22 June 2010.
59   Cassidy p. 43.

60 Lenore Taylor 'How Rudd's ETS was killed from within Labor ranks' *Age* 5 April 2011.
61 Chubb p. 112.
62 Mark Danner 'How, and What, Obama Won' *NYRB* 20 December 2012.
63 Joe Hildebrand 'Railroaded by 10 years of Labor lies' *DT* 27 October 2008.
64 Cavalier 2012, p. 166.
65 Ross Gittins 'Iemma writhes as victim of virtual government' *SMH* 27 March 2006.
66 Franklin 1999, pp. 19–20.
67 Stephen Wall 'Uncivil Servants' *New Statesman* 17 October 2005.
68 Patrick Wintour 'Whitehall chiefs hit out at Downing Street' *G* 27 September 2004.
69 Patrick Wintour 'Sack the chancellor. Cherie Blair's repeated advice to her husband' *G* 19 June 2007.
70 McKnight 2016, p. 8.
71 Kelly 2014, p. 175.
72 Swan pp. 181–2.
73 Ferguson p. 82.
74 Kuhn 2002, p. 47.
75 Laura Tingle 'There is wisdom in argument rather than authority' *AFR* 29 August 2014.
76 Laura Tingle 'There is wisdom in argument rather than authority' *AFR* 29 August 2014.
77 Cassidy p. 119.
78 Cassidy p. 128.
79 Cassidy p. 129.
80 Robert Reich 'Bush Administration paradox explained' *San Francisco Chronicle* 19 September 2005.
81 Kelly 2014, p. 144.
82 Kelly 2014, p. 153.
83 Chubb pp. 15–16.
84 Chubb pp. 19–20.
85 Edwards 1996, p. 644.
86 Kuhn 2005, p. 95.
87 Brown 2002, p. 81.
88 Matthew Knott 'The power index: spinners, the most powerful is ... Peta Credlin, *Crikey* 24 February 2012.
89 Heath Aston and Chris Johnson 'Accusations of meddling by Prime Minister Tony Abbott's chief of staff Peta Credlin' *Age* 8 December 2013.
90 Heath Aston and Jonathan Swan '"Control freak" Peta Credlin accused of pulling Coalition strings' *SMH* 5 December 2013.
91 Judith Ireland 'Tony Abbott's chief of staff Peta Credlin gets mixed reviews from government insiders' *Age* 13 December 2014.
92 Miranda Devine 'Desperate defence of Credlin is humiliating' *Sunday Telegraph* 1 February 2015.
93 Katharine Murphy 'Bidding farewell to Peta Credlin, the woman who broke all Canberra's rules' *G* 23 September 2015.
94 James Massola 'What will happen to Peta Credlin and Brian Loughnane, Liberal

power couple' *SMH* 16 September 2015.

95   Katharine Murphy 'Bidding farewell to Peta Credlin, the woman who broke all Canberra's rules' *G* 23 September 2015.

96   Ferguson p. 134.

97   *The Killing Season.*

98   Chubb p. 70.

99   Swan p. 174.

100   Chubb p. 70.

101   Swan p. 174.

102   Sean Kelly 'The drip feed' *The Monthly* March 2014.

103   Ferguson p. 116.

104   Ferguson p. 76.

105   Andrew Crook 'Bitar's email bombshell on the "Lindsay test"' *Crikey* 25 February 2011.

106   Cavalier 2012, p. 128.

107   Cavalier 2012, p. 128.

108   Benson p. 111.

109   Cavalier 2012, p. 127.

110   Sartor p. 59.

111   Goot p. 281.

112   Goot p. 274.

113   Collins p. 309.

114   Collins pp. 300–5.

115   Peter Brent 'How gay marriage fell victim to Labor's Stockholm Syndrome' *IS* 25 May 2015.

116   Kevin Maguire 'You know when you've been Campbelled' *G* 29 March 2003.

117   Matthew Knott 'The McTernan Curse: when the spin doctor becomes the story' *Crikey* 25 June 2013.

118   Latika Bourke 'Leaked John McTernan emails reveal aggressive approach of Julia Gillard's spin doctor' *ABC News* 11 December 2013.

119   Joe Aston 'Rear Window's 2012' *AFR* 27 December 2012.

120   Andrew Crook 'Election deciders, the spinners at #3' *Crikey* 5 June 2013.

121   Grattan p. 42.

122   Anon 'John Lyons: hatchet man on the make' *Crikey* 26 August 2005.

123   Alan Ramsey 'Stop the presses: the story Rudd tried to kill' *SMH* 31 March 2007.

124   Cassidy pp. 89–90.

125   Richard Farmer 'A few drinks and a bit of big noting?' *Crikey* 19 April 2013.

126   Nixon p. 354.

Chapter 11: The Doctrine of the Disposable Leader

1   William Bowe 'Liberal lords defend their fiefdoms, crush preselection reform' *Crikey* 16 October 2016.

2   Errington p. 16.

3   Button 2002, pp. 21–4.

4   Button 2002, p. 32.

5   Miragliotta pp. 64–5.

6   Cavalier 2012, p. ix.

7   Economou 2015, p. 1; Miragliotta pp. 62, 67.

8   Button 2002, p. 42.
9   Brown, Archie, 2014, pp. 355, 98.
10   Brown, Archie, 2014, p. 355.
11   Smith, p. 18.
12   Vanessa Desloires 'Lord Mayor Robert Doyle warns state Liberals against a lurch to the right or risk decade in opposition' *Age* 10 December 2014.
13   Miragliotta p. 69.
14   Brown, Archie, 2014, p. 62.
15   Brown, Archie, 2014, p. 69.
16   McAllister 2003, p. 260.
17   Heffernan p. 583.
18   Meyer 2002.
19   Pringle p. 89.
20   Hasluck p. 171.
21   Tingle p. 10.
22   Walter and Strangio p. 49.
23   Walter and Strangio p. 53.
24   Walter and Strangio p. 24.
25   Tingle.
26   Tiernan.
27   Bynander and 't Hart p. 61.
28   Brown, Archie, 2014, p. vii.
29   Mariano Heyden and Dimitrios Georgakakis 'Australia has embraced the outsider CEO, but they can't always save the day' *Conv* 9 February 2016.

Appendix A
1   Dunstan, p. 133; Bannon.
2   Lowe p. 51.
3   Ian Smith 'Former South Australian Liberal Party leader Dale Baker dies' *Advertiser* 28 March 2012.
4   Parkin p. 439.
5   Tiffen 1999, pp. 6–7.
6   Collins p. 207.
7   Tony Jones 'WA Liberals in disarray' *Lateline* ABC TV 21 February 2001.
8   Kennedy p. 285.
9   Kennedy p. 286.
10   Latham p. 8.
11   Latham pp. 405, 411.
12   Kelly 2014, p. 99.
13   McCall and Hay pp. 236–7.
14   Herr p. 646.
15   Wear p. 118.
16   Kelly 1992, pp. 297, 301.
17   Tiffen 2014, pp. 151–2.
18   Howard 2010, p. 157.
19   Kelly 1992, p. 303.
20   Kelly 1992, pp. 407, 410.

Bibliography

Abbott, Tony (2010) *Battlelines* (Melbourne, Melbourne University Press [MUP])

Abjorensen, Norman (2006) 'Lewis, Thomas Lancelot' in David Clune and Ken Turner (eds) *The Premiers of New South Wales 1856–2005*, vol. 2, 1901–2005 (Sydney, Federation Press)

Atkinson, Joe (2005) 'The panic over "spin": Neo-liberalism, insider populism, and media cynicism' (Paper to IAMCR conference, Taipei, July)

Aubin, Tracey (1999) *Peter Costello. A Biography* (Sydney, HarperCollins)

Ayres, Philip (1987) *Malcolm Fraser. A Biography* (Melbourne, William Heinemann Australia)

Bannon, John (2002) 'Walsh, Francis Henry (1897–1968)' *Australian Dictionary of Biography*, vol. 16, (Melbourne, MUP)

Barns, Greg (2005) *Selling the Australian Government. Politics and Propaganda from Whitlam to Howard* (Sydney, UNSW Press)

Benson, Simon (2010) *Betrayal. The Underbelly of Australian Labor* (Sydney, Pantera Press)

Blumler, Jay G and Gurevitch, Michael (1995) *The Crisis of Public Communication* (London, Routledge)

Blumler, Jay G and Kavanagh, Dennis (1999) 'The Third Age of Political Communication: Influences and Features', *Political Communication* 16, 209–30

Brett, Judith (2007) 'Exit Right. The Unravelling of John Howard', *Quarterly Essay* No. 28 (Melbourne, Black Inc)

Brown, Archie (2014) *The Myth of the Strong Leader. Political Leadership in the Modern Age* (London, Basic Books)

Brown, Wallace (2002) *Ten Prime Ministers. Life Among the Politicians* (Sydney, Longueville Books)

Burton, Bob (2007) *Inside Spin. The Dark Underbelly of the PR Industry* (Sydney, Allen & Unwin)

Button, John (1998) *As It Happened* (Melbourne, Text Publishing)

Button, John (2002) 'Beyond Belief. What Future for Labor?', *Quarterly Essay* No. 6 (Melbourne, Black Inc)

Bynander, Fredrik and 't Hart, Paul (2007) 'The Politics of Party Leader Survival and Succession: Australia in Comparative Perspective', *Australian Journal of Political Science* 42, 1, 47–72

Cain, John (1995) *John Cain's Years. Power, Parties and Politics* (Melbourne, MUP)

Calwell, Arthur (1972) *Be Just and Fear Not* (Melbourne, Lloyd O'Neil)

Carney, Shaun (2001) *Peter Costello. The New Liberal* (Sydney, Allen & Unwin)

Carr, Bob (2007) 'Diary Keeping: A Personal Perspective' in David Clune and Ken Turner (eds) *Writing Party History* (Sydney, Parliament of New South Wales)

Cassidy, Barrie (2010) *The Party Thieves. The Real Story of the 2010 Election* (Melbourne, MUP)

Cavalier, Rodney (2010) *Power Crisis. The Self-Destruction of a State Labor Party* (Melbourne, Cambridge University Press [CUP])

Cavalier, Rodney (2012) 'Preface' in David Clune and Rodney Smith (eds) *From Carr to Keneally. Labor in Office in NSW 1995–2011* (Sydney, Allen & Unwin)

Chubb, Philip (2014) *Power Failure. The Inside Story of Climate Politics under Rudd and Gillard* (Melbourne, Black Inc)

Clune, David (2005) 'Bob Carr: The unexpected Colossus' in John Wanna and Paul Williams (eds) *Yes, Premier. Labor Leadership in Australia's States and Territories* (Sydney, UNSW Press)

Clune, David (2012a) 'NSW politics, 2007–10' in David Clune and Rodney Smith (eds) *From Carr to Keneally. Labor in Office in NSW 1995–2011* (Sydney, Allen & Unwin)

Clune, David (2012b) 'The Campaign' in David Clune and Rodney

Smith (eds) *From Carr to Keneally. Labor in Office in NSW 1995–2011* (Sydney, Allen & Unwin)

Coaldrake, Peter (1989) *Working the System. Government in Queensland* (Brisbane, UQP)

Colebatch, Tim (2015) *Dick Hamer. The Liberal Liberal* (Melbourne, Scribe)

Collins, Peter (2000) *The Bear Pit. A Life in Politics* (Sydney, Allen & Unwin)

Costello, Peter with Coleman, Peter (2008) *The Costello Memoirs* (Melbourne, MUP)

Crabb, Annabel (2005) *Losing It. The Inside Story of the Labor Party in Opposition* (Sydney, Pan Macmillan)

Crabb, Annabel (2009) 'Stop at Nothing. The Life and Adventures of Malcolm Turnbull', *Quarterly Essay* No. 34 (Melbourne, Black Inc)

Dale, Brian (1985) *Ascent to Power* (Sydney, Allen & Unwin)

Davis, Aeron (2002) *Public Relations Democracy. Public Relations, Politics and the Mass Media in Britain* (Manchester, Manchester University Press)

Davis, Glyn (2011) 'Leader of the Gang. How Political Parties Choose Numero Uno', *Griffith Review* (Melbourne, Text Publishing)

Deacon, David and Golding, Peter (1994) *Taxation and Representation. The Media, Political Representation and the Poll Tax* (London, John Libbey)

Dodkin, Marilyn (2003) *Bob Carr. The Reluctant Leader* (Sydney, UNSW Press)

Dunstan, Don (1981) *Felicia. The Political Memoirs of Don Dunstan* (Melbourne, Macmillan)

Economou, Nick (2006) 'Jeff Kennett: The larrikin metropolitan' in Paul Strangio and Brian Costar (eds) *The Victorian Premiers 1856–2006* (Sydney, Federation Press)

Economou, Nick (2015) 'Democracy, Oligarchy or Polyarchy? Intra Party Politics and the Australian Labor Party Drift' in Narelle Miragliotta, Anika Gauja and Rodney Smith (eds) *Contemporary*

Australian Political Party Organisations (Melbourne, Monash University Publishing)

Edwards, John (1977) *Life Wasn't Meant to be Easy. A Political Profile of Malcolm Fraser* (Sydney, Hale & Iremonger)

Edwards, John (1996) *Keating. The Inside Story* (Melbourne, Viking)

Errington, Wayne (2015) 'The Liberal Party: Electoral Success Despite Organisational Drift' in Narelle Miragliotta, Anika Gauja and Rodney Smith (eds) *Contemporary Australian Political Party Organisations* (Melbourne, Monash University Publishing)

Errington, Wayne and van Onselen, Peter (2007) *John Winston Howard. The Biography* (Melbourne, MUP)

Errington, Wayne and van Onselen, Peter (2015) *Battleground. Why the Liberal Party Shirtfronted Tony Abbott* (Melbourne, MUP)

Esser, Frank, Reinemann, Carsten and Fan, David (2001) 'Spin Doctors in the United States, Great Britain and Germany. Metacommunication about Media Manipulation', *Press/Politics* 6, 1, 16–45

Ferguson, Sarah (2016) *The Killing Season Uncut* (Melbourne, MUP)

Fitzgerald, Julian (2006) *Lobbying in Australia: You Can't Expect to Change Anything if You Don't Speak Up* (Dural, NSW, Rosenberg Publishing)

Fitzgerald, Ross and Holt, Stephen (2010) *Alan Reid. The Red Fox* (Sydney, NewSouth Publishing)

Foley, Kevin (1983) 'The Liberal Party Campaign' in Brian Costar and Colin A Hughes *Labor to Office. The Victorian State Election 1982* (Melbourne, Drummond)

Franklin, Bob (1999) *Social Policy, the Media and Misrepresentation* (London, Routledge)

Franklin, Bob (2003) '"A Good Day to Bury Bad News?": Journalists, Sources and the Packaging of Politics' in Simon Cottle (ed.) *News, public relations and power* (London, Sage)

Fraser, Malcolm and Simons, Margaret (2010) *Malcolm Fraser. The Political Memoirs* (Melbourne, The Miegunyah Press)

Freudenberg, Graham (1977) *A Certain Grandeur. Gough Whitlam in Politics* (Melbourne, Sun Books)

Goot, Murray (2012) 'The polls and voter attitudes' in David Clune and

Rodney Smith (eds) *From Carr to Keneally. Labor in Office in NSW 1995–2011* (Sydney, Allen & Unwin)

Grattan, Michelle (1998) 'The Politics of Spin', *Australian Studies in Journalism* No. 7, 32–45

Griffen-Foley, Bridget (2003) *Party Games. Australian Politicians and the Media from War to Dismissal* (Melbourne, Text Publishing)

Hancock, Ian (2002) *John Gorton. He Did It His Way* (Sydney, Hodder)

Hartcher, Peter (2009) *To the Bitter End. The Dramatic Story Behind the Fall of John Howard and the Rise of Kevin Rudd* (Sydney, Allen & Unwin)

Hasluck, Paul (1997) *The Chance of Politics* (Melbourne, Text Publishing)

Haupt, Robert (with Michelle Grattan) (1983) *31 Days to Power. Hawke's Victory* (Sydney, Allen & Unwin)

Hawke, Bob (1994) *The Hawke Memoirs* (Melbourne, William Heinemann)

Hawker, Bruce (2013) *The Rudd Rebellion. The Campaign to Save Labor* (Melbourne, MUP)

Hayward, David (2006) 'Steve Bracks: The Quiet Achiever' in Paul Strangio and Brian Costar (eds) *The Victorian Premiers 1856–2006* (Sydney, Federation Press)

Heffernan, Richard (2006) 'The Prime Minister and the News Media: Political Communication as a Leadership Resource', *Parliamentary Affairs* 59, 4, 582–98

Henderson, Gerard (2000) 'Sir John Grey Gorton' in Michelle Grattan (ed.) *Australian Prime Ministers* (Sydney, New Holland Publishers)

Herr, Richard (2008) 'Tasmania. January to June 2008', *Australian Journal of Politics and History* 54, 4, December

Hobbs, Mitchell (2015) 'The Sociology of Spin: An Investigation into the Uses, Practices and Consequences of Political Communication', *Journal of Sociology*, 52, N2, 371–86, 1–16

Hobbs, Mitchell and McKnight, David (2016) '"Kick this mob out": The Murdoch Media and the Australian Labor Government (2007 to 2013)', *Global Media Journal Australian Edition* 10, 1

Howard, John (2010) *Lazarus Rising. A Personal and Political Autobiography* (Sydney, HarperCollins)

Howard, John (2014) *The Menzies Era. The Years that Shaped Modern Australia* (Sydney, HarperCollins)

Howard Years, The (2008) (ABC DVD)

Howson, Peter (1984) *The Life of Politics. The Howson Diaries* (Melbourne, The Viking Press)

Illich, Ivan (1975) *Medical Nemesis. The Expropriation of Health* (London, Calder & Boyars Ltd)

Kelly, Paul (1976) *The Unmaking of Gough* (Sydney, Angus & Robertson)

Kelly, Paul (1984) *The Hawke Ascendancy* (Sydney, Angus & Robertson)

Kelly, Paul (1992) *The End of Certainty. The Story of the 1980s* (Sydney, Allen & Unwin)

Kelly, Paul (2009) *The March of Patriots. The Struggle for Modern Australia* (Melbourne, MUP)

Kelly, Paul (2014) *Triumph and Demise. The Broken Promise of a Labor Generation* (Melbourne, MUP)

Kennedy, Peter (2014) *Tales from Boomtown. Western Australian Premiers from Brand to Barnett* (Perth, UWA Publishing)

Kent, Jacqueline (2014) *The Making of Julia Gillard* (Melbourne, Penguin Books)

Killing Season, The (2015) (ABC DVD)

Kuhn, Raymond (2002) 'The First Blair Government and Political Journalism' in Raymond Kuhn and Erik Neveu (eds) *Political Journalism. New Challenges, New Practices* (London, Routledge)

Kuhn, Raymond (2005) 'Media Management' in Anthony Seldon and Dennis Kavanagh (eds) *The Blair Effect 2001–5* (Cambridge, CUP)

Kurtz, Howard (1998) *Spin Cycle. Inside the Clinton Propaganda Machine* (New York, The Free Press)

Labor in Power (1993) (ABC DVD)

Latham, Mark (2005) *The Latham Diaries* (Melbourne, MUP)

Leser, David (1994) *Bronwyn Bishop. A Woman in Pursuit of Power* (Melbourne, Text Publishing)

Lowe, Doug (1984) *The Price of Power. The Politics Behind the Tasmanian Dams Case* (Melbourne, Macmillan)

Mackerras, Malcolm (2006) 'Willis, Sir Eric Archibald' in David Clune and Ken Turner (eds) *The Premiers of New South Wales 1856–2005*, vol. 2, 1901–2005 (Sydney, Federation Press)

Major, John (2003) *The Erosion of Parliamentary Government* (London, Centre for Policy Studies)

Manning, Haydon (2005) 'Mike Rann: A Fortunate "King of Spin"' in John Wanna and Paul Williams (eds) *Yes, Premier. Labor Leadership in Australia's States and Territories* (Sydney, UNSW Press)

Manning, Paddy (2015) *Born to Rule. The Unauthorised Biography of Malcolm Turnbull* (Melbourne, MUP)

Marr, David (2012) 'Political Animal. The Making of Tony Abbott', *Quarterly Essay* No. 47 (Melbourne, Black Inc)

Martin, AW and Hardy, Patsy (eds) (1993) *Dark and Hurrying Days. Menzies' 1941 Diary* (Canberra, National Library of Australia)

McAllister, Ian (2003) 'Prime Ministers, Opposition Leaders and Government Popularity in Australia', *Australian Journal of Political Science* 38, 2, 259–78

McAllister, Ian (2007) 'The Personalisation of Politics' in RJ Dalton and H-D Klingemann *Oxford Handbook of Political Behaviour* (Oxford, Oxford University Press) 571–88

McCall, Tony and Hay, Peter (2005) 'Jim Bacon/Paul Lennon: The Changing of the Guard – from "the Emperor" to "Big Red"' in John Wanna and Paul Williams (eds) *Yes, Premier. Labor Leadership in Australia's States and Territories* (Sydney, UNSW Press)

McClymont, Kate and Besser, Linton (2014) *He Who Must Be Obeid. The Untold Story* (Sydney, Vintage Books)

McKnight, David (2015) 'Shaping the News: Media Advisers Under the Howard and Rudd Governments', *Australian Journalism Review* 37, 1, 21–31

McKnight, David (2016) 'The Rudd Labor Government and the Limitations of Spin', *Media International Australia* 1–10

McKnight, David and Hobbs, Mitchell (2013) 'Public Contest Through the Popular Media: The Mining Industry's Advertising War Against the Australian Labor Government', *Australian Journal of Political Science* 48, 3, 307–19

McNair, Brian (2000) *Journalism and Democracy. An Evaluation of the Political Public Sphere* (London, Routledge)

McNair, Brian (2004) 'PR Must Die: Spin, Anti-Spin and Political Public Relations in the UK, 1997–2004', *Journalism Studies* 5, 3, 325–38

Megalogenis, George (2010) 'Trivial Pursuit. Leadership and the End of the Reform Era', *Quarterly Essay* No. 40 (Melbourne, Black Inc)

Meyer, Thomas (2002) *Media Democracy. How the Media Colonize Politics* (Cambridge, Polity Press)

Mills, Stephen (1993) *The Hawke Years. The Story from the Inside* (Melbourne, Viking)

Mills, Stephen (2014) *The Professionals. Strategy, Money and the Rise of the Political Campaigner in Australia* (Melbourne, Black Inc)

Miragliotta, Narelle (2015) 'Parties and Mass Membership' in Narelle Miragliotta, Anika Gauja and Rodney Smith (eds) *Contemporary Australian Political Party Organisations* (Melbourne, Monash University Publishing)

Nixon, Richard (1978) *The Memoirs of Richard Nixon* (New York, Grosset & Dunlap)

Oakes, Laurie (1973) *Whitlam. PM* (Sydney, Angus & Robertson)

Oakes, Laurie (1976) *Crash Through or Crash. The Unmaking of a Prime Minister* (Melbourne, Drummond)

Oakes, Laurie (2008) *Power Plays. The Real Stories of Australian Politics* (Sydney, Hachette Australia)

Paluszek, John L (2002) 'Propaganda, Public Relations, and Journalism: When Bad Things Happen to Good Words', *Journalism Studies* 3, 3, November, 441–6

Parker, Derek (1991) *The Courtesans: The Press Gallery in the Hawke Era* (Sydney, Allen & Unwin)

Parkin, Andrew (1992) 'South Australia', *Australian Journal of Politics and History* 38, 3, December, 436–41

Parkinson, Tony (2000) *Jeff. The Rise and Fall of a Political Phenomenon* (Melbourne, Viking)

Patrick, Aaron (2016) *Credlin and Co. How the Abbott Government Destroyed Itself* (Melbourne, Black Inc)

Pringle, John Douglas (1973) *Have Pen: Will Travel* (London, Chatto & Windus)

Ramsey, Alan (2009) *A Matter of Opinion* (Sydney, Allen & Unwin)

Ramsey, Alan (2011) *The Way They Were. The View from the Hill of the 25 Years that Remade Australia* (Sydney, UNSW Press)

Reid, Alan (1971) *The Gorton Experiment* (Sydney, Shakespeare Head Press)

Richardson, Graham (1994) *Whatever It Takes* (Sydney, Bantam Books)

Rodan, Paul (2006) 'Rupert "Dick" Hamer: The Urbane Liberal' in Paul Strangio and Brian Costar (eds) *The Victorian Premiers 1856–2006* (Sydney, Federation Press)

Roshco, Bernard (1975) *Newsmaking* (Chicago, University of Chicago Press)

Sartor, Frank (2011) *The Fog on the Hill. How NSW Labor Lost Its Way* (Melbourne, MUP)

Savva, Niki (2010) *So Greek. Confessions of a Conservative Leftie* (Melbourne, Scribe)

Savva, Niki (2016) *The Road to Ruin. How Tony Abbott and Peta Credlin Destroyed their Own Government* (Melbourne, Scribe)

Schneider, Russell (1981) *The Colt from Kooyong: Andrew Peacock, a Political Biography* (Sydney, Angus & Robertson)

Smith, Rodney (2012) 'The Liberal Party' in David Clune and Rodney Smith (eds) *From Carr to Keneally. Labor in Office in NSW 1995–2011* (Sydney, Allen & Unwin)

Stanyer, James (2003) 'Intraparty Conflict and the Struggle to Shape News Agendas. Television News and the Coverage of Annual British Party Conferences', *International Journal of Press/Politics* 8, 2, 71–89

Strangio, Paul (2006) 'John Cain Jnr: The Burden of History' in Paul Strangio and Brian Costar (eds) *The Victorian Premiers 1856–2006* (Sydney, Federation Press)

Stuart, Nicholas (2007) *What Goes Up ... Behind the 2007 Election* (Melbourne, Scribe)

Stuart, Nicholas (2010) *Rudd's Way. November 2007 – June 2010* (Melbourne, Scribe)

Summers, Anne (1983) *Gamble for Power* (Melbourne, Thomas Nelson)

Summers, Anne (2013) *The Misogyny Factor* (Sydney, NewSouth Publishing)

Swan, Wayne (2014) *The Good Fight* (Sydney, Allen & Unwin)

Tanner, Stephen (1995) 'The Rise and Fall of Edmund Rouse', *Australian Studies in Journalism* 4, 72–89

Tiernan, Anne (2016) 'Beyond the Nadir of Political Leadership' in Julianne Schultz and Ann Tiernan *Fixing the System*, *Griffith Review* 51

Tiffen, Rodney (1988) 'A Politician's Experiences with the Press. Insights from the Howson Diaries', *Media Information Australia* 49, August, 25–29

Tiffen, Rodney (1989) *News and Power* (Sydney, Allen & Unwin)

Tiffen, Rodney (1999) *Scandals. Media, Politics and Corruption in Contemporary Australia* (Sydney, UNSW Press)

Tiffen, Rodney (2002) 'Media Escalation and Political Anti-Climax in Australia's *Cash for Comment* Scandal' in Raymond Kuhn and Erik Neveu (eds) *Political Journalism. New Challenges, New Practices* (London, Routledge) 131–48

Tiffen, Rodney (2012) 'Spin Doctors, News Values and Public Interest – the Bermuda Triangle of Policy Debate' in Matthew Ricketson (ed.) *Australian Journalism Today* (Melbourne, Palgrave Macmillan)

Tiffen, Rodney (2014) *Rupert Murdoch. A Reassessment* (Sydney, NewSouth Publishing)

Tingle, Laura (2015) 'Political Amnesia. How We Forgot How to Govern', *Quarterly Essay* No. 60 (Melbourne, Black Inc)

Tumber, Howard (2001) 'Public Relations in Media', *International Encyclopaedia of the Social and Behaviourial Sciences* (Elsevier Science Ltd) 12758–61

Turner, Graeme, Bonner, Frances and Marshall, P David (2000) *Fame Games: The Production of Celebrity in Australia* (Cambridge, CUP)

Walsh, Kerry-Anne (2013) *The Stalking of Julia Gillard* (Sydney, Allen & Unwin)

Walter, James and Strangio, Paul (2007) *No, Prime Minister. Reclaiming Politics from Leaders* (Sydney, UNSW Press)

Wanna, John and Arklay, Tracey (2010) *The Ayes Have It. The History of the Queensland Parliament 1957–1989* (Canberra, ANU Press)

Ward, Ian (2003) 'An Australian PR State?', *Australian Journal of Communication* 30, 1, 25–42

Wear, Rae (2002) *Johannes Bjelke-Petersen. The Lord's Premier* (Brisbane, UQP)

Weller, Pat (2014) *Kevin Rudd. Twice Prime Minister* (Melbourne, MUP)

Williams, Evan (2006) 'Heffron, Robert James' in David Clune and Ken Turner (eds) *The Premiers of New South Wales 1856–2005*, vol. 2, 1901–2005 (Sydney, Federation Press)

Young, Sally (2007a) 'A History of Government Advertising in Australia' in Sally Young (ed.) *Government Communication in Australia* (Melbourne, CUP)

Young, Sally (2007b) 'Conclusion: the Present and Future of Government Communication' in Sally Young (ed.) *Government Communication in Australia* (Melbourne, CUP)

Index

Index

www.ingramcontent.com/pod-product-compliance
Lightning Source LLC
Chambersburg PA
CBHW020503270326
41926CB00008B/720